YOUR 15-MONT
COMPLETE AND INDI

CANCER
June 21 - July 20

1992
SUPER HOROSCOPE

ARROW BOOKS LIMITED
20 Vauxhall Bridge Road
London SW1V 2SA

CONTENTS

THE PUBLISHERS REGRET THAT THEY CANNOT ANSWER INDIVIDUAL LETTERS REQUESTING PERSONAL HOROSCOPE INFORMATION.

FIRST PUBLISHED IN GREAT BRITAIN BY ARROW BOOKS 1991
© GROSSET & DUNLAP, INC., 1974, 1978, 1979, 1980, 1981, 1982
© CHARTER COMMUNICATIONS, INC., 1983, 1984, 1985
COPYRIGHT © 1986, 1987, 1988, 1989, 1990, 1991 THE BERKLEY PUBLISHING GROUP
THIS EDITION PUBLISHED BY AGREEMENT WITH THE BERKLEY PUBLISHING GROUP

PRINTED IN GREAT BRITAIN BY
GUERNSEY PRESS CO. LTD
GUERNSEY C.I.
ISBN 0 09 980690 8

NOTE TO THE CUSP-BORN

First find the year of your birth, and then find the sign under which you were born according to your day of birth. Thus, you can determine if you are a true Cancer (or Gemini or Leo), according to the variations of the dates of the Zodiac. (See also page 7.)

Are you *really* a Cancer? If your birthday falls during the fourth week of June, at the beginning of Cancer, will you still retain the traits of Gemini, the sign of the Zodiac before Cancer? And what if you were born late in July—are you more Leo than Cancer? Many people born at the edge, or cusp, of a sign have difficulty determining exactly what sign they are. If you are one of these people, here's how you can figure it out, once and for all.

Consult the following table. It will tell you the precise days on which the Sun entered and left your sign for the year of your birth. If you were born at the beginning or end of Cancer, yours is a lifetime reflecting a process of subtle transformation. Your life on Earth will symbolize a significant change in consciousness, for you are either about to enter a whole new way of living or are leaving one behind.

If you were born during the fourth week of June, you may want to read the Gemini book as well as Cancer. Because Gemini holds the keys to the more hidden sides of your personality; many of your dilemmas and uncertainties about the world and people around you, your secret wishes, and your potential for cosmic unfoldment.

Although you feel you have a lot to say, you will often withdraw and remain silent. Sometimes, the more you say the more confused a situation can get. Talking can drain you, and you are vulnerable to gossip. You feel secure surrounded by initimates you can trust, but sometimes the neighbors—even your own relatives—seem to be talking behind your back and you sense a vague plot in the air.

You symbolize the birth of feeling, the silent but rich condition of a fertilized seed growing full with life. The family is always an issue. At best you are a "feeling" type whose power of sensing things remains a force behind everything you think and do.

If you were born the fourth week of July, you may want to read the horoscope book for Leo as well as Cancer, for Leo could be your greatest asset. You need a warm embrace, the comfort and safety of being cared for, protected, fed. You need strong ties to the past, to the family. Attachments are natural for you. You want to be your own person, yet you often find ties and attachments prohibiting you from the rebirth you are anticipating. You may find it hard to separate yourself from dependencies without being drawn backward again and again.

You symbolize the fullness of growth, the condition of being *nearly* ripe, the new life about to emerge from the shadows into the sunshine.

DATES SUN ENTERS CANCER (LEAVES GEMINI)

June 21 every year from 1900 to 2000, except for the following:

June 20:	June 22:		
1988	1902	1915	1931
92	03	18	35
96	06	19	39
	07	22	43
	10	23	47
	11	26	51
	14	27	55

DATES SUN LEAVES CANCER (ENTERS LEO)

July 23 every year from 1900 to 2000, except for the following:

July 22:				
1928	1953	1968	1981	1992
32	56	69	84	93
36	57	72	85	94
40	60	73	86	96
44	61	76	88	97
48	64	77	89	98
52	65	80	90	

HISTORY AND USES
OF ASTROLOGY

Does astrology have a place in the fast-moving, ultra-scientific world we live in today? Can it be justified in a sophisticated society whose outriders are already preparing to step off the moon into the deep space of the planets themselves? Or is it just a hangover of ancient superstition, a psychological dummy for neurotics and dreamers of every historical age?

These are the kind of questions that any inquiring person can be expected to ask when they approach a subject like astrology which goes beyond, but never excludes, the materialistic side of life.

The simple, single answer is that astrology works. It works for tens of millions of people in the western world alone. In the United States there are 10 million followers and in Europe, an estimated 25 million. America has more than 4000 practicing astrologers, Europe nearly three times as many. Even down-under Australia has its hundreds of thousands of adherents. The importance of such vast numbers of people from diverse backgrounds and cultures is recognized by the world's biggest newspapers and magazines who probably devote more of their space to this subject in a year than to any other. In the eastern countries, astrology has enormous followings, again, because it has been proved to work. In countries like India, brides and grooms for centuries have been chosen on the basis of astrological compatibility. The low divorce rate there, despite today's heavy westernizing influence, is attributed largely to this practice.

In the western world, astrology today is more vital than ever before; more practicable because it needs a sophisticated society like ours to understand and develop its contribution to the full; more valid because science itself is confirming the precepts of astrological knowledge with every new exciting step. The ordinary person who daily applies astrology intelligently does not have to wonder whether it is true nor believe in it blindly. He can see it working for himself. And, if he can use it—and this book is designed to help the reader to do just that—he can make living a far richer experience, and become a more developed personality and a better person.

Astrology is the science of relationships. It is not just a study of planetary influences on man and his environment. It is the study of man himself.

We are at the center of our personal universe, of all our rela-

1

tionships. And our happiness or sadness depends on how we act, how we relate to the people and things that surround us. The emotions that we generate have a distinct affect—for better or worse—on the world around us. Our friends and our enemies will confirm this. Just look in the mirror the next time you are angry. In other words, each of us is a kind of sun or planet or star and our influence on our personal universe, whether loving, helpful or destructive, varies with our changing moods, expressed through our individual character.

And to an extent that includes the entire galaxy, this is true of the planetary bodies. Their radiations affect each other, including the earth and all the things on it. And in comparatively recent years, giant constellations called "quasars" have been discovered. These exist far beyond the night stars that we can observe, and science says these quasars are emitting radiating influences more powerful and different than ever recorded on earth. Their effect on man from an astrological point of view is under deep study. Compared with these inter-stellar forces, our personal "radiations" are negligible on the planetary scale. But ours are just as potent in the way they affect our moods, and our ability to control them. To this extent they determine much of the happiness and satisfaction in our lives. For instance, if we were bound and gagged and had to hold some strong emotion within us without being able to move, we would soon start to feel very uncomfortable. We are obviously pretty powerful radiators inside, in our own way. But usually, we are able to throw off our emotion in some sort of action—we have a good cry, walk it off, or tell someone our troubles—before it can build up too far and make us physically ill. Astrology helps us to understand the universal forces working on us, and through this understanding, we can become more properly adjusted to our surroundings and find ourselves coping where others may flounder.

Closely related to our emotions is the "other side" of our personal universe, our physical welfare. Our body, of course, is largely influenced by things around us over which we have very little control. The phone rings, we hear it. The train runs late. We snag our stocking or cut our face shaving. Our body is under a constant bombardment of events that influence our lives to varying degrees.

The question that arises from all this is, what makes each of us act so that we have to involve other people and keep the ball of activity and evolution rolling? This is the question that both science and astrology are involved with. The scientists have attacked it from different angles: anthropology, the study of human evolution as body, mind and response to environment; anatomy, the study of bodily structure; psychology, the science of the human mind; and so on. These studies have produced very impressive classifications and valuable information, but because the approach to the problem is fragmented, so is the result. They remain "branches" of science. Science generally studies effects. It keeps turning up wonderful answers but no lasting solutions. Astrology, on the other hand approaches the question from the broader viewpoint. Astrology began its inquiry with the totality of human experience and saw it as an effect. It then looked to find the cause, or at least the prime movers, and during thousands of years of observation of man and his *universal* environment, came up with the extraordinary principle of planetary influence—or astrology, which, from the Greek, means the science of the stars.

Modern science, as we shall see, has confirmed much of astrology's foundations—most of it unintentionally, some of it reluctantly, but still, indisputably.

It is not difficult to imagine that there must be a connection between outer space and the earth. Even today, scientists are not too sure how our earth was created, but it is generally agreed that it is only a tiny part of the universe. And as a part of the universe, people on earth see and feel the influence of heavenly bodies in almost every aspect of our existence. There is no doubt that the sun has the greatest influence on life on this planet. Without it there would be no life, for without it there would be no warmth, no division into day and night, no cycles of time or season at all. This is clear and easy to see. The influence of the moon, on the other hand, is more subtle, though no less definite.

There are many ways in which the influence of the moon manifests itself here on earth, both on human and animal life. It is a well-known fact, for instance, that the large movements of water on our planet—that is the ebb and flow of the tides—are caused by the moon's gravitational pull. Since this is so, it follows that these water movements do not occur only in the oceans, but that all bodies of water are affected, even down to the tiniest puddle.

The human body, too, which consists of about 70 percent water, falls within the scope of this lunar influence. For example the menstrual cycle of most women corresponds to the lunar month; the period of pregnancy in humans is 273 days, or equal to nine lunar months. Similarly, many illnesses reach a crisis at the change of the moon, and statistics in many countries have shown that the crime rate is highest at the time of the full moon. Even human sexual desire has been associated with the phases of the moon. But, it is in the movement of the tides that we get the clearest demonstration of planetary influence, and the irresistible correspondence between the so-called metaphysical and the physical.

Tide tables are prepared years in advance by calculating the future positions of the moon. Science has known for a long time that the moon is the main cause of tidal action. But only in the last few years has it begun to realize the possible extent of this influence on mankind. To begin with, the ocean tides do not rise and fall as we might imagine from our personal observations of them. The moon as it orbits around the earth, sets up a circular wave of attraction which pulls the oceans of the world after it, broadly in an east to west direction. This influence is like a phantom wave crest, a loop of power stretching from pole to pole which passes over and around the earth like an invisible shadow. It travels with equal effect across the land masses and, as scientists were recently amazed to observe, caused oysters placed in the dark in the middle of the United States where there is no sea, to open their shells to receive the non-existent tide. If the land-locked oysters react to this invisible signal, what effect does it have on us who not so long ago in evolutionary time, came out of the sea and still have its salt in our blood and sweat?

Less well known is the fact that the moon is also the primary force behind the circulation of blood in human beings and animals, and the movement of sap in trees and plants. Agriculturists have established that the moon has a distinct influence on crops, which explains why for centuries people have planted according to moon cycles. The habits of many animals, too, are directed by the movement of the moon. Migratory birds, for instance, depart only at or near the time of the full moon. Just as certain fish, eels in particular, move only in accordance with certain phases of the moon.

Know Thyself—Why?

In today's fast-changing world, everyone still longs to know what the future holds. It is the one thing that everyone has in common: rich and poor, famous and infamous, all are deeply concerned about tomorrow.

But the key to the future, as every historian knows, lies in the past. This is as true of individual people as it is of nations. You cannot understand your future without first understanding your past, which is simply another way of saying that you must first of all know yourself.

The motto "know thyself" seems obvious enough nowadays, but it was originally put forward as the foundation of wisdom by the ancient Greek philosophers. It was then adopted by the "mystery religions" of the ancient Middle East, Greece and Rome, and is still used in all genuine schools of mind training or mystical discipline, both in those of the East, based on yoga, and those of the West. So it is universally accepted now, and has been through the ages.

But how do you go about discovering what sort of person you are? The first step is usually classification into some sort of system of types. Astrology did this long before the birth of Christ. Psychology has also done it. So has modern medicine, in its way.

One system classifies men according to the source of the impulses they respond to most readily: the muscles, leading to direct bodily action; the digestive organs, resulting in emotion, or the brain and nerves. Another such system says that character is determined by the endocrine glands, and gives us labels like "pituitary," "thyroid" and "hyperthyroid" types. These different systems are neither contradictory nor mutually exclusive. In fact, they are very often different ways of saying the same thing.

Very popular and useful classifications were devised by Dr. C. G. Jung, the eminent disciple of Freud. Jung observed among the different faculties of the mind, four which have a predominant influence on character. These four faculties exist in all of us without exception, but not in perfect balance. So when we say, for instance, that a man is a "thinking type," it means that in any situation he tries to be rational. It follows that emotion, which some say is the opposite of thinking, will be his weakest function. This type can be sensible and reasonable, or calculating and unsympathetic. The emotional type, on the other hand, can often be recognized by exaggerated language—everything is either marvelous or terrible—and in extreme cases they even invent dramas and quarrels out of nothing just to make life more interesting.

The other two faculties are intuition and physical sensation. The sensation type does not only care for food and drink, nice clothes and furniture; he is also interested in all forms of physical experience. Many scientists are sensation types as are athletes and naturelovers. Like sensation, intuition is a form of perception and we all possess it. But it works through that part of the mind which is not under conscious control—consequently it sees meanings and connections which are not obvious to thought or emotion. Inventors and original thinkers are always intuitive, but so, too, are superstitious people who see meanings where none exist.

Thus, sensation tells us what is going on in the world, feeling (that is, emotion) tells us how important it is to ourselves, thinking enables us to interpret it and work out what we should do about it, and intuition tells us what it means to ourselves and others. All four faculties are essential, and all are present in every one of us. But some people are guided chiefly by one, others by another.

Besides these four types, Jung observed a division into extrovert and introvert, which cuts across them. By and large, the introvert is one who finds truth inside himself rather than outside. He is not, therefore, ideally suited to a religion or a political party which tells him what to believe. Original thinkers are almost necessarily introverts. The extrovert, on the other hand, finds truth coming to him from outside. He believes in experts and authorities, and wants to think that nature and the laws of nature really exists, that they are what they appear to be and not just generalities made by men.

A disadvantage of all these systems of classification, is that one cannot tell very easily where to place oneself. Some people are reluctant to admit that they act to please their emotions. So they deceive themselves for years by trying to belong to whichever type they think is the "best." Of course, there is no best; each has its faults and each has its good points.

The advantage of the signs of the Zodiac is that they simplify classification. Not only that, but your date of birth is personal—it is unarguably yours. What better way to know yourself than by going back as far as possible to the very moment of your birth? And this is precisely what your horoscope is all about.

What Is a Horoscope?

If you had been able to take a picture of the heavens at the moment of your birth, that photograph would be your horoscope. Lacking such a snapshot, it is still possible to recreate the picture—and this is at the basis of the astrologer's art. In other words, your horoscope is a representation of the skies with the planets in the exact positions they occupied at the time you were born.

This information, of course, is not enough for the astrologer. He has to have a background of significance to put the photograph on. You will get the idea if you imagine two balls—one inside the other. The inner one is transparent. In the center of both is the astrologer, able to look up, down and around in all directions. The outer sphere is the Zodiac which is divided into twelve approximately equal segments, like the segments of an orange. The inner ball is our photograph. It is transparent except for the images of the planets. Looking out from the center, the astrologer sees the planets in various segments of the Zodiac. These twelve segments are known as the signs or houses.

The position of the planets when each of us is born is always different. So the photograph is always different. But the Zodiac and its signs are fixed.

Now, where in all this are you, the subject of the horoscope?

Your character is largely determined by the sign the sun is in. So that is where the astrologer looks first in your horoscope.

There are twelve signs in the Zodiac and the sun spends approximately one month in each. As the sun's motion is almost perfectly regular, the astrologers have been able to fix the dates governing each sign. There are not many people who do not know which sign of the Zodiac they were born under or who have not been amazed at some time or other at the accuracy of the description of their own character. Here are the twelve signs, the ancient zodiacal symbol, and their dates for the year 1992.*

ARIES	Ram	March 20–April 19
TAURUS	Bull	April 19–May 20
GEMINI	Twins	May 20–June 20
CANCER	Crab	June 20–July 22
LEO	Lion	July 22–August 22
VIRGO	Virgin	August 22–September 22
LIBRA	Scales	September 22–October 22
SCORPIO	Scorpion	October 22–November 21
SAGITTARIUS	Archer	November 21–December 21
CAPRICORN	Sea-Goat	December 21–January 20
AQUARIUS	Water-Bearer	January 20–February 19
PISCES	Fish	February 19–March 20

The time of birth—apart from the date—is important in advanced astrology because the planets travel at such great speed that the patterns they form change from minute to minute. For this reason, each person's horoscope is his and his alone. Further on we will see that the practicing astrologer has ways of determining and reading these minute time changes which dictate the finer character differences in us all.

However, it is still possible to draw significant conclusions and make meaningful predictions based simply on the sign of the Zodiac a person is born under. In a horoscope, the signs do not necessarily correspond with the divisions of the houses. It could be that a house begins halfway across a sign. It is the interpretation of such combinations of different influences that distinguishes the professional astrologer from the student and the follower.

However, to gain a workable understanding of astrology, it is not necessary to go into great detail. In fact, the beginner is likely to find himself confused if he attempts to absorb too much too quickly. It should be remembered that this is a science and to become proficient at it, and especially to grasp the tremendous scope of possibilities in man and his affairs and direct them into a worthwhile reading, takes a great deal of study and experience.

*These dates are fluid and change with the motion of the Earth from year to year.

If you do intend to pursue it seriously you will have to learn to figure the exact moment of birth against the degrees of longitude and latitude of the planets at that precise time. This involves adapting local time to Greenwich Mean Time (G.M.T.), reference to tables of houses to establish the Ascendant, as well as making calculations from Ephemeris—the tables of the planets' positions.

After reading this introduction, try drawing up a rough horoscope to get the "feel" of reading some elementary characteristics and natal influences.

Draw a circle with twelve equal segments. Write in counterclockwise the names of the signs—Aries, Taurus, Gemini etc.— one for each segment. Look up an ephemeris for the year of the person's birth and note down the sign each planet was in on the birthday. Do not worry about the number of degrees (although if a planet is on the edge of a sign its position obviously should be considered). Write the name of the planet in the segment/sign on your chart. Write the number 1 in the sign where the sun is. This is the first house. Number the rest of the houses, counterclockwise till you finish at 12. Now you can investigate the probable basic expectation of experience of the person concerned. This is done first of all by seeing what planet or planets is/are in what sign and house. (See also page 72.)

The 12 houses control these functions:

1st.	Individuality, body appearance, general outlook on life	(Personality house)
2nd.	Finance, business	(Money house)
3rd.	Relatives, education, correspondence	(Relatives house)
4th.	Family, neighbors	(Home house)
5th.	Pleasure, children, attempts, entertainment	(Pleasure house)
6th.	Health, employees	(Health house)
7th.	Marriage, partnerships	(Marriage house)
8th.	Death, secret deals, difficulties	(Death house)
9th.	Travel, intellectual affairs	(Travel house)
10th.	Ambition, social standing	(Business and Honor house)
11th.	Friendship, social life, luck	(Friends house)
12th.	Troubles, illness, loss	(Trouble house)

The characteristics of the planets modify the influence of the Sun according to their natures and strengths.

Sun: Source of life. Basic temperament according to sun sign. The will.
Moon: Superficial nature. Moods. Changeable. Adaptive. Mother.
Mercury: Communication. Intellect. Reasoning power. Curiosity. Short travels.
Venus: Love. Delight. Art. Beautiful possessions.
Mars: Energy. Initiative. War. Anger. Destruction. Impulse.
Jupiter: Good. Generous. Expansive. Opportunities. Protection.
Saturn: Jupiter's opposite. Contraction. Servant. Delay. Hardwork. Cold. Privation. Research. Lasting rewards after long struggle.
Uranus: Fashion. Electricity. Revolution. Sudden changes. Modern science.
Neptune: Sensationalism. Mass emotion. Devastation. Delusion.
Pluto: Creates and destroys. Lust for power. Strong obsessions.

Superimpose the characteristics of the planets on the functions of the house in which they appear. Express the result through the character of the birth (sun) sign, and you will get the basic idea of how astrology works.

Of course, many other considerations have been taken into account in producing the carefully worked out predictions in this book: The aspects of the planets to each other; their strength according to position and sign; whether they are in a house of exaltation or decline; whether they are natural enemies or not; whether a planet occupies his own sign; the position of a planet in relation to its own house or sign; whether the planet is male, female or neuter; whether the sign is a fire, earth, water or air sign. These are only a few of the colors on the astrologer's pallet which he must mix with the inspiration of the artist and the accuracy of the mathematician.

The Problem of Love

Love, of course, is never a problem. The problem lies in recognizing the difference between infatuation, emotion, sex and, sometimes, the downright deceit of the other person. Mankind, with its record of broken marriages, despair and disillusionment, is obviously not very good at making these distinctions.

Can astrology help?

Yes. In the same way that advance knowledge can usually help in any human situation. And there is probably no situation as human, as poignant, as pathetic and universal, as the failure of man's love.

Love, of course, is not just between man and woman. It involves love of children, parents, home and so on. But the big problems usually involve the choice of partner.

Astrology has established degrees of compatibility that exist between people born under the various signs of the Zodiac. Because people are individuals, there are numerous variations and modifications and the astrologer, when approached on mate and marriage matters makes allowances for them. But the fact remains that some groups of people are suited for each other and some are not and astrology has expressed this in terms of characteristics which all can study and use as a personal guide.

No matter how much enjoyment and pleasure we find in the different aspects of each other's character, if it is not an overall compatibility, the chances of our finding fulfillment or enduring happiness in each other are pretty hopeless. And astrology can help us to find someone compatible.

History of Astrology

The origins of astrology have been lost far back in history, but we do know that reference is made to it as far back as the first written records of the human race. It is not hard to see why. Even in primitive times, people must have looked for an explanation for the various happenings in their lives. They must have wanted to know why people were different from one to another. And in their search they turned to the regular movements of the sun, moon and stars to see if they could provide an answer.

It is interesting to note that as soon as man learned to use his tools in any type of design, or his mind in any kind of calculation, he turned his attention to the heavens. Ancient cave dwellings reveal dim crescents and circles representative of the sun and moon, rulers of day and night. Mesopotamia and the civilization of Chaldea, in itself the foundation of those of Babylonia and Assyria, show a complete picture of astronomical observation and well-developed astrological interpretation.

Humanity has a natural instinct for order. The study of anthropology reveals that primitive people—even as far back as prehistoric times—were striving to achieve a certain order in their lives. They tried to organize the apparent chaos of the universe. They had the desire to attach meaning to things. This demand for order has persisted throughout the history of man. So that observing the regularity of the heavenly bodies made it logical that primitive peoples should turn heavenwards in their search for an understanding of the world in which they found themselves so random and alone.

And they did find a significance in the movements of the stars. Shepherds tending their flocks, for instance, observed that when the cluster of stars now known as the constellation Aries was in sight, it was the time of fertility and they associated it with the Ram. And they noticed that the growth of plants and plant life corresponded with different phases of the moon, so that certain times were favorable for the planting of crops, and other times were not. In this way, there grew up a tradition of seasons and causes connected with the passage of the sun through the twelve signs of the Zodiac.

Astrology was valued so highly that the king was kept informed of the daily and monthly changes in the heavenly bodies, and the results of astrological studies regarding events of the future. Head astrologers were clearly men of great rank and position, and the office was said to be a hereditary one.

Omens were taken, not only from eclipses and conjunctions of the moon or sun with one of the planets, but also from storms and earthquakes. In the eastern civilizations, particularly, the reverence inspired by astrology appears to have remained unbroken since the very earliest days. In ancient China, astrology, astronomy and religion went hand in hand. The astrologer, who was also an astronomer, was part of the official government service and had his own corner in the Imperial Palace. The duties of the Imperial astrologer, whose office was one of the most important in the land, were clearly defined, as this extract from early records shows:

"This exalted gentleman must concern himself with the stars in the heavens, keeping a record of the changes and movements of the Planets, the Sun and the Moon, in order to examine the movements of the terrestial world with the object of prognosticating good and bad fortune. He divides the territories of the nine regions of the empire in accordance with their dependence on particular celestial bodies. All the fiefs and principalities are connected with the stars and from this their prosperity or misfortune should be ascertained. He makes prognostications according to the twelve years of the Jupiter cycle of good and evil of the terrestial world. From the colors of the five kinds of clouds, he determines the coming of floods or droughts, abundance or famine. From the twelve winds, he draws conclusions about the state of harmony of heaven and earth, and takes note of good and bad signs that result from their accord or disaccord. In general, he concerns himself with five kinds of phenomena so as to warn the Emperor to come to the aid of the government and to allow for variations in the ceremonies according to their circumstances."

The Chinese were also keen observers of the fixed stars, giving them such unusual names as Ghost Vehicle, Sun of Imperial Concubine, Imperial Prince, Pivot of Heaven, Twinkling Brilliance or Weaving Girl. But, great astrologers though they may have been, the Chinese lacked one aspect of mathematics that the Greeks applied to astrology—deductive geometry. Deductive geometry was the basis of much classical astrology in and after the time of the Greeks, and this explains the different methods of prognostication used in the East and West.

Down through the ages the astrologer's art has depended, not so much on the uncovering of new facts, though this is important, as on the interpretation of the facts already known. This is the essence of his skill. Obviously one cannot always tell how people will react (and this underlines the very important difference between astrology and predestination which will be discussed later on) but one can be prepared, be forewarned, to know what to expect.

But why should the signs of the zodiac have any effect at all on the formation of human character? It is easy to see why people thought they did, and even now we constantly use astrological expressions in our everyday speech. The thoughts of "lucky star," "ill-fated," "star-crossed," "mooning around," are interwoven into the very structure of our language.

In the same way that the earth has been created by influences from outside, there remains an indisputable togetherness in the working of the universe. The world, after all, is a coherent structure, for if it were not, it would be quite without order and we would never know what to expect. A dog could turn into an apple, or an elephant sprout wings and fly at any moment without so much as a by your leave. But nature, as we know, functions according to laws, not whims, and the laws of nature are certainly not subject to capricious exceptions.

This means that no part of the universe is ever arbitrarily cut off from any other part. Everything is therefore to some extent linked with everything else. The moon draws an imperceptible tide on every puddle; tiny and trivial events can be effected by outside forces (such as the fall of a feather by the faintest puff of wind). And so it is fair to think that the local events at any moment reflect to a very small extent the evolution of the world as a whole.

From this principle follows the possibility of divination, and also knowledge of events at a distance, provided one's mind were always as perfectly undisturbed, as ideally smooth, as a mirror or unruffled lake. Provided, in other words, that one did not confuse the picture with hopes, guesses, and expectations. When people try to foretell the future by cards or crystal ball gazing they find it much easier to confuse the picture with expectations than to reflect it clearly.

But the present does contain a good deal of the future to which it leads—not all, but a good deal. The diver halfway between bridge and water is going to make a splash; the train whizzing towards the station will pass through it unless interfered with; the burglar breaking a pane of glass has exposed himself to the possibility of a prison sentence. Yet this is not a doctrine of determinism, as was emphasized earlier. Clearly, there are forces already at work in the present, and any one of them could alter the situation in some way. Equally, a change of decision could alter the whole situation as well. So the future depends, not on an irresistible force, but on a small act of free will.

An individual's age, physique, and position on the earth's surface are remote consequences of his birth. Birth counts as the original cause for all that happens subsequently. The horoscope, in this case, means "this person represents the further evolution of the state of the universe pictured in this chart." Such a chart can apply equally to man or woman, dog, ship or even limited company.

If the evolution of an idea, or of a person, is to be understood as a totality, it must continue to evolve from its own beginnings, which is to say, in the terms in which it began. The brown-eyed person will be faithful to brown eyes all his life; the traitor is being faithful to some complex of ideas which has long been evolving in him; and the person born at sunset will always express, as he evolves, the psychological implications or analogies of the moment when the sun sinks out of sight.

This is the doctrine that an idea must continue to evolve in terms of its origin. It is a completely non-materialist doctrine, though it never fails to apply to material objects. And it implies, too, that the individual will continue to evolve in terms of his moment of origin, and therefore possibly of the sign of the Zodiac rising on the eastern horizon at his birth. It also implies that the signs of the Zodiac themselves will evolve in the collective mind of the human race in the same terms that they were first devised and not in the terms in which modern astrologers consciously think they ought to work.

For the human race, like every other kind of animal, has a collective mind, as Professor Jung discovered in his investigation of dreams. If no such collective mind existed, no infant could ever learn anything, for communication would be impossible. Furthermore, it is absurd to suggest that the conscious mind could be older than the "unconscious," for an infant's nervous system functions correctly before it has discovered the difference between "myself" and "something else" or discovered what eyes and hands are for. Indeed, the involuntary muscles function correctly even before birth, and will never be under conscious control. They are part of what we call the "unconscious" which is not really "unconscious" at all. To the contrary, it is totally aware of itself and everything else; it is merely that part of the mind that cannot be controlled by conscious effort.

And human experience, though it varies in detail with every individual, is basically the same for each one of us, consisting of sky and earth, day and night, waking and sleeping, man and woman, birth and death. So there is bound to be in the mind of the human race a very large number of inescapable ideas, which are called our natural archetypes.

There are also, however, artificial or cultural archetypes which are not universal or applicable to everyone, but are nevertheless inescapable within the limits of a given culture. Examples of these are the cross in Christianity, and the notion of "escape from the wheel of rebirth" in India. There was a time when these ideas did not exist. And there was a time, too, when the scheme of the Zodiac did not exist. One would not expect the Zodiac to have any influence on remote and primitive peoples, for example, who have never heard of it. If the Zodiac is only an archetype, their horoscopes probably would not work and it would not matter which sign they were born under.

But where the Zodiac is known, and the idea of it has become worked into the collective mind, then there it could well appear to have an influence, even if it has no physical existence. For ideas do not have a physical existence, anyway. No physical basis has yet been discovered for the telepathy that controls an anthill; young swallows migrate before, not after, their parents; and the weaver-bird builds its intricate nest without being taught. Materialists suppose, but cannot prove, that "instinct" (as it is called, for no one knows how it works) is controlled by nucleic acid in the chromosomes. This is not a genuine explanation, though, for it only pushes the mystery one stage further back.

Does this mean, then, that the human race, in whose civilization the idea of the twelve signs of the Zodiac has long been embedded, is divided into only twelve types? Can we honestly believe that it is really as simple as that? If so, there must be pretty wide ranges of variation within each type. And if, to explain the variation, we call in heredity and environment, experiences in early childhood, the thyroid and other glands, and also the four functions of the mind mentioned at the beginning of this introduction, and extroversion and introversion, then one begins to wonder if the original classification was worth making at all. No sensible person believes that his favorite system explains everything. But even so, he will not find it much use at all if it does not even save him the trouble of bothering with the others.

Under the Jungian system, everyone has not only a dominant or principal function, but also a secondary or subsidiary one, so that the four can be arranged in order of potency. In the intuitive type, sensation is always the most inefficient function, but the second most inefficient function can be either thinking (which tends to make original thinkers such as Jung himself) or else feeling (which tends to make artistic people). Therefore, allowing for introversion and extroversion, there are at least four kinds of intuitive types, and sixteen types in all. Furthermore, one can see how the sixteen types merge into each other, so that there are no unrealistic or unconvincingly rigid divisions.

In the same way, if we were to put every person under only one sign of the Zodiac, the system becomes too rigid and unlike life. Besides, it was never intended to be used like that. It may be convenient to have only twelve types, but we know that in practice there is every possible gradation between aggressiveness and timidity, or between conscientiousness and laziness. How, then, do we account for this?

The Tyrant and the Saint

Just as the thinking type of man is also influenced to some extent by sensation and intuition, but not very much by emotion, so a person born under Leo can be influenced to some extent by one or two (but not more) of the other signs. For instance, famous persons born under the sign of Gemini include Henry VIII, whom nothing and no-one could have induced to abdicate, and Edward VIII, who did just that. Obviously, then, the sign Gemini does not fully explain the complete character of either of them.

Again, under the opposite sign, Sagittarius, were both Stalin, who was totally consumed with the notion of power, and Charles V, who freely gave up an empire because he preferred to go into a monastery. And we find under Scorpio, many uncompromising characters such as Luther, de Gaulle, Indira Gandhi and Montgomery, but also Petain, a successful commander whose name later became synonymous with collaboration.

A single sign is therefore obviously inadequate to explain the differences between people; it can only explain resemblances, such as the combativeness of the Scorpio group, or the far-reaching devotion of Charles V and Stalin to their respective ideals—the Christian heaven and the Communist utopia.

But very few people are born under one sign only. As well as the month of birth, as was mentioned earlier, the day matters, and, even more, the hour, which ought, if possible, to be noted to the nearest minute. Without this, it is impossible to have an actual horoscope, for the word horoscope means literally, "a consideration of the hour."

The month of birth tells you only which sign of the Zodiac was occupied by the sun. The day and hour tell you what sign was occupied by the moon. And the minute tells you which sign was rising on the eastern horizon. This is called the Ascendant, and it is supposed to be the most important thing in the whole horoscope.

If you were born at midnight, the sun is then in an important position, although invisible. But at one o'clock in the morning the sun is not important, so the moment of birth will not matter much. The important thing then will be the Ascendant, and possibly one or two of the planets. At a given day and hour, say, dawn on January 1st, or 9:00 p.m. on the longest day, the Ascendant will always be the same at any given place. But the moon and planets alter from day to day, at different speeds and have to be looked up in an astronomical table.

The sun is said to signify one's heart, that is to say, one's deepest desires and inmost nature. This is quite different from the moon, which, as we have seen, signifies one's superficial way of behaving. When the ancient Romans referred to the Emperor Augustus as a Capricornian, they meant that he had the moon in Capricorn; they did not pay much attention to the sun, although he was born at sunrise. Or, to take another example, a modern astrologer would call Disraeli a Scorpion because he had Scorpio rising, but most people would call him Sagittarian because he had the sun there. The Romans would have called him Leo because his moon was in Leo.

The sun, as has already been pointed out, is important if one is born near sunrise, sunset, noon or midnight, but is otherwise not reckoned as the principal influence. So if one does not seem to fit one's birth month, it is always worthwhile reading the other signs, for one may have been born at a time when any of them were rising or occupied by the moon. It also seems to be the case that the influence of the sun develops as life goes on, so that the month of birth is easier to guess in people over the age of forty. The young are supposed to be influenced mainly by their Ascendant which characterizes the body and physical personality as a whole.

It should be clearly understood that it is nonsense to assume that all people born at a certain time will exhibit the same characteristics, or that they will even behave in the same manner. It is quite obvious that, from the very moment of its birth, a child is subject to the effects of its environment, and that this in turn will influence its character and heritage to a decisive extent. Also to be taken into account are education and economic conditions, which play a very important part in the formation of one's character as well.

However, it is clearly established that people born under one sign of the Zodiac do have certain basic traits in their character which are different from those born under other signs. It is obvious to every thinking person that certain events produce different reactions in various people. For instance, if a man slips on a banana skin and falls heavily on the pavement, one passer-by may laugh and find this extremely amusing, while another may just walk on, thinking: "What a fool falling down like that. He should look where he is going." A third might also walk away saying to himself: "It's none of my business—I'm glad it wasn't me." A fourth might walk past and think: "I'm sorry for that man, but I haven't the time to be bothered with helping him." And a fifth might stop to help the fallen man to his feet, comfort him and take him home. Here is just one event which could produce entirely different reactions in different people. And, obviously, there are many more. One that comes to mind immediately is the violently opposed views to events such as wars, industrial strikes, and so on. The fact that people have different attitudes to the same event is simply another way of saying that they have different characters. And this is not something that can be put down to background, for people of the same race, religion, or class, very often express quite different reactions to happenings or events. Similarly, it is often the case that members of the same family, where there is clearly uniform background of economic and social standing, education, race and religion, often argue bitterly among themselves over political and social issues.

People have, in general, certain character traits and qualities which, according to their environment, develop in either a positive or a negative manner. Therefore, selfishness (inherent selfishness, that is) might emerge as unselfishness; kindness and consideration as cruelty and lack of consideration towards others. In the same way, a naturally constructive person, may, through frustration, become destructive, and so on. The latent characteristics with which people are born can, therefore, through environment and good or bad training, become something that would appear to be its opposite, and so give the lie to the astrologer's description of their character. But this is not the case. The true character is still there, but it is buried deep beneath these external superficialities.

Careful study of the character traits of different signs can be immeasurable help, and can render beneficial service to the intelligent person. Undoubtedly, the reader will already have discovered that, while he is able to get on very well with some people, he just "cannot stand" others. The causes sometimes seem inexplicable. At times there is intense dislike, at other times immediate sympathy. And there is, too, the phenomenon of love at first sight, which is also apparently inexplicable. People appear to be either sympathetic or unsympathetic towards each other for no apparent reason.

Now if we look at this in the light of the Zodiac, we find that people born under different signs are either compatible or incompatible with each other. In other words, there are good and bad interrelating factors among the various signs. This does not, of course, mean that humanity can be divided into groups of hostile camps. It would be quite wrong to be hostile or indifferent toward people who happen to be born under an incompatible sign. There is no reason why everybody should not, or cannot, learn to control and adjust their feelings and actions, especially after they are aware of the positive qualities of other people by studying their character analyses, among other things.

Every person born under a certain sign has both positive and negative qualities, which are developed more or less according to his free will. Nobody is entirely good or entirely bad, and it is up to each one of us to learn to control himself on the one hand, and at the same time to endeavor to learn about himself and others.

It cannot be repeated often enough that, though the intrinsic nature of man and his basic character traits are born in him, nevertheless it is his own free will that determines whether he will make really good use of his talents and abilities—whether, in other words, he will overcome his vices or allow them to rule him. Most of us are born with at least a streak of laziness, irritability, or some other fault in our nature, and it is up to each one of us to see that we exert sufficient willpower to control our failings so that they do not harm ourselves or others.

Astrology can reveal our inclinations and tendencies. Our weaknesses should not be viewed as shortcomings that are impossible to change. The horoscope of a man may show him to have criminal leanings, for instance, but this does not mean he will definitely become a criminal.

The ordinary man usually finds it difficult to know himself. He is often bewildered. Astrology can frequently tell him more about himself than the different schools of psychology are able to do. Knowing his failings and shortcomings, he will do his best to overcome them, and make himself a better and more useful member of society and a helpmate to his family and friends. It can also save him a great deal of unhappiness and remorse.

And yet it may seem absurd that an ancient philosophy, something that is known as a "pseudo-science," could be a prop to the men and women of the twentieth century. But below the materialistic surface of modern life, there are hidden streams of feeling and thought. Symbology is reappearing as a study worthy of the scholar; the psychosomatic factor in illness has passed from the writings of the crank to those of the specialist; spiritual healing in all its forms is no longer a pious hope but an accepted phenomenon. And it is into this context that we consider astrology, in the sense that it is an analysis of human types.

Astrology and medicine had a long journey together, and only parted company a couple of centuries ago. There still remain in medical language such astrological terms as "saturnine," "choleric," and "mercurial," used in the diagnosis of physical tendencies. The herbalist, for long the handyman of the medical profession, has been dominated by astrology since the days of the Greeks. Certain herbs traditionally respond to certain planetary influences, and diseases must therefore be treated to ensure harmony between the medicine and the disease.

No one expects the most eccentric of modern doctors to go back to the practices of his predecessors. We have come a long way since the time when phases of the moon were studied in illness. Those days were a medical nightmare, with epidemics that were beyond control, and an explanation of the Black Death sought in conjunction with the planets. Nowadays, astrological diagnosis of disease has literally no parallel in modern life. And yet, age-old symbols of types and of the vulnerability of, say, the Saturnian to chronic diseases or the choleric to apoplexy and blood pressure and so on, are still applicable.

But the stars are expected to foretell and not only to diagnose. The astrological forecaster has a counterpart on a highly conventional level in the shape of the weather prophet, racing tipster and stock market forecaster, to name just three examples. All in their own way are aiming at the same result. They attempt to look a little further into the pattern of life and also try to determine future patterns accurately.

Astrological forecasting has been remarkably accurate, but often it is wide of the mark. The brave man who cares to predict world events takes dangerous chances. Individual forecasting is less clear cut; it can be a help or a disillusionment. Then welcome to the nagging question: if it is possible to foreknow, is it right to foretell? A complex point of ethics on which it is hard to pronounce judgment. The doctor faces the same dilemma if he finds that symptoms of a mortal disease are present in his patient and that he can only prognosticate a steady decline. How much to tell an individual in a crisis is a problem that has perplexed many distinguished scholars. Honest and conscientious astrologers in this modern world, where so many people are seeking guidance, face the same problem.

The ancient cults, the symbols of old religions, are eclipsed for the moment. They may return with their old force within a decade or two. But at present the outlook is dark. Human beings badly need assurance, as they did in the past, that all is not chaos. Somewhere, somehow, there is a pattern that must be worked out. As to the why and wherefore, the astrologer is not expected to give judgment. He is just someone who, by dint of talent and training, can gaze into the future.

Five hundred years ago it was customary to call in a learned man who was an astrologer who was probably also a doctor and a philosopher. By his knowledge of astrology, his study of planetary influences, he felt himself qualified to guide those in distress. The world has moved forward at a fantastic rate since then, and in this twentieth century speed has been the keyword everywhere. Tensions have increased, the spur of ambition has been applied indiscriminately. People are uncertain of themselves. At first sight it seems fantastic in the light of modern thinking that they turn to the most ancient of all studies, and get someone to calculate a horoscope for them. But is it *really* so fantastic if you take a second look? For astrology is concerned with tomorrow, with survival. And in a world such as ours, those two things are the keywords of the time in which we live.

HOW TO USE
THESE PREDICTIONS

A person reading the predictions in this book should understand that they are produced from the daily position of the planets for a group of people and are not, of course, individually specialized. To get the full benefit of them he should relate the predictions to his own character and circumstances, co-ordinate them, and draw his own conclusions from them.

If he is a serious observer of his own life he should find a definite pattern emerge that will be a helpful and reliable guide.

The point is that we always retain our free will. The stars indicate certain directional tendencies but we are not compelled to follow. We can do or not do, and wisdom must make the choice.

We all have our good and bad days. Sometimes they extend into cycles of weeks. It is therefore advisable to study daily predictions in a span ranging from the day before to several days ahead; also to re-read the monthly predictions for similar cycles.

Daily predictions should be taken very generally. The word "difficult" does not necessarily indicate a whole day of obstruction or inconvenience. It is a warning to you to be cautious. Your caution will often see you around the difficulty before you are involved. This is the correct use of astrology.

In another section, detailed information is given about the influence of the moon as it passes through the various signs of the Zodiac. It includes instructions on how to use the Moon Tables. This information should be used in conjunction with the daily forecasts to give a fuller picture of the astrological trends.

THE MOON

Moon is the nearest planet to the earth. It exerts more observable influence on us from day to day than any other planet. The effect is very personal, very intimate, and if we are not aware of how it works it can make us quite unstable in our ideas. And the annoying thing is that at these times we often see our own instability but can do nothing about it. A knowledge of what can be expected may help considerably. We can then be prepared to stand strong against the moon's negative influences and use its positive ones to help us to get ahead. Who has not heard of going with the tide?

Moon reflects, has no light of its own. It reflects the sun—the life giver—in the form of vital movement. Moon controls the tides, the blood rhythm, the movement of sap in trees and plants. Its nature is inconstancy and change so it signifies our moods, our superficial behavior—walking, talking and especially thinking. Being a true reflector of other forces, moon is cold, watery like the surface of a still lake, brilliant and scintillating at times, but easily ruffled and disturbed by the winds of change.

The moon takes 28½ days to circle the earth and the Zodiac. It spends just over 2¼ days in each sign. During that time it reflects the qualities, energies and characteristics of the sign and, to a degree, the planet which rules the sign. While the moon in its transit occupies a sign incompatible with our own birth sign, we can expect to feel a vague uneasiness, perhaps a touch of irritableness. We should not be discouraged nor let the feeling get us down, or, worse still, allow ourselves to take the discomfort out on others. Try to remember that the moon has to change signs within 55 hours and, provided you are not physically ill, your mood will probably change with it. It is amazing how frequently depression lifts with the shift in the moon's position. And, of course, when the moon is transiting a sign compatible or sympathetic to yours you will probably feel some sort of stimulation or just plain happy to be alive.

In the horoscope, the moon is such a powerful indicator that competent astrologers often use the sign it occupied at birth as the birth sign of the person. This is done particularly when the sun is on the cusp, or edge, of two signs. Most experienced astrologers, however, coordinate both sun and moon signs by reading and confirming from one to the other and secure a far more accurate and personalized analysis.

For these reasons, the moon tables which follow this section (see pages 28–35) are of great importance to the individual. They show the days and the exact times the moon will enter each sign of the Zodiac for the year. Remember, you have to adjust the indicated times to local time. The corrections, already calculated for most of the main cities, are at the beginning of the tables. What follows now is a guide to the influences that will be reflected to the earth by the moon while it transits each of the twelve signs. The influence is at its peak about 26 hours after the moon enters a sign.

MOON IN ARIES

This is a time for action, for reaching out beyond the usual self-imposed limitations and faint-hearted cautions. If you have plans in your head or on your desk, put them into practice. New ventures, applications, new jobs, new starts of any kind—all have a good chance of success. This is the period when original and dynamic impulses are being reflected onto the earth. The energies are extremely vital and favor the pursuit of pleasure and adventure in practically every form. Sick people should feel an improvement. Those who are well will probably find themselves exuding confidence and optimism. People fond of physical exercise should find their bodies growing with tone and well-being. Boldness, strength, determination should characterize most of your activities with a readiness to face up to old challenges. Yesterday's problems may seem petty and exaggerated—so deal with them. Strike out alone. Self-reliance will attract others to you. This is a good time for making friends. Business and marriage partners are more likely to be impressed with the man and woman of action. Opposition will be overcome or thrown aside with much less effort than usual. CAUTION: Be dominant but not domineering.

MOON IN TAURUS

The spontaneous, action-packed person of yesterday gives way to the cautious, diligent, hardworking "thinker." In this period ideas will probably be concentrated on ways of improving finances. A great deal of time may be spent figuring out and going over schemes and plans. It is the right time to be careful with detail. People will find themselves working longer than usual at their desks. Or devoting more time to serious thought about the future. A strong desire to put order into business and financial arrangements may cause extra work. Loved ones may complain of being neglected and may fail to appreciate that your efforts are for their ultimate benefit. Your desire for system may extend to criticism of arrangements in the home and lead to minor upsets. Health may be affected through overwork. Try to secure a reasonable amount of rest and relaxation, although the tendency will be to "keep going" despite good advice. Work done conscientiously in this period should result in a solid contribution to your future security. CAUTION: Try not to be as serious with people as the work you are engaged in.

MOON IN GEMINI

The humdrum of routine and too much work should suddenly end. You are likely to find yourself in an expansive, quicksilver world of change and self-expression. Urges to write, to paint, to experience the freedom of some sort of artistic outpouring, may be very strong. Take full advantage of them. You may find yourself finishing something you began and put aside long ago. Or embarking on something new which could easily be prompted by a chance meeting, a new acquaintance, or even an advertisement. There may be a yearning for a change of scenery, the feeling to visit another country (not too far away), or at least to get away for a few days. This may result in short, quick journeys. Or, if you are planning a single visit, there may be some unexpected changes or detours on the way. Familiar activities will seem to give little satisfaction unless they contain a fresh element of excitement or expectation. The inclination will be towards untried pursuits, particularly those that allow you to express your inner nature. The accent is on new faces, new places. CAUTION: Do not be too quick to commit yourself emotionally.

MOON IN CANCER

Feelings of uncertainty and vague insecurity are likely to cause problems while the moon is in Cancer. Thoughts may turn frequently to the warmth of the home and the comfort of loved ones. Nostalgic impulses could cause you to bring out old photographs and letters and reflect on the days when your life seemed to be much more rewarding and less demanding. The love and understanding of parents and family may be important, and, if it is not forthcoming you may have to fight against a bit of self-pity. The cordiality of friends and the thought of good times with them that are sure to be repeated will help to restore you to a happier frame of mind. The feeling to be alone may follow minor setbacks or rebuffs at this time, but solitude is unlikely to help. Better to get on the telephone or visit someone. This period often causes peculiar dreams and up-surges of imaginative thinking which can be very helpful to authors of occult and mystical works. Preoccupation with the more person-al world of simple human needs should overshadow any material strivings. CAUTION: Do not spend too much time thinking—seek the company of loved ones or close friends.

MOON IN LEO

New horizons of exciting and rather extravagant activity open up. This is the time for exhilarating entertainment, glamorous and lavish parties, and expensive shopping sprees. Any merrymaking that relies upon your generosity as a host has every chance of being a spectacular success. You should find yourself right in the center of the fun, either as the life of the party or simply as a person whom happy people like to be with. Romance thrives in this heady at-mosphere and friendships are likely to explode unexpectedly into serious attachments. Children and younger people should be at-tracted to you and you may find yourself organizing a picnic or a visit to a fun-fair, the cinema or the seaside. The sunny company and vitality of youthful companions should help you to find some unsuspected energy. In career, you could find an opening for pro-motion or advancement. This should be the time to make a direct approach. The period favors those engaged in original research. CAUTION: Bask in popularity but not in flattery.

MOON IN VIRGO

Off comes the party cap and out steps the busy, practical worker. He wants to get his personal affairs straight, to rearrange them, if necessary, for more efficiency, so he will have more time for more work. He clears up his correspondence, pays outstanding bills, makes numerous phone calls. He is likely to make inquiries, or sign up for some new insurance and put money into gilt-edged invest-ment. Thoughts probably revolve around the need for future secur-ity—to tie up loose ends and clear the decks. There may be a ten-dency to be "finicky," to interfere in the routine of others, particu-larly friends and family members. The motive may be a genuine desire to help with suggestions for updating or streamlining their affairs, but these will probably not be welcomed. Sympathy may be felt for less fortunate sections of the community and a flurry of some sort of voluntary service is likely. This may be accompanied by strong feelings of responsibility on several fronts and health may suffer from extra efforts made. CAUTION: Everyone may not want your help or advice.

MOON IN LIBRA

These are days of harmony and agreement and you should find yourself at peace with most others. Relationships tend to be smooth and sweet-flowing. Friends may become closer and bonds deepen in mutual understanding. Hopes will be shared. Progress by cooperation could be the secret of success in every sphere. In business, established partnerships may flourish and new ones get off to a good start. Acquaintances could discover similar interests that lead to congenial discussions and rewarding exchanges of some sort. Love, as a unifying force, reaches its optimum. Marriage partners should find accord. Those who wed at this time face the prospect of a happy union. Cooperation and tolerance are felt to be stronger than dissension and impatience. The argumentative are not quite so loud in their bellowings, nor as inflexible in their attitudes. In the home, there should be a greater recognition of the other point of view and a readiness to put the wishes of the group before selfish insistence. This is a favorable time to join an art group. CAUTION: Do not be too independent—let others help you if they want to.

MOON IN SCORPIO

Driving impulses to make money and to economize are likely to cause upsets all round. No area of expenditure is likely to be spared the axe, including the household budget. This is a time when the desire to cut down on extravagance can become near fanatical. Care must be exercised to try to keep the aim in reasonable perspective. Others may not feel the same urgent need to save and may retaliate. There is a danger that possessions of sentimental value will be sold to realize cash for investment. Buying and selling of stock for quick profit is also likely. The attention may turn to having a good clean up round the home and at the office. Neglected jobs could suddenly be done with great bursts of energy. The desire for solitude may intervene. Self-searching thoughts could disturb. The sense of invisible and mysterious energies at work could cause some excitability. The reassurance of loves ones may help. CAUTION: Be kind to the people you love.

MOON IN SAGITTARIUS

These are days when you are likely to be stirred and elevated by discussions and reflections of a religious and philosophical nature. Ideas of far-away places may cause unusual response and excitement. A decision may be made to visit someone overseas, perhaps a person whose influence was important to your earlier character development. There could be a strong resolution to get away from present intellectual patterns, to learn new subjects and to meet more interesting people. The superficial may be rejected in all its forms. An impatience with old ideas and unimaginative contacts could lead to a change of companions and interests. There may be an upsurge of religious feeling and metaphysical inquiry. Even a new insight into the significance of astrology and other occult studies is likely under the curious stimulus of the moon in Sagittarius. Physically, you may express this need for fundamental change by spending more time outdoors: sports, gardening or going for long walks. CAUTION: Try to channel any restlessness into worthwhile study.

MOON IN CAPRICORN

Life in these hours may seem to pivot around the importance of gaining prestige and honor in the career, as well as maintaining a spotless reputation. Ambitious urges may be excessive and could be accompanied by quite acquisitive drives for money. Effort should be directed along strictly ethical lines where there is no possibility of reproach or scandal. All endeavors are likely to be characterized by great earnestness, and an air of authority and purpose which should impress those who are looking for leadership or reliability. The desire to conform to accepted standards may extend to sharp criticism of family members. Frivolity and unconventional actions are unlikely to amuse while the moon is in Capricorn. Moderation and seriousness are the orders of the day. Achievement and recognition in this period could come through community work or organizing for the benefit of some amateur group. CAUTION: Dignity and esteem are not always self-awarded.

MOON IN AQUARIUS

Moon in Aquarius is in the second last sign of the Zodiac where ideas can become disturbingly fine and subtle. The result is often a mental "no-man's land" where imagination cannot be trusted with the same certitude as other times. The dangers for the individual are the extremes of optimism and pessimism. Unless the imgination is held in check, situations are likely to be misread, and rosy conclusions drawn where they do not exist. Consequences for the unwary can be costly in career and business. Best to think twice and not speak or act until you think again. Pessimism can be a cruel self-inflicted penalty for delusion at this time. Between the two extremes are strange areas of self-deception which, for example, can make the selfish person think he is actually being generous. Eerie dreams which resemble the reality and even seem to continue into the waking state are also possible. CAUTION: Look for the fact and not just for the image in your mind.

MOON IN PISCES

Everything seems to come to the surface now. Memory may be crystal clear, throwing up long-forgotten information which could be valuable in the career or business. Flashes of clairvoyance and intuition are possible along with sudden realizations of one's own nature, which may be used for self-improvement. A talent, never before suspected, may be discovered. Qualities not evident before in friends and marriage partners are likely to be noticed. As this is a period in which the truth seems to emerge, the discovery of false characteristics is likely to lead to disenchantment or a shift in attachments. However, where qualities are realized it should lead to happiness and deeper feeling. Surprise solutions could bob up for old problems. There may be a public announcement of the solving of a crime or mystery. People with secrets may find someone has "guessed" correctly. The secrets of the soul or the inner self also tend to reveal themselves. Religious and philosophical groups may make some interesting discoveries. CAUTION: Not a time for activities that depend on secrecy.

MOON TABLES

TIME CORRECTIONS FOR GREENWICH MOON TABLES

London, Glasgow, Dublin, Lisbon, Gibraltar........Same time

Vienna, Prague, Rome, Kinshasa, Frankfurt,
  Stockholm, Brussels, Amsterdam, Warsaw,
  Zurich..Add 1 hour

Bucharest, Istanbul, Beirut, Cairo, Johannesburg,
  Athens, Cape Town, Helsinki, Tel Aviv........Add 2 hours

Dhahran, Baghdad, Moscow, Leningrad, Nairobi,
  Addis Ababa, Zanzibar.......................Add 3 hours

Delhi, Calcutta, Bombay, Colombo ....Add 5½ hours

Rangoon ....Add 6½ hours

Saigon, Bangkok, Chungking....................Add 7 hours

Canton, Manila, Hong Kong, Shanghai, Peking ...Add 8 hours

Tokyo, Pusan, Seoul, Vladivostok, Yokohama ....Add 9 hours

Sydney, Melbourne, Guam, Port Moresby ....Add 10 hours

Azores, Reykjavik.............................Deduct 1 hour

Rio de Janeiro, Montevideo, Buenos Aires,
  Sao Paulo, Recife ....Deduct 3 hours

LaPaz, San Juan, Santiago, Bermuda, Caracas,
  Halifax ....Deduct 4 hours

New York, Washington, Boston, Detroit, Lima,
  Havana, Miami, Bogota....................Deduct 5 hours

Mexico, Chicago, New Orleans, Houston ......Deduct 6 hours

San Francisco, Seattle, Los Angeles, Hollywood,
  Ketchikan, Juneau.........................Deduct 8 hours

Honolulu, Fairbanks, Anchorage, Papeete.....Deduct 10 hours

1992 MOON TABLES—GREENWICH TIME

JANUARY		FEBRUARY		MARCH	
Day Moon Enters		**Day Moon Enters**		**Day Moon Enters**	
1. Sagitt.	7:30 am	1. Capric.		1. Aquar.	
2. Sagitt.		2. Aquar.	2:09 pm	2. Aquar.	
3. Capric.	7:09 pm	3. Aquar.		3. Pisces	9:11 am
4. Capric.		4. Aquar.		4. Pisces	
5. Capric.		5. Pisces	2:51 am	5. Aries	8:07 pm
6. Aquar.	7:59 am	6. Pisces		6. Aries	
7. Aquar.		7. Aries	2:15 pm	7. Aries	
8. Pisces	8:52 pm	8. Aries		8. Taurus	5:05 am
9. Pisces		9. Taurus	11:36 pm	9. Taurus	
10. Pisces		10. Taurus		10. Gemini	12:03 pm
11. Aries	8:22 am	11. Taurus		11. Gemini	
12. Aries		12. Gemini	6:08 am	12. Cancer	4:50 pm
13. Taurus	5:00 pm	13. Gemini		13. Cancer	
14. Taurus		14. Cancer	9:31 am	14. Leo	7:20 pm
15. Gemini	9:55 pm	15. Cancer		15. Leo	
16. Gemini		16. Leo	10:15 am	16. Virgo	8:13 pm
17. Cancer	11:26 pm	17. Leo		17. Virgo	
18. Cancer		18. Virgo	9:47 am	18. Libra	8:55 pm
19. Leo	10:57 pm	19. Virgo		19. Libra	
20. Leo		20. Libra	10:04 am	20. Scorpio	11:20 pm
21. Virgo	10:22 pm	21. Libra		21. Scorpio	
22. Virgo		22. Scorpio	1:11 pm	22. Scorpio	
23. Libra	11:42 pm	23. Scorpio		23. Sagitt.	5:13 am
24. Libra		24. Sagitt.	8:26 pm	24. Sagitt.	
25. Libra		25. Sagitt.		25. Capric.	3:08 pm
26. Scorpio	4:32 am	26. Sagitt.		26. Capric.	
27. Scorpio		27. Capric.	7:33 am	27. Capric.	
28. Sagitt.	1:20 pm	28. Capric.		28. Aquar.	3:44 am
29. Sagitt.		29. Aquar.	8:34 pm	29. Aquar.	
30. Sagitt.				30. Pisces	4:23 pm
31. Capric.	1:07 am			31. Pisces	

Summer time to be considered where applicable.

1992 MOON TABLES—GREENWICH TIME

APRIL		MAY		JUNE	
Day Moon Enters		**Day Moon Enters**		**Day Moon Enters**	
1. Pisces		1. Taurus	7:09 pm	1. Gemini	
2. Aries	3:04 am	2. Taurus		2. Cancer	11:58 am
3. Aries		3. Taurus		3. Cancer	
4. Taurus	11:18 am	4. Gemini	0:28 am	4. Leo	1:35 pm
5. Taurus		5. Gemini		5. Leo	
6. Gemini	5:33 pm	6. Cancer	4:09 am	6. Virgo	3:28 pm
7. Gemini		7. Cancer		7. Virgo	
8. Cancer	10:18 pm	8. Leo	7:07 am	8. Libra	6:33 pm
9. Cancer		9. Leo		9. Libra	
10. Cancer		10. Virgo	9:56 am	10. Scorpio	11:27 pm
11. Leo	1:46 am	11. Virgo		11. Scorpio	
12. Leo		12. Libra	1:05 pm	12. Scorpio	
13. Virgo	4:09 am	13. Libra		13. Sagitt.	6:29 am
14. Virgo		14. Scorpio	5:15 pm	14. Sagitt.	
15. Libra	6:10 am	15. Scorpio		15. Capric.	3:50 pm
16. Libra		16. Sagitt.	11:22 pm	16. Capric.	
17. Scorpio	9:10 am	17. Sagitt.		17. Capric.	
18. Scorpio		18. Sagitt.		18. Aquar.	3:19 am
19. Sagitt.	2:40 pm	19. Capric.	8:13 am	19. Aquar.	
20. Sagitt.		20. Capric.		20. Pisces	4:00 pm
21. Capric.	11:41 pm	21. Aquar.	7:43 pm	21. Pisces	
22. Capric.		22. Aquar.		22. Pisces	
23. Capric.		23. Aquar.		23. Aries	4:03 am
24. Aquar.	11:38 am	24. Pisces	8:25 am	24. Aries	
25. Aquar.		25. Pisces		25. Taurus	1:28 pm
26. Aquar.		26. Aries	7:53 pm	26. Taurus	
27. Pisces	0:20 am	27. Aries		27. Gemini	7:14 pm
28. Pisces		28. Aries		28. Gemini	
29. Aries	11:13 am	29. Taurus	4:16 am	29. Cancer	9:42 pm
30. Aries		30. Taurus		30. Cancer	
		31. Gemini	9:19 am		

Summer time to be considered where applicable.

1992 MOON TABLES—GREENWICH TIME

JULY		AUGUST		SEPTEMBER	
Day Moon Enters		**Day Moon Enters**		**Day Moon Enters**	
1. Leo	10:15 pm	1. Virgo		1. Scorpio	
2. Leo		2. Libra	8:17 am	2. Scorpio	
3. Virgo	10:37 pm	3. Libra		3. Sagitt.	0:50 am
4. Virgo		4. Scorpio	11:16 am	4. Sagitt.	
5. Virgo		5. Scorpio		5. Capric.	10:06 am
6. Libra	0:27 am	6. Sagitt.	5:57 pm	6. Capric.	
7. Libra		7. Sagitt.		7. Aquar.	10:08 pm
8. Scorpio	4:53 am	8. Sagitt.		8. Aquar.	
9. Scorpio		9. Capric.	4:00 am	9. Aquar.	
10. Sagitt.	12:17 pm	10. Capric.		10. Pisces	10:56 am
11. Sagitt.		11. Aquar.	4:07 pm	11. Pisces	
12. Capric.	10:16 pm	12. Aquar.		12. Aries	11:02 pm
13. Capric.		13. Aquar.		13. Aries	
14. Capric.		14. Pisces	4:51 am	14. Aries	
15. Aquar.	10:03 am	15. Pisces		15. Taurus	9:47 am
16. Aquar.		16. Aries	5:11 pm	16. Taurus	
17. Pisces	10:33 pm	17. Aries		17. Gemini	6:40 pm
18. Pisces		18. Aries		18. Gemini	
19. Pisces		19. Taurus	4:10 am	19. Gemini	
20. Aries	11:07 am	20. Taurus		20. Cancer	0:59 am
21. Aries		21. Gemini	12:36 pm	21. Cancer	
22. Taurus	9:36 pm	22. Gemini		22. Leo	4:19 am
23. Taurus		23. Cancer	5:36 pm	23. Leo	
24. Taurus		24. Cancer		24. Virgo	5:08 am
25. Gemini	4:44 am	25. Leo	7:15 pm	25. Virgo	
26. Gemini		26. Leo		26. Libra	4:55 am
27. Cancer	8:08 am	27. Virgo	6:46 pm	27. Libra	
28. Cancer		28. Virgo		28. Scorpio	5:44 am
29. Leo	8:39 am	29. Libra	6:11 pm	29. Scorpio	
30. Leo		30. Libra		30. Sagitt.	9:33 am
31. Virgo	8:01 am	31. Scorpio	7:38 pm		

Summer time to be considered where applicable.

1992 MOON TABLES—GREENWICH TIME

OCTOBER Day Moon Enters		NOVEMBER Day Moon Enters		DECEMBER Day Moon Enters	
1. Sagitt.		1. Aquar.	12:43 pm	1. Pisces	9:23 am
2. Capric.	5:29 pm	2. Aquar.		2. Pisces	
3. Capric.		3. Aquar.		3. Aries	9:49 pm
4. Capric.		4. Pisces	1:13 am	4. Aries	
5. Aquar.	4:53 am	5. Pisces		5. Aries	
6. Aquar.		6. Aries	1:19 pm	6. Taurus	8:16 am
7. Pisces	5:38 pm	7. Aries		7. Taurus	
8. Pisces		8. Taurus	11:16 pm	8. Gemini	3:37 pm
9. Pisces		9. Taurus		9. Gemini	
10. Aries	5:36 am	10. Taurus		10. Cancer	8:05 pm
11. Aries		11. Gemini	6:49 am	11. Cancer	
12. Taurus	3:48 pm	12. Gemini		12. Leo	10:47 pm
13. Taurus		13. Cancer	12:19 pm	13. Leo	
14. Taurus		14. Cancer		14. Leo	
15. Gemini	0:08 am	15. Leo	4:23 pm	15. Virgo	0:56 am
16. Gemini		16. Leo		16. Virgo	
17. Cancer	6:36 am	17. Virgo	7:28 pm	17. Libra	3:33 am
18. Cancer		18. Virgo		18. Libra	
19. Leo	11:01 am	19. Libra	10:03 pm	19. Scorpio	7:20 am
20. Leo		20. Libra		20. Scorpio	
21. Virgo	1:27 pm	21. Libra		21. Sagitt.	12:47 pm
22. Virgo		22. Scorpio	0:52 am	22. Sagitt.	
23. Libra	2:39 pm	23. Scorpio		23. Capric.	8:04 pm
24. Libra		24. Sagitt.	5:01 am	24. Capric.	
25. Scorpio	4:04 pm	25. Sagitt.		25. Capric.	
26. Scorpio		26. Capric.	11:38 am	26. Aquar.	5:43 am
27. Sagitt.	7:29 pm	27. Capric.		27. Aquar.	
28. Sagitt.		28. Aquar.	9:19 pm	28. Pisces	5:28 pm
29. Sagitt.		29. Aquar.		29. Pisces	
30. Capric.	2:18 am	30. Aquar.		30. Pisces	
31. Capric.				31. Aries	6:07 am

Summer time to be considered where applicable.

1992 PHASES OF THE MOON—GREENWICH TIME

New Moon	First Quarter	Full Moon	Last Quarter
Jan. 4	Jan. 13	Jan. 19	Jan. 26
Feb. 3	Feb. 11	Feb. 18	Feb. 25
Mar. 4	Mar. 12	Mar. 18	Mar. 26
Apr. 3	Apr. 10	Apr. 17	Apr. 24
May 2	May 9	May 16	May 24
June 1	June 7	June 15	June 23
June 30	July 7	July 14	July 22
July 29	Aug. 5	Aug. 13	Aug. 21
Aug. 28	Sep. 3	Sep. 12	Sep. 19
Sep. 26	Oct. 3	Oct. 11	Oct. 19
Oct. 25	Nov. 2	Nov. 10	Nov. 17
Nov. 24	Dec. 2	Dec. 9	Dec. 16
Dec. 24	(1993)	(1993)	(1993)

Summer time to be considered where applicable.

1992 PLANTING GUIDE

	Aboveground Crops	Root Crops	Pruning	Weeds Pests
January	1-4-9-10-11-18-19	24-25-26	12-13	20-21
February	6-7-15-16	1-2-21-22-28-29	13-14	17-18
March	4-5-13-14-17	19-20-26-27-28	12-15-16	29-30
April	9-10-11-14-15	17-22-23-24	12-13	25-26-27
May	7-8-11-12--15-16	20-21-30-31	9-10	24
June	3-4-7-8-11-12-13	16-17-18-26-27	14-15	28-29
July	18-19-20-28-29	14-15-23-24-25	11-12	13-14-15
August	15-16-24-25-28	20-21	7-8-9	12-13
September	12-21-22-25-26	16-17-27-28	4-5	9-10
October	18-19-22-23	13-14-15-24	11-12	6-7
November	14-15-18-19-23	13-20-21-22	7-8	2-3-4
December	11-12-16-17-20-21	18-19	4-5-6	1-9-10

1992 FISHING GUIDE

	Good	Best
January	3-5-8-10-15-21-28	1-9-18-27
February	1-7-11-14-19-24-29	6-15-23
March	5-7-12-14-20-25-27	4-13-21-31
April	1-6-10-12-14-20-25-27	1-9-18-28
May	3-5-10-11-18-21-26	7-15-25
June	1-6-12-17-20-22	3-11-21-30
July	5-10-20-21-25-30	1-9-18-28
August	1-4-10-18-25-27-29-31	5-15-24
September	7-10-17-22-24-25-30	1-11-21-29
October	5-16-19-21-23-27	8-18-26
November	6-10-15-19-24	5-14-23
December	3-8-12-16-19-21-22-25	2-11-20-29

MOON'S INFLUENCE OVER DAILY AFFAIRS

The Moon makes a complete transit of the Zodiac every 27 days 7 hours and 43 minutes. In making this transit the Moon forms different aspects with the planets and consequently has favorable or unfavorable bearings on affairs and events for persons according to the sign of the Zodiac under which they were born. Whereas the Sun exclusively represents fire, the Moon rules water. The action of the Moon may be described as fluctuating, variable, absorbent and receptive.

When the Moon is in conjunction with the Sun it is called a New Moon; when the Moon and Sun are in opposition it is called a Full Moon. From New Moon to Full Moon, first and second quarter—which takes about two weeks—the Moon is increasing or waxing. From Full Moon to New Moon, third and fourth quarter, the Moon is decreasing or waning. The Moon Table indicates the New Moon and Full Moon and the quarters.

ACTIVITY	MOON IN
Business:	
buying and selling	Sagittarius, Aries, Gemini, Virgo
new, requiring public support	1st and 2nd quarter
meant to be kept quiet	3rd and 4th quarter
Investigation	3rd and 4th quarter
Signing documents	1st & 2nd quarter, Cancer, Scorpio, Pisces
Advertising	2nd quarter, Sagittarius
Journeys and trips	1st & 2nd quarter, Gemini, Virgo
Renting offices, etc.	Taurus, Leo, Scorpio, Aquarius
Painting of house/apartment	3rd & 4th quarter, Taurus, Scorpio, Aquarius
Decorating	Gemini, Libra, Aquarius
Buying clothes and accessories	Taurus, Virgo
Beauty salon or barber shop visit	1st & 2nd quarter, Taurus, Leo, Libra, Scorpio, Aquarius
Weddings	1st & 2nd quarter

MOON'S INFLUENCE OVER YOUR HEALTH

ARIES	Head, brain, face, upper jaw
TAURUS	Throat, neck, lower jaw
GEMINI	Hands, arms, lungs, shoulders, nervous system
CANCER	Esophagus, stomach, breasts, womb, liver
LEO	Heart, spine
VIRGO	Intestines, liver
LIBRA	Kidneys, lower back
SCORPIO	Sex and eliminative organs
SAGITTARIUS	Hips, thighs, liver
CAPRICORN	Skin, bones, teeth, knees
AQUARIUS	Circulatory system, lower legs
PISCES	Feet, tone of being

Try to avoid work being done on that part of the body when the Moon is in the sign governing that part.

MOON'S INFLUENCE OVER PLANTS

Centuries ago it was established that seeds planted when the Moon is in certain signs and phases called Fruitful will produce more growth than seeds planted when the Moon is in a Barren sign.

FRUITFUL SIGNS	BARREN SIGNS	DRY SIGNS
Taurus	Aries	Aries
Cancer	Gemini	Gemini
Libra	Leo	Sagittarius
Scorpio	Virgo	Aquarius
Capricorn	Sagittarius	
Pisces	Aquarius	

ACTIVITY	MOON IN
Mow lawn, trim plants	**Fruitful sign:** 1st & 2nd quarter
Plant flowers	**Fruitful sign:** 2nd quarter; best in Cancer and Libra
Prune	**Fruitful sign:** 3rd & 4th quarter
Destroy pests; spray	**Barren sign:** 4th quarter
Harvest potatoes, root crops	**Dry sign:** 3rd & 4th quarter; Taurus, Leo, and Aquarius

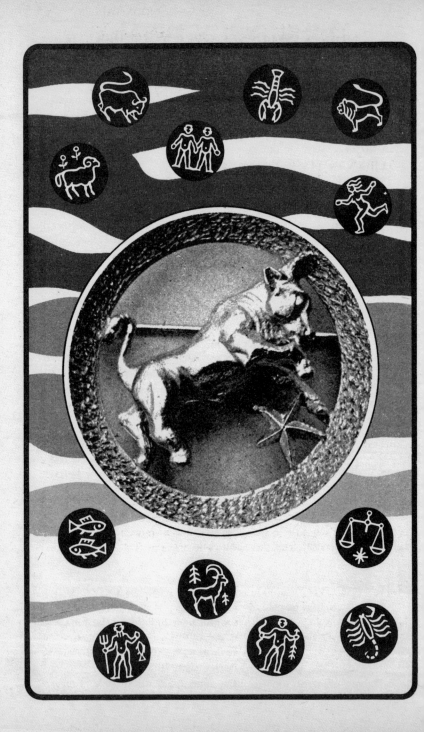

THE SIGNS: DOMINANT CHARACTERISTICS

March 21–April 20

The Positive Side of Aries

The Arien has many positive points to his character. People born under this first sign of the Zodiac are often quite strong and enthusiastic. On the whole, they are forward-looking people who are not easily discouraged by temporary setbacks. They know what they want out of life and they go out after it. Their personalities are strong. Others are usually quite impressed by the Arien's way of doing things. Quite often they are sources of inspiration for others traveling the same route. Aries men and women have a special zest for life that is often contagious; for others, they are often the example of how life should be lived.

The Aries person usually has a quick and active mind. He is imaginative and inventive. He enjoys keeping busy and active. He generally gets along well with all kinds of people. He is interested in mankind, as a whole. He likes to be challenged. Some would say he thrives on opposition, for it is when he is set against that he often does his best. Getting over or around obstacles is a challenge he generally enjoys. All in all, the Arien is quite positive and young-thinking. He likes to keep abreast of new things that are happening in the world. Ariens are often fond of speed. They like things to be done quickly and this sometimes aggravates their slower colleagues and associates.

The Aries man or woman always seems to remain young. Their whole approach to life is youthful and optimistic. They never say die, no matter what the odds. They may have an occasional setback, but it is not long before they are back on their feet again.

The Negative Side of Aries

Everybody has his less positive qualities—and Aries is no exception. Sometimes the Aries man or woman is not very tactful in communicating with others; in his hurry to get things done he is apt to

be a little callous or inconsiderate. Sensitive people are likely to find him somewhat sharp-tongued in some situations. Often in his eagerness to achieve his aims, he misses the mark altogether. At times the Arien is too impulsive. He can occasionally be stubborn and refuse to listen to reason. If things do not move quickly enough to suit the Aries man or woman, he or she is apt to become rather nervous or irritable. The uncultivated Arien is not unfamiliar with moments of doubt and fear. He is capable of being destructive if he does not get his way. He can overcome some of his emotional problems by steadily trying to express himself as he really is, but this requires effort.

April 21–May 20

The Positive Side of Taurus

The Taurus person is known for his ability to concentrate and for his tenacity. These are perhaps his strongest qualities. The Taurus man or woman generally has very little trouble in getting along with others; it's his nature to be helpful toward people in need. He can always be depended on by his friends, especially those in trouble.

The Taurean generally achieves what he wants through his ability to persevere. He never leaves anything unfinished but works on something until it has been completed. People can usually take him at his word; he is honest and forthright in most of his dealings. The Taurus person has a good chance to make a success of his life because of his many positive qualities. The Taurean who aims high seldom falls short of his mark. He learns well by experience. He is thorough and does not believe in short-cuts of any kind. The Taurean's thoroughness pays off in the end, for through his deliberateness he learns how to rely on himself and what he has learned. The Taurus person tries to get along with others, as a rule. He is not overly critical and likes people to be themselves. He is a tolerant person and enjoys peace and harmony—especially in his home life.

The Taurean is usually cautious in all that he does. He is not a person who believes in taking unnecessary risks. Before adopting any one line of action, he will weigh all of the pros and cons. The

Taurus person is steadfast. Once his mind is made up it seldom changes. The person born under this sign usually is a good family person—reliable and loving.

The Negative Side of Taurus

Sometimes the Taurus man or woman is a bit too stubborn. He won't listen to other points of view if his mind is set on something. To others, this can be quite annoying. The Taurean also does not like to be told what to do. He becomes rather angry if others think him not too bright. He does not like to be told he is wrong, even when he is. He dislikes being contradicted.

Some people who are born under this sign are very suspicious of others—even of those persons close to them. They find it difficult to trust people fully. They are often afraid of being deceived or taken advantage of. The Taurean often finds it difficult to forget or forgive. His love of material things sometimes makes him rather avaricious and petty.

May 21–June 20

The Positive Side of Gemini

The person born under this sign of the Heavenly Twins is usually quite bright and quick-witted. Some of them are capable of doing many different things. The Gemini person very often has many different interests. He keeps an open mind and is always anxious to learn new things.

The Geminian is often an analytical person. He is a person who enjoys making use of his intellect. He is governed more by his mind than by his emotions. He is a person who is not confined to one view; he can often understand both sides to a problem or question. He knows how to reason; how to make rapid decisions if need be.

He is an adaptable person and can make himself at home almost anywhere. There are all kinds of situations he can adapt to. He is a person who seldom doubts himself; he is sure of his talents and his

ability to think and reason. The Geminian is generally most satisfied when he is in a situation where he can make use of his intellect. Never short of imagination, he often has strong talents for invention. He is rather a modern person when it comes to life; the Geminian almost always moves along with the times—perhaps that is why he remains so youthful throughout most of his life.

Literature and art appeal to the person born under this sign. Creativity in almost any form will interest and intrigue the Gemini man or woman.

The Geminian is often quite charming. A good talker, he often is the center of attraction at any gathering. People find it easy to like a person born under this sign because he can appear easygoing and usually has a good sense of humor.

The Negative Side of Gemini

Sometimes the Gemini person tries to do too many things at one time—and as a result, winds up finishing nothing. Some Geminians are easily distracted and find it rather difficult to concentrate on one thing for too long a time. Sometimes they give in to trifling fancies and find it rather boring to become too serious about any one thing. Some of them are never dependable, no matter what they promise.

Although the Gemini man or woman often appears to be well-versed on many subjects, this is sometimes just a veneer. His knowledge may be only superficial, but because he speaks so well he gives people the impression of erudition. Some Geminians are sharp-tongued and inconsiderate; they think only of themselves and their own pleasure.

June 21–July 20

The Positive Side of Cancer

The Cancerians's most positive point is his understanding nature. On the whole, he is a loving and sympathetic person. He would never go out of his way to hurt anyone. The Cancer man or woman

is often very kind and tender; they give what they can to others. They hate to see others suffering and will do what they can to help someone in less fortunate circumstances than themselves. They are often very concerned about the world. Their interest in people generally goes beyond that of just their own families and close friends; they have a deep sense of brotherhood and respect humanitarian values. The Cancerian means what he says, as a rule; he is honest about his feelings.

The Cancer man or woman is a person who knows the art of patience. When something seems difficult, he is willing to wait until the situation becomes manageable again. He is a person who knows how to bide his time. The Cancerian knows how to concentrate on one thing at a time. When he has made his mind up he generally sticks with what he does, seeing it through to the end.

The Cancerian is a person who loves his home. He enjoys being surrounded by familiar things and the people he loves. Of all the signs, Cancer is the most maternal. Even the men born under this sign often have a motherly or protective quality about them. They like to take care of people in their family—to see that they are well loved and well provided for. They are usually loyal and faithful. Family ties mean a lot to the Cancer man or woman. Parents and in-laws are respected and loved. The Cancerian has a strong sense of tradition. He is very sensitive to the moods of others.

The Negative Side of Cancer

Sometimes the Cancerian finds it rather hard to face life. It becomes too much for him. He can be a little timid and retiring, when things don't go too well. When unfortunate things happen, he is apt to just shrug and say, "Whatever will be will be." He can be fatalistic to a fault. The uncultivated Cancerian is a bit lazy. He doesn't have very much ambition. Anything that seems a bit difficult he'll gladly leave to others. He may be lacking in initiative. Too sensitive, when he feels he's been injured, he'll crawl back into his shell and nurse his imaginary wounds. The Cancer woman often is given to crying when the smallest thing goes wrong.

Some Cancerians find it difficult to enjoy themselves in environments outside their homes. They make heavy demands on others, and need to be constantly reassured that they are loved.

July 21–August 21

The Positive Side of Leo

Often Leos make good leaders. They seem to be good organizers and administrators. Usually they are quite popular with others. Whatever group it is that he belongs to, the Leo man is almost sure to be or become the leader.

The Leo person is generous most of the time. It is his best characteristic. He or she likes to give gifts and presents. In making others happy, the Leo person becomes happy himself. He likes to splurge when spending money on others. In some instances it may seem that the Leo's generosity knows no boundaries. A hospitable person, the Leo man or woman is very fond of welcoming people to his house and entertaining them. He is never short of company.

The Leo person has plenty of energy and drive. He enjoys working toward some specific goal. When he applies himself correctly, he gets what he wants most often. The Leo person is almost never unsure of himself. He has plenty of confidence and aplomb. He is a person who is direct in almost everything he does. He has a quick mind and can make a decision in a very short time.

He usually sets a good example for others because of his ambitious manner and positive ways. He knows how to stick to something once he's started. Although the Leo person may be good at making a joke, he is not superficial or glib. He is a loving person, kind and thoughtful.

There is generally nothing small or petty about the Leo man or woman. He does what he can for those who are deserving. He is a person others can rely upon at all times. He means what he says. An honest person, generally speaking, he is a friend that others value.

The Negative Side of Leo

Leo, however, does have his faults. At times, he can be just a bit too arrogant. He thinks that no one deserves a leadership position except him. Only he is capable of doing things well. His opinion of himself is often much too high. Because of his conceit, he is sometimes rather unpopular with a good many people. Some Leos are too materialistic; they can only think in terms of money and profit.

Some Leos enjoy lording it over others—at home or at their place of business. What is more, they feel they have the right to. Egocentric to an impossible degree, this sort of Leo cares little about how others think or feel. He can be rude and cutting.

August 22–September 22

The Positive Side of Virgo

The person born under the sign of Virgo is generally a busy person. He knows how to arrange and organize things. He is a good planner. Above all, he is practical and is not afraid of hard work.

The person born under this sign, Virgo, knows how to attain what he desires. He sticks with something until it is finished. He never shirks his duties, and can always be depended upon. The Virgo person can be thoroughly trusted at all times.

The man or woman born under this sign tries to do everything to perfection. He doesn't believe in doing anything half-way. He always aims for the top. He is the sort of a person who is constantly striving to better himself—not because he wants more money or glory, but because it gives him a feeling of accomplishment.

The Virgo man or woman is a very observant person. He is sensitive to how others feel, and can see things below the surface of a situation. He usually puts this talent to constructive use.

It is not difficult for the Virgoan to be open and earnest. He believes in putting his cards on the table. He is never secretive or under-handed. He's as good as his word. The Virgo person is generally plain-spoken and down-to-earth. He has no trouble in expressing himself.

The Virgo person likes to keep up to date on new developments in his particular field. Well-informed, generally, he sometimes has a keen interest in the arts or literature. What he knows, he knows well. His ability to use his critical faculties is well-developed and sometimes startles others because of its accuracy.

The Virgoan adheres to a moderate way of life; he avoids excesses. He is a responsible person and enjoys being of service.

The Negative Side of Virgo

Sometimes a Virgo person is too critical. He thinks that only he can do something the way it should be done. Whatever anyone else does is inferior. He can be rather annoying in the way he quibbles over insignificant details. In telling others how things should be done, he can be rather tactless and mean.

Some Virgos seem rather emotionless and cool. They feel emo-

tional involvement is beneath them. They are sometimes too tidy, too neat. With money they can be rather miserly. Some try to force their opinions and ideas on others.

September 23–October 22

The Positive Side of Libra

Librans love harmony. It is one of their most outstanding character traits. They are interested in achieving balance; they admire beauty and grace in things as well as in people. Generally speaking, they are kind and considerate people. Librans are usually very sympathetic. They go out of their way not to hurt another person's feelings. They are outgoing and do what they can to help those in need.

People born under the sign of Libra almost always make good friends. They are loyal and amiable. They enjoy the company of others. Many of them are rather moderate in their views; they believe in keeping an open mind, however, and weighing both sides of an issue fairly before making a decision.

Alert and often intelligent, the Libran, always fair-minded, tries to put himself in the position of the other person. They are against injustice; quite often they take up for the underdog. In most of their social dealings, they try to be tactful and kind. They dislike discord and bickering, and most Libras strive for peace and harmony in all their relationships.

The Libra man or woman has a keen sense of beauty. They appreciate handsome furnishings and clothes. Many of them are artistically inclined. Their taste is usually impeccable. They know how to use color. Their homes are almost always attractively arranged and inviting. They enjoy entertaining people and see to it that their guests always feel at home and welcome.

The Libran gets along with almost everyone. He is well-liked and socially much in demand.

The Negative Side of Libra

Some people born under this sign tend to be rather insincere. So eager are they to achieve harmony in all relationships that they will even go so far as to lie. Many of them are escapists. They find facing

the truth an ordeal and prefer living in a world of make-believe.

In a serious argument, some Librans give in rather easily even when they know they are right. Arguing, even about something they believe in, is too unsettling for some of them.

Librans sometimes care too much for material things. They enjoy possessions and luxuries. Some are vain and tend to be jealous.

October 23–November 22

The Positive Side of Scorpio

The Scorpio man or woman generally knows what he or she wants out of life. He is a determined person. He sees something through to the end. The Scorpion is quite sincere, and seldom says anything he doesn't mean. When he sets a goal for himself he tries to go about achieving it in a very direct way.

The Scorpion is brave and courageous. They are not afraid of hard work. Obstacles do not frighten them. They forge ahead until they achieve what they set out for. The Scorpio man or woman has a strong will.

Although the Scorpion may seem rather fixed and determined, inside he is often quite tender and loving. He can care very much for others. He believes in sincerity in all relationships. His feelings about someone tend to last; they are profound and not superficial.

The Scorpio person is someone who adheres to his principles no matter what happens. He will not be deterred from a path he believes to be right.

Because of his many positive strengths, the Scorpion can often achieve happiness for himself and for those that he loves.

He is a constructive person by nature. He often has a deep understanding of people and of life, in general. He is perceptive and unafraid. Obstacles often seem to spur him on. He is a positive person who enjoys winning. He has many strengths and resources; challenge of any sort often brings out the best in him.

The Negative Side of Scorpio

The Scorpio person is sometimes hypersensitive. Often he imagines injury when there is none. He feels that others do not bother to

recognize him for his true worth. Sometimes he is given to excessive boasting in order to compensate for what he feels is neglect

The Scorpio person can be rather proud and arrogant. They can be rather sly when they put their minds to it and they enjoy outwitting persons or institutions noted for their cleverness.

Their tactics for getting what they want are sometimes devious and ruthless. They don't care too much about what others may think. If they feel others have done them an injustice, they will do their best to seek revenge. The Scorpion often has a sudden, violent temper; and this person's interest in sex is sometimes quite unbalanced or excessive.

November 23–December 20

The Positive Side of Sagittarius

People born under this sign are often honest and forthright. Their approach to life is earnest and open. The Sagittarian is often quite adult in his way of seeing things. They are broadminded and tolerant people. When dealing with others the person born under the sign of Sagittarius is almost always open and forthright. He doesn't believe in deceit or pretension. His standards are high. People who associate with the Sagittarian, generally admire and respect him.

The Sagittarian trusts others easily and expects them to trust him. He is never suspicious or envious and almost always thinks well of others. People always enjoy his company because he is so friendly and easy-going. The Sagittarius man or woman is often good-humored. He can always be depended upon by his friends, family, and co-workers.

The person born under this sign of the Zodiac likes a good joke every now and then; he is keen on fun and this makes him very popular with others.

A lively person, he enjoys sports and outdoor life. The Sagittarian is fond of animals. Intelligent and interesting, he can begin an animated conversation with ease. He likes exchanging ideas and discussing various views.

He is not selfish or proud. If someone proposes an idea or plan that is better than his, he will immediately adopt it. Imaginative yet practical, he knows how to put ideas into practice.

He enjoys sport and game, and it doesn't matter if he wins or loses. He is a forgiving person, and never sulks over something that has not worked out in his favor.

He is seldom critical, and is almost always generous.

The Negative Side of Sagittarius

Some Sagittarians are restless. They take foolish risks and seldom learn from the mistakes they make. They don't have heads for money and are often mismanaging their finances. Some of them devote much of their time to gambling.

Some are too outspoken and tactless, always putting their feet in their mouths. They hurt others carelessly by being honest at the wrong time. Sometimes they make promises which they don't keep. They don't stick close enough to their plans and go from one failure to another. They are undisciplined and waste a lot of energy.

December 21–January 19

The Positive Side of Capricorn

The person born under the sign of Capricorn is usually very stable and patient. He sticks to whatever tasks he has and sees them through. He can always be relied upon and he is not averse to work.

An honest person, the Capricornian is generally serious about whatever he does. He does not take his duties lightly. He is a practical person and believes in keeping his feet on the ground.

Quite often the person born under this sign is ambitious and knows how to get what he wants out of life. He forges ahead and never gives up his goal. When he is determined about something, he almost always wins. He is a good worker—a hard worker. Although things may not come easy to him, he will not complain, but continue working until his chores are finished.

He is usually good at business matters and knows the value of money. He is not a spendthrift and knows how to put something away for a rainy day; he dislikes waste and unnecessary loss.

The Capricornian knows how to make use of his self-control. He

can apply himself to almost anything once he puts his mind to it. His ability to concentrate sometimes astounds others. He is diligent and does well when involved in detail work.

The Capricorn man or woman is charitable, generally speaking, and will do what is possible to help others less fortunate. As a friend, he is loyal and trustworthy. He never shirks his duties or responsibilities. He is self-reliant and never expects too much of the other fellow. He does what he can on his own. If someone does him a good turn, then he will do his best to return the favor.

The Negative Side of Capricorn

Like everyone, the Capricornian, too, has his faults. At times, he can be over-critical of others. He expects others to live up to his own high standards. He thinks highly of himself and tends to look down on others.

His interest in material things may be exaggerated. The Capricorn man or woman thinks too much about getting on in the world and having something to show for it. He may even be a little greedy.

He sometimes thinks he knows what's best for everyone. He is too bossy. He is always trying to organize and correct others. He may be a little narrow in his thinking.

January 20–February 18

The Positive Side of Aquarius

The Aquarius man or woman is usually very honest and forthright. These are his two greatest qualities. His standards for himself are generally very high. He can always be relied upon by others. His word is his bond.

The Aquarian is perhaps the most tolerant of all the Zodiac personalities. He respects other people's beliefs and feels that everyone is entitled to his own approach to life.

He would never do anything to injure another's feelings. He is never unkind or cruel. Always considerate of others, the Aquarian is always willing to help a person in need. He feels a very strong tie between himself and all the other members of mankind.

The person born under this sign is almost always an individualist. He does not believe in teaming up with the masses, but prefers going his own way. His ideas about life and mankind are often quite advanced. There is a saying to the effect that the average Aquarian is fifty years ahead of his time.

He is broadminded. The problems of the world concern him greatly. He is interested in helping others no matter what part of the globe they live in. He is truly a humanitarian sort. He likes to be of service to others.

Giving, considerate, and without prejudice, Aquarians have no trouble getting along with others.

The Negative Side of Aquarius

The Aquarian may be too much of a dreamer. He makes plans but seldom carries them out. He is rather unrealistic. His imagination has a tendency to run away with him. Because many of his plans are impractical, he is always in some sort of a dither.

Others may not approve of him at all times because of his unconventional behavior. He may be a bit eccentric. Sometimes he is so busy with his own thoughts, that he loses touch with the realities of existence.

Some Aquarians feel they are more clever and intelligent than others. They seldom admit to their own faults, even when they are quite apparent. Some become rather fanatic in their views. Their criticism of others is sometimes destructive and negative.

February 19–March 20

The Positive Side of Pisces

The Piscean can often understand the problems of others quite easily. He has a sympathetic nature. Kindly, he is often dedicated in the way he goes about helping others. The sick and the troubled often turn to him for advice and assistance.

He is very broadminded and does not criticize others for their faults. He knows how to accept people for what they are. On the whole, he is a trustworthy and earnest person. He is loyal to his

friends and will do what he can to help them in time of need. Generous and good-natured, he is a lover of peace; he is often willing to help others solve their differences. People who have taken a wrong turn in life often interest him and he will do what he can to persuade them to rehabilitate themselves.

He has a strong intuitive sense and most of the time he knows how to make it work for him; the Piscean is unusually perceptive and often knows what is bothering someone before that person, himself, is aware of it. The Pisces man or woman is an idealistic person, basically, and is interested in making the world a better place in which to live. The Piscean believes that everyone should help each other. He is willing to do more than his share in order to achieve cooperation with others.

The person born under this sign often is talented in music or art. He is a receptive person; he is able to take the ups and downs of life with philosophic calm.

The Negative Side of Pisces

Some Pisceans are often depressed; their outlook on life is rather glum. They may feel that they have been given a bad deal in life and that others are always taking unfair advantage of them. The Piscean sometimes feel that the world is a cold and cruel place. He is easily discouraged. He may even withdraw from the harshness of reality into a secret shell of his own where he dreams and idles away a good deal of his time.

The Piscean can be rather lazy. He lets things happen without giving the least bit of resistance. He drifts along, whether on the high road or on the low. He is rather short on willpower.

Some Pisces people seek escape through drugs or alcohol. When temptation comes along they find it hard to resist. In matters of sex, they can be rather permissive.

THE SIGNS AND
THEIR KEY WORDS

		POSITIVE	NEGATIVE
ARIES	self	courage, initiative, pioneer instinct	brash rudeness, selfish impetuosity
TAURUS	money	endurance, loyalty, wealth	obstinacy, gluttony
GEMINI	mind	versatility	capriciousness, unreliability
CANCER	family	sympathy, homing instinct	clannishness, childishness
LEO	children	love, authority, integrity	egotism, force
VIRGO	work	purity, industry, analysis	fault-finding, cynicism
LIBRA	marriage	harmony, justice	vacillation, superficiality
SCORPIO	sex	survival, regeneration	vengeance, discord
SAGITTARIUS	travel	optimism, higher learning	lawlessness
CAPRICORN	career	depth	narrowness, gloom
AQUARIUS	friends	human fellowship, genius	perverse unpredictability
PISCES	confine-ment	spiritual love, universality	diffusion, escapism

THE ELEMENTS AND QUALITIES OF THE SIGNS

ELEMENT	SIGN	QUALITY	SIGN
FIRE..................	ARIES LEO SAGITTARIUS	CARDINAL.........	ARIES LIBRA CANCER CAPRICORN
EARTH...............	TAURUS VIRGO CAPRICORN	FIXED................	TAURUS LEO SCORPIO AQUARIUS
AIR.....................	GEMINI LIBRA AQUARIUS	MUTABLE.........	GEMINI VIRGO SAGITTARIUS PISCES
WATER..............	CANCER SCORPIO PISCES		

Every sign has both an element and a quality associated with it. The element indicates the basic makeup of the sign, and the quality describes the kind of activity associated with each.

Signs can be grouped together according to their *element* and *quality*. Signs of the same element share many basic traits in common. They tend to form stable configurations and ultimately harmonious relationships. Signs of the same quality are often less harmonious, but they share many dynamic potentials for growth as well as profound fulfillment.

THE FIRE SIGNS

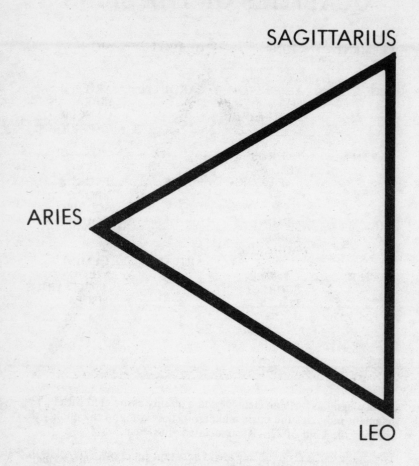

This is the fire group. On the whole these are emotional, volatile types, quick to anger, quick to forgive. They are adventurous, powerful people and act as a source of inspiration for everyone. They spark into action with immediate exuberant impulses. They are intelligent, self-involved, creative and idealistic. They all share a certain vibrancy and glow that outwardly reflects an inner flame and passion for living.

THE EARTH SIGNS

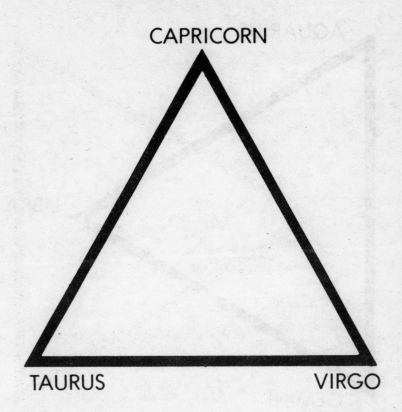

CAPRICORN

TAURUS

VIRGO

This is the earth group. They are in constant touch with the material world and tend to be conservative. Although they are all capable of spartan self-discipline, they are earthy, sensual people who are stimulated by the tangible, elegant and luxurious. The thread of their lives is always practical, but they do fantasize and are often attracted to dark, mysterious, emotional people. They are like great cliffs overhanging the sea, forever married to the ocean but always resisting erosion from the dark, emotional forces that thunder at their feet.

THE AIR SIGNS

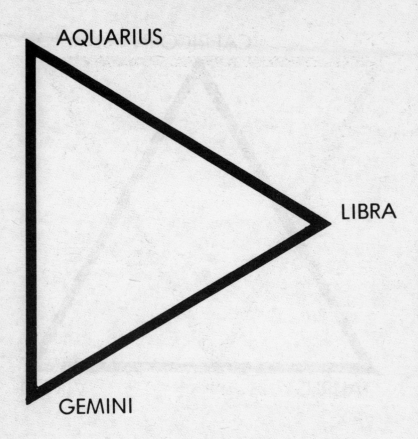

AQUARIUS

LIBRA

GEMINI

This is the air group. They are light, mental creatures desirous of contact, communication and relationship. They are involved with people and the forming of ties on many levels. Original thinkers, they are the bearers of human news. Their language is their sense of word, color, style and beauty. They provide an atmosphere suitable and pleasant for living. They add change and versatility to the scene, and it is through them that we can explore new territory of human intelligence and experience.

THE WATER SIGNS

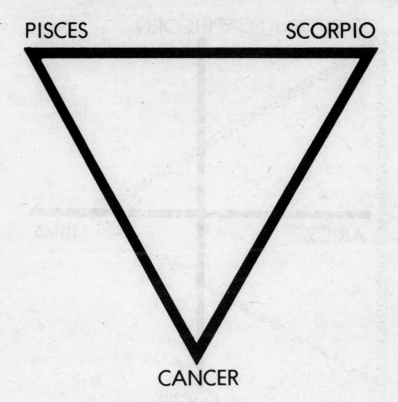

PISCES

SCORPIO

CANCER

This is the water group. Through the water people, we are all joined together on emotional, non-verbal levels. They are silent, mysterious types whose magic hypnotizes even the most determined realist. They have uncanny perceptions about people and are as rich as the oceans when it comes to feeling, emotion or imagination. They are sensitive, mystical creatures with memories that go back beyond time. Through water, life is sustained. These people have the potential for the depths of darkness or the heights of mysticism and art.

THE CARDINAL SIGNS

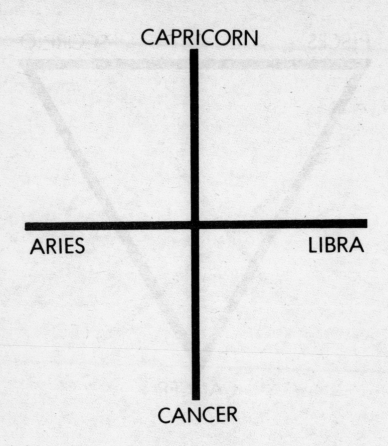

Put together, this is a clear-cut picture of dynamism, activity, tremendous stress and remarkable achievement. These people know the meaning of great change since their lives are often characterized by significant crises and major successes. This combination is like a simultaneous storm of summer, fall, winter and spring. The danger is chaotic diffusion of energy; the potential is irrepressible growth and victory.

THE FIXED SIGNS

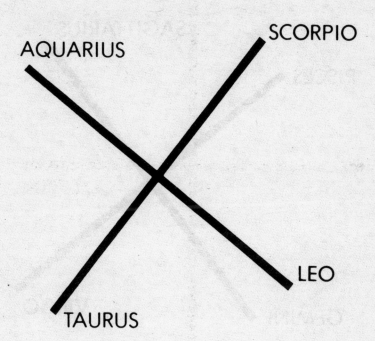

Fixed signs are always establishing themselves in a given place or area of experience. Like explorers who arrive and plant a flag, these people claim a position from which they do not enjoy being deposed. They are staunch, stalwart, upright, trusty, honorable people, although their obstinacy is well-known. Their contribution is fixity, and they are the angels who support our visible world.

THE MUTABLE SIGNS

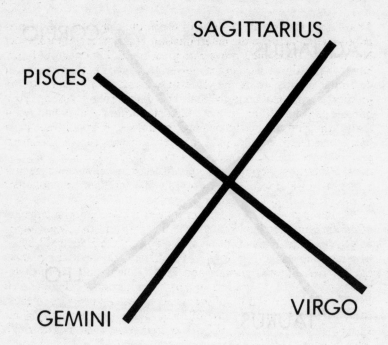

Mutable people are versatile, sensitive, intelligent, nervous and deeply curious about life. They are the translators of all energy. They often carry out or complete tasks initiated by others. Combinations of these signs have highly developed minds; they are imaginative and jumpy and think and talk a lot. At worst their lives are a Tower of Babel. At best they are adaptable and ready creatures who can assimilate one kind of experience and enjoy it while anticipating coming changes.

HOW TO APPROXIMATE YOUR RISING SIGN

Apart from the month and day of birth, the exact *time* of birth is another vital factor in the determination of an accurate horoscope. Not only do the planets move with great speed, but one must know how far the Earth has turned during the day. That way you can determine exactly where the planets are located with respect to the precise birthplace of an individual. This makes *your* horoscope *your* horoscope. In addition to these factors, another grid is laid upon that of the Zodiac and the planets: the houses. After all three have been considered, specific planetary relationships can be measured and analyzed in accordance with certain ordered procedures. It is the skillful translation of all this complex astrological language that a serious astrologer strives for in his attempt at coherent astrological synthesis. Keep this in mind.

The horoscope sets up a kind of framework around which the life of an individual grows like wild ivy, this way and that, weaving its way around the trellis of the natal positions of the planets. The year of birth tells us the positions of the distant, slow-moving planets like Jupiter, Saturn, Uranus and Pluto. The month of birth indicates the Sun sign, or birth sign as it is commonly called, as well as indicating the positions of the rapidly moving planets like Venus, Mercury and Mars. The day of birth locates the position of our Moon, and the moment of birth determines the houses through what is called the Ascendant, or Rising Sign.

As the Earth rotates on its axis once every 24 hours, each one of the twelve signs of the Zodiac appears to be "rising" on the horizon, with a new one appearing about every two hours. Actually it is the turning of the Earth that exposes each sign to view, but you will remember that in much of our astrological work we are discussing "apparent" motion. This *Rising Sign* marks the Ascendant and it colors the whole orientation of a horoscope. It indicates the sign governing the first house of the chart, and will thus determine which signs will govern all the other houses. The idea is a bit complicated at first, and we needn't dwell on complications in this introduction, but if you can imagine two color wheels with twelve divisions superimposed upon each other, one moving slowly and the other remaining still, you will have some idea of how the signs keep shifting the "color" of the houses as the Rising Sign continues to change every two hours.

The important point is that the birth chart, or horoscope, actually does define specific factors of a person's makeup. It contains a picture of being, much the way the nucleus of a tiny cell contains the potential for an entire elephant, or a packet of seeds contains a rosebush. If there were no order or continuity to the world, we could plant roses and get elephants. This same order that gives continuous flow to our lives often annoys people if it threatens to determine too much of their lives. We must grow from what we were planted, and there's no reason why we can't do that magnificently. It's all there in the horoscope. Where there is limitation, there is breakthrough; where there is crisis, there is transformation. Accurate analysis of a horoscope can help you find these points of breakthrough and transformation, and it requires knowledge of subtleties and distinctions that demand skillful judgment in order to solve even the simplest kind of personal question.

It is still quite possible, however, to draw some conclusions based upon the sign occupied by the Sun alone. In fact, if you're just being introduced to this vast subject, you're better off keeping it simple. Otherwise it seems like an impossible jumble, much like trying to read a novel in a foreign language without knowing the basic vocabulary. As with anything else, you can progress in your appreciation and understanding of astrology in direct proportion to your interest. To become really good at it requires study, experience, patience and above all—and maybe simplest of all—a fundamental understanding of what is actually going on right up there in the sky over your head. It is a vital living process you can observe, contemplate and ultimately understand. You can start by observing sunrise, or sunset, or even the full Moon.

In fact you can do a simple experiment after reading this introduction. You can erect a rough chart by following the simple procedure below:

1. Draw a circle with twelve equal segments.

2. Starting at what would be the nine o'clock position on a clock, number the segments, or houses, from 1 to 12 in a *counterclockwise direction*.

3. Label house number 1 in the following way: 4 A.M.-6 A.M.

4. In a counterclockwise direction, label the rest of the houses: 2 A.M.-4 A.M., MIDNIGHT-2 A.M., 10 P.M-MIDNIGHT, 8 P.M.-10 P.M., 6 P.M.-8 P.M., 4 P.M.-6 P.M., 2 P.M.-4 P.M., NOON-2 P.M., 10 A.M.-NOON, 8 A.M.-10 A.M., and 6 A.M.-8 A.M.

5. Now find out what time you were born and place the sun in the appropriate house.

6. Label the edge of that house with your Sun sign. You now have a description of your basic character and your fundamental drives. You can also see in what areas of life on Earth you will be most likely to focus your constant energy and center your activity.

7. If you are really feeling ambitious, label the rest of the houses with the signs, starting with your Sun sign, in order, still in a *counterclockwise direction.* When you get to Pisces, start over with Aries and keep going until you reach the house behind the Sun.

8. Look to house number 1. The sign that you have now labeled and attached to house number 1 is your Rising sign. It will color your self-image, outlook, physical constitution, early life and whole orientation to life. Of course this is a mere approximation, since there are many complicated calculations that must be made with respect to adjustments for birth time, but if you read descriptions of the sign preceding and the sign following the one you have calculated in the above manner, you may be able to identify yourself better. In any case, when you get through labeling all the houses, your drawing should look something like this:

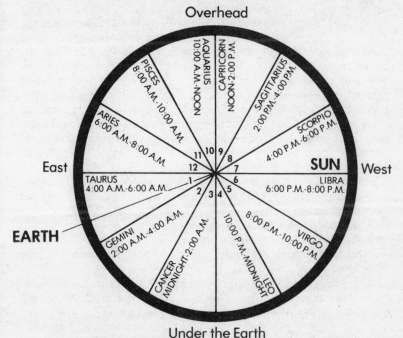

Basic chart illustrating the position of the Sun in Scorpio, with the Ascendant Taurus as the Rising Sign.

This individual was born at 5:15 P.M. on October 31 in New York City. The Sun is in Scorpio and is found in the 7th house. The Rising sign, or the sign governing house number 1, is Taurus, so this person is a blend of Scorpio and Taurus.

Any further calculation would necessitate that you look in an ephemeris, or table of planetary motion, for the positions of the rest of the planets for your particular birth year. But we will take the time to define briefly all the known planets of our Solar System and the Sun to acquaint you with some more of the astrological vocabulary that you will be meeting again and again. (See page 21 for a full explanation of the Moon in all the Signs.)

THE PLANETS AND SIGNS THEY RULE

The signs of the Zodiac are linked to the planets in the following way. Each sign is governed or ruled by one or more planets. No matter where the planets are located in the sky at any given moment, they still rule their respective signs, and when they travel through the signs they rule, they have special dignity and their effects are stronger.

Following is a list of the planets and the signs they rule. After looking at the list, go back over the definitions of the planets and see if you can determine how the planet ruling *your* Sun sign has affected your life.

SIGNS	RULING PLANETS
Aries	Mars, Pluto
Taurus	Venus
Gemini	Mercury
Cancer	Moon
Leo	Sun
Virgo	Mercury
Libra	Venus
Scorpio	Mars, Pluto
Sagittarius	Jupiter
Capricorn	Saturn
Aquarius	Saturn, Uranus
Pisces	Jupiter, Neptune

THE PLANETS
OF THE
SOLAR SYSTEM

Here are the planets of the Solar System. They all travel around the Sun at different speeds and different distances. Taken with the Sun, they all distribute individual intelligence and ability throughout the entire chart.

The planets modify the influence of the Sun in a chart according to their own particular natures, strengths and positions. Their positions must be calculated for each year and day, and their function and expression in a horoscope will change as they move from one area of the Zodiac to another.

Following, you will find brief statements of their pure meanings.

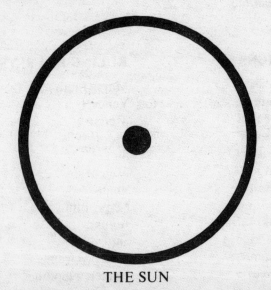

THE SUN

SUN

This is the center of existence. Around this flaming sphere all the planets revolve in endless orbits. Our star is constantly sending out its beams of light and energy without which no life on Earth would be possible. In astrology it symbolizes everything we are trying to become, the center around which all of our activity in life will always revolve. It is the symbol of our basic nature and describes the natural and constant thread that runs through everything that we do from birth to death on this planet.

To early astrologers, the sun seemed to be another planet because it crossed the heavens every day, just like the rest of the bodies in the sky.

It is the only star near enough to be seen well—it is, in fact, a dwarf star. Approximately 860,000 miles in diameter, it is about ten times as wide as the giant planet Jupiter. The next nearest star is nearly 300,000 times as far away, and if the Sun were located as far away as most of the bright stars, it would be too faint to be seen without a telescope.

Everything in the horoscope ultimately revolves around this singular body. Although other forces may be prominent in the charts of some individuals, still the Sun is the total nucleus of being and symbolizes the complete potential of every human being alive. It is vitality and the life force. Your whole essence comes from the position of the Sun.

You are always trying to express the Sun according to its position by house and sign. Possibility for all development is found in the Sun, and it marks the fundamental character of your personal radiations all around you.

It is the symbol of strength, vigor, wisdom, dignity, ardor and generosity, and the ability for a person to function as a mature individual. It is also a creative force in society. It is consciousness of the gift of life.

The underdeveloped solar nature is arrogant, pushy, undependable and proud, and is constantly using force.

MERCURY

Mercury is the planet closest to the Sun. It races around our star, gathering information and translating it to the rest of the system. Mercury represents your capacity to understand the desires of your own will and to translate those desires into action.

In other words it is the planet of Mind and the power of communication. Through Mercury we develop an ability to think, write, speak and observe—to become aware of the world around us. It colors our attitudes and vision of the world, as well as our capacity to communicate our inner responses to the outside world. Some people who have serious disabilities in their power of verbal communication have often wrongly been described as people lacking intelligence.

Although this planet (and its position in the horoscope) indicates your power to communicate your thoughts and perceptions to the world, intelligence is something deeper. Intelligence is distributed throughout all the planets. It is the relationship of the planets to each other that truly describes what we call intelligence. Mercury rules speaking, language, mathematics, draft and design, students, messengers, young people, offices, teachers and any pursuits where the mind of man has wings.

VENUS

Venus is beauty. It symbolizes the harmony and radiance of a rare and elusive quality: beauty itself. It is refinement and delicacy, softness and charm. In astrology it indicates grace, balance and the aesthetic sense. Where Venus is we see beauty, a gentle drawing in of energy and the need for satisfaction and completion. It is a special touch that finishes off rough edges. It is sensitivity, and affection, and it is always the place for that other elusive phenomenon: love. Venus describes our sense of what is beautiful and loving. Poorly developed, it is vulgar, tasteless and self-indulgent. But its ideal is the flame of spiritual love—Aphrodite, goddess of love, and the sweetness and power of personal beauty.

MARS

This is raw, crude energy. The planet next to Earth but outward from the Sun is a fiery red sphere that charges through the horoscope with force and fury. It represents the way you reach out for new adventure and new experience. It is energy and drive, initiative, courage and daring. The power to start something and see it through. It can be thoughtless, cruel and wild, angry and hostile, causing cuts, burns, scalds and wounds. It can stab its way through a chart, or it can be the symbol of healthy spirited adventure, well-channeled constructive power to begin and keep up the drive. If you have trouble starting things, if you lack the get-up-and-go to start the ball rolling, if you lack aggressiveness and self-confidence, chances are there's another planet influencing your Mars. Mars rules soldiers, butchers, surgeons, salesmen—any field that requires daring, bold skill, operational technique or self-promotion.

JUPITER

This is the largest planet of the Solar System. Scientists have recently learned that Jupiter reflects more light than it receives from the Sun. In a sense it is like a star itself. In astrology it rules good luck and good cheer, health, wealth, optimism, happiness, success and joy. It is the symbol of opportunity and always opens the way for new possibilities in your life. It rules exuberance, enthusiasm, wisdom, knowledge, generosity and all forms of expansion in general. It rules actors, statesmen, clerics, professional people, religion, publishing and the distribution of many people over large areas.

Sometimes Jupiter makes you think you deserve everything, and you become sloppy, wasteful, careless and rude, prodigal and lawless, in the illusion that nothing can ever go wrong. Then there is the danger of over-confidence, exaggeration, undependability and over-indulgence.

Jupiter is the minimization of limitation and the emphasis on spirituality and potential. It is the thirst for knowledge and higher learning.

SATURN

Saturn circles our system in dark splendor with its mysterious rings, forcing us to be awakened to whatever we have neglected in the past. It will present real puzzles and problems to be solved, causing delays, obstacles and hindrances. By doing so, Saturn stirs our own sensitivity to those areas where we are laziest.

Here we must patiently develop *method,* and only through painstaking effort can our ends be achieved. It brings order to a horoscope and imposes reason just where we are feeling least reasonable. By creating limitations and boundary, Saturn shows the consequences of being human and demands that we accept the changing cycles inevitable in human life. Saturn rules time, old age and sobriety. It can bring depression, gloom, jealousy and greed, or serious acceptance of responsibilities out of which success will develop. With Saturn there is nothing to do but face facts. It rules laborers, stones, granite, rocks and crystals of all kinds.

The Outer Planets

The following three are the outer planets. They liberate human beings from cultural conditioning, and in that sense are the law breakers. In early times it was thought that Saturn was the last planet of the system—the outer limit beyond which we could never go. The discovery of the next three planets ushered in new phases of human history, revolution and technology.

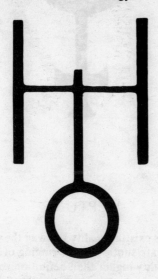

URANUS

Uranus rules unexpected change, upheaval, revolution. It is the symbol of total independence and asserts the freedom of an individual from all restriction and restraint. It is a breakthrough planet and indicates talent, originality and genius in a horoscope. It usually causes last-minute reversals and changes of plan, unwanted separations, accidents, catastrophes and eccentric behavior. It can add irrational rebelliousness and perverse bohemianism to a personality or a streak of unaffected brilliance in science and art. It rules technology, aviation and all forms of electrical and electronic advancement. It governs great leaps forward and topsy-turvy situations, and *always* turns things around at the last minute. Its effects are difficult to ever really predict, since it rules sudden last-minute decisions and events that come like lightning out of the blue.

NEPTUNE

Neptune dissolves existing reality the way the sea erodes the cliffs beside it. Its effects are subtle like the ringing of a buoy's bell in the fog. It suggests a reality higher than definition can usually describe. It awakens a sense of higher responsibility often causing guilt, worry, anxieties or delusions. Neptune is associated with all forms of escape and can make things seem a certain way so convincingly that you are absolutely sure of something that eventually turns out to be quite different.

It is the planet of illusion and therefore governs the invisible realms that lie beyond our ordinary minds, beyond our simple factual ability to prove what is "real." Treachery, deceit, disillusionment and disappointment are linked to Neptune. It describes a vague reality that promises eternity and the divine, yet in a manner so complex that we cannot really fathom it at all. At its worst Neptune is a cheap intoxicant; at its best it is the poetry, music and inspiration of the higher planes of spiritual love. It has dominion over movies, photographs and much of the arts.

PLUTO

Pluto lies at the outpost of our system and therefore rules finality in a horoscope—the final closing of chapters in your life, the passing of major milestones and points of development from which there is no return. It is a final wipeout, a closeout, an evacuation. It is a distant, subtle but powerful catalyst in all transformations that occur. It creates, destroys, then recreates. Sometimes Pluto starts its influence with a minor event or insignificant incident that might even go unnoticed. Slowly but surely, little by little, everything changes, until at last there has been a total transformation in the area of your life where Pluto has been operating. It rules mass thinking and the trends that society first rejects, then adopts and finally outgrows.

Pluto rules the dead and the underworld—all the powerful forces of creation and destruction that go on all the time beneath, around and above us. It can bring a lust for power with strong obsessions.

It is the planet that rules the metamorphoses of the caterpillar into a butterfly, for it symbolizes the capacity to change totally and forever a person's life style, way of thought and behavior.

FAMOUS PERSONALITIES

ARIES: Hans Christian Andersen, Pearl Bailey, Marlon Brando, Wernher Von Braun, Charlie Chaplin, Joan Crawford, Da Vinci, Bette Davis, Doris Day, W. C. Fields, Alec Guinness, Adolf Hitler, William Holden, Thomas Jefferson, Nikita Khrushchev, Elton John, Arturo Toscanini, J. P. Morgan, Paul Robeson, Gloria Steinem, Lowell Thomas, Vincent van Gogh, Tennessee Williams

TAURUS: Fred Astaire, Charlote Brontë, Carol Burnett, Irving Berlin, Bing Crosby, Salvador Dali, Tchaikovsky, Queen Elizabeth II, Duke Ellington, Ella Fitzgerald, Henry Fonda, Sigmund Freud, Orson Welles, Joe Louis, Lenin, Karl Marx, Golda Meir, Eva Peron, Bertrand Russell, Shakespeare, Kate Smith, Benjamin Spock, Barbra Streisand, Shirley Temple, Harry Truman

GEMINI: Mikhail Baryshnikov, Boy George, Igor Stravinsky, Carlos Chavez, Walt Whitman, Bob Dylan, Ralph Waldo Emerson, Judy Garland, Paul Gauguin, Allen Ginsberg, Benny Goodman, Bob Hope, Burl Ives, John F. Kennedy, Peggy Lee, Marilyn Monroe, Joe Namath, Cole Porter, Laurence Olivier, Harriet Beecher Stowe, Queen Victoria, John Wayne, Frank Lloyd Wright

CANCER: "Dear Abby," David Brinkley, Yul Brynner, Pearl Buck, Marc Chagall, Jack Dempsey, Mildred (Babe) Zaharias, Mary Baker Eddy, Henry VIII, John Glenn, Ernest Hemingway, Lena Horne, Oscar Hammerstein, Helen Keller, Ann Landers, George Orwell, Nancy Reagan, Rembrandt, Richard Rodgers, Ginger Rogers, Rubens, Jean-Paul Sartre, O. J. Simpson

LEO: Neil Armstrong, Russell Baker, James Baldwin, Emily Brontë, Wilt Chamberlain, Julia Child, Cecil B. De Mille, Ogden Nash, Amelia Earhart, Edna Ferber, Arthur Goldberg, Dag Hammarskjöld, Alfred Hitchcock, Mick Jagger, George Meany, George Bernard Shaw, Napoleon, Jacqueline Onassis, Henry Ford, Francis Scott Key, Andy Warhol, Mae West, Orville Wright

VIRGO: Ingrid Bergman, Warren Burger, Maurice Chevalier, Agatha Christie, Sean Connery, Lafayette, Peter Falk, Greta Garbo, Althea Gibson, Arthur Godfrey, Goethe, Buddy Hackett, Michael Jackson, Lyndon Johnson, D. H. Lawrence, Sophia Loren, Grandma Moses, Arnold Palmer, Queen Elizabeth I, Walter Reuther, Peter Sellers, Lily Tomlin, George Wallace

LIBRA: Brigitte Bardot, Art Buchwald, Truman Capote, Dwight D. Eisenhower, William Faulkner, F. Scott Fitzgerald, Gandhi, George Gershwin, Micky Mantle, Helen Hayes, Vladimir Horowitz, Doris Lessing, Martina Navratalova, Eugene O'Neill, Luciano Pavarotti, Emily Post, Eleanor Roosevelt, Bruce Springsteen, Margaret Thatcher, Gore Vidal, Barbara Walters, Oscar Wilde

SCORPIO: Vivien Leigh, Richard Burton, Art Carney, Johnny Carson, Billy Graham, Grace Kelly, Walter Cronkite, Marie Curie, Charles de Gaulle, Linda Evans, Indira Gandhi, Theodore Roosevelt, Rock Hudson, Katherine Hepburn, Robert F. Kennedy, Billie Jean King, Martin Luther, Georgia O'Keeffe, Pablo Picasso, Jonas Salk, Alan Shepard, Robert Louis Stevenson

SAGITTARIUS: Jane Austen, Louisa May Alcott, Woody Allen, Beethoven, Willy Brandt, Mary Martin, William F. Buckley, Maria Callas, Winston Churchill, Noel Coward, Emily Dickinson, Walt Disney, Benjamin Disraeli, James Doolittle, Kirk Douglas, Chet Huntley, Jane Fonda, Chris Evert Lloyd, Margaret Mead, Charles Schulz, John Milton, Frank Sinatra, Steven Spielberg

CAPRICORN: Muhammad Ali, Isaac Asimov, Pablo Casals, Dizzy Dean, Marlene Dietrich, James Farmer, Ava Gardner, Barry Goldwater, Cary Grant, J. Edgar Hoover, Howard Hughes, Joan of Arc, Gypsy Rose Lee, Martin Luther King, Jr., Rudyard Kipling, Mao Tse-tung, Richard Nixon, Gamal Nasser, Louis Pasteur, Albert Schweitzer, Stalin, Benjamin Franklin, Elvis Presley

AQUARIUS: Marian Anderson, Susan B. Anthony, Jack Benny, Charles Darwin, Charles Dickens, Thomas Edison, John Barrymore, Clark Gable, Jascha Heifetz, Abraham Lincoln, John McEnroe, Yehudi Menuhin, Mozart, Jack Nicklaus, Ronald Reagan, Jackie Robinson, Norman Rockwell, Franklin D. Roosevelt, Gertrude Stein, Charles Lindbergh, Margaret Truman

PISCES: Edward Albee, Harry Belafonte, Alexander Graham Bell, Frank Borman, Chopin, Adelle Davis, Albert Einstein, Jackie Gleason, Winslow Homer, Edward M. Kennedy, Victor Hugo, Mike Mansfield, Michelangelo, Edna St. Vincent Millay, Liza Minelli, John Steinbeck, Linus Pauling, Ravel, Diana Ross, William Shirer, Elizabeth Taylor, George Washington

CANCER

CHARACTER ANALYSIS

The Cancerian is generally speaking a rather sensitive person. He is quite often a generous person by nature, and he is willing to help almost anyone in need. He is emotional and often feels sorry for persons less fortunate than he. He could never refuse to answer someone's call for help. It is because of his sympathetic nature that others take advantage of him now and again.

In spite of his willingness to help others, the Cancer man or woman may seem difficult to approach by people not well acquainted with his character. On the whole, he seems rather subdued and reserved. Others may feel there is a wall between them and the Cancerian while this may not be the case at all. The person born under this sign is careful not to let others hurt him; he has learned through hard experience that protection of some sort is necessary in order to get along in life. The person who wins his confidence and is able to get beyond this barrier will find him a warm and loving person.

With his family and close friends, he is a very faithful and dependable person. In his quiet way, he can be affectionate and loving. He is generally not one given to demonstrative behavior. He can be fond of someone without telling them so a dozen times a day. With people he is close to, the Cancerian is bound to be more open about his own need for affection, and he enjoys being made over by his loved ones. He likes to feel wanted and protected.

When he has made up his mind about something, he sticks to it, and is generally a very constant person. He knows how to hold his ground. He never wavers. People who don't know him may think him weak and easily managed, because he is so quiet and modest, but this is far from true. He can take a lot of punishment for an idea or a cause he believes in. For the Cancerian, right is right. In order to protect himself, the person born under this sign will sometimes put up a pose as someone bossy and domineering. Sometimes he is successful in fooling others with his brash front. People who have known him for a while, however, are seldom taken in.

Many people born under this sign are rather shy and seemingly lacking confidence. They know their own minds, though, even if they do not seem to. He responds to kindness and encouragement. He will be himself with people he trusts. A good person can bring out the best in this person. Disagreeable or unfeeling people can send him scurrying back into his shell. He is a person who does not appreciate sharp criticism. Some people born under this sign are worriers. They are very concerned about what others may think of them. This may bother them so much that they develop a deep feeling of inferiority. Sometimes this reaches the point where he is so unsure of himself in some matters that he allows himself to be influenced by someone who has a stronger personality. The Cancerian is sometimes afraid that people will talk behind his back if he doesn't comply to their wishes. However, this does not stop him from doing what he feels is right. The cultivated Cancerian learns to think for himself and has no fear of disapproval.

The Cancer man or woman is most himself at home. The person born under this sign is a real lover of domesticity. He likes a place where he can relax and feel properly sheltered. Cancerians like things to stay as they are; they are not fond of changes of any sort. They are not very adaptable people. When visiting others or going to unfamiliar places, they are not likely to feel very comfortable. They are not the most talkative people at a party. In the comfort of their own homes, however, they blossom and bloom.

The Cancer man or woman sticks by the rules, whatever the game. He is not a person who would ever think of going against an established grain. He is conventional and moderate in almost all things. In a way he likes the old-fashioned things; however, in spite of this, he is interested in new things and does what he can to keep up with the times. In a way, he has two sides to his character. He is seldom forgetful. He has a memory like an elephant and can pick out any detail from the past with no trouble at all. He often reflects on things that have happened. He prefers the past to the future, which sometimes fills him with a feeling of apprehension.

This fourth sign of the Zodiac is a motherly one. Even the Cancer man has something maternal about him. He is usually kind and considerate; ready to help and protect. Others are drawn to them because of these gentle qualities. People in trouble often turn to him for advice and sympathy. People find him easy to confide in.

The Cancer person in general is a very forgiving person. He almost never holds a grudge. Still, it would not be wise to anger him. Treat him fairly and he will treat you the same. He does not appreciate people who lose patience with him. The Cancerian is usually proud of his mind and does not like to be considered unintelligent. Even if others feel that he is somewhat slow in some areas, he would rather not have this opinion expressed in his presence. He's not a person to be played with; he can tell when someone is treating him like a fool.

Quite often people born under this sign are musically inclined. Some of them have a deep interest in religious matters. They are apt to be interested in mystical matters, as well. Although they are fascinated by these things, they may be somewhat afraid of being overwhelmed if they go into them too deeply. In spite of this feeling of apprehension, they try to satisfy their curiosity in these matters.

Health

For the person born under the sign of Cancer, the stomach is his weak point. Chances are that the Cancerian is very susceptible most of the time to infectious diseases. Sometimes his health is affected by nervousness. He can be quite a worrier; even little things eat at him from time to time and this is apt to lower his resistance to infectious illnesses. He is often upset by small matters.

The Cancerian as a child is sometimes rather sickly and weak. His physique during this period of growth can be described in most cases as fragile. Some develop into physically strong adults, others may have the remnants of childhood ailments with them for a good part of their adult lives. They are rather frightened of being sick. Illness is a word they would rather not mention. Pain is also a thing they fear.

They are given to quick-changing moods at times and this often has an effect on their overall health. Worry or depression can have a subliminal effect on their general health. Usually their illnesses are not as serious as they imagine them to be. They sometimes find it easy to feel sorry for themselves.

On the whole, the Cancer man or woman is a quiet person. He is not one to brag or push his weight around. However, let it not be thought that he lacks the force that others have. He can be quite purposeful and energetic when the situation calls for it. However, when it comes to tooting their own horn, they can be somewhat shy and reticent. They may lack the get-up-and-go that others have when it comes to pushing their personal interests ahead.

Some Cancerians are quite aware of the fact that they are not what one would call sturdy in physique or temperament, and often they go through life rather painfully trying to cover up the weak side of their nature.

The man or woman born under the sign of Cancer is not apt to be very vigorous or active. As a rule, they are not too fond of physical exercise, and they have a weakness for rich and heavy foods. As a result, in later life they could end up overweight. Some Cancerians have trouble with their kidneys and intestines. Others digest their food poorly. The wise Cancer man or woman, however, adheres to a strict and well-balanced diet with plenty of fresh fruit and vegetables. Moreover, they see to it that they properly exercise their bodies daily. The Cancer man or woman who learns to cut down on rich foods and worry, often lives to a ripe old age.

Occupation

The Cancer person generally has no trouble at all establishing himself in the business world. He has all those qualities that generally make one a success professionally. He is careful with his equipment as well as his money. He is patient and he knows how to persevere. Any job where he has a chance to use his mind instead of his body is usually a job in which he has no trouble succeeding. He can work well with people—especially persons situated in dire straits. Welfare work is the kind of occupation in which he usually excels. He can really be quite a driving person if his job calls for it. The Cancerian is surprisingly resourceful. In spite of his retiring disposition, he is capable of accomplishing some very difficult tasks.

The Cancerian can put on an aggressive front, and in some cases it can carry him far. Quite often he is able to develop leadership qualities and make good use of them. He generally knows how to direct his energy so that he never becomes immediately exhausted. He'll work away at a difficult chore gradually; seldomly approaching anything head on. By working at something obliquely he often finds advantages along the way that are not apparent to others. In spite of his cautious approach, the Cancerian is often taxed by work that is too demanding of his energy. He may put up a good front of being strong and courageous while actually he is at the end of his emotional rope. Risks sometimes frighten the person born under this sign. It is often this fear which exhausts him. The possible dangers in the world of business set him to worrying.

The Cancerian does not boast about what he is going to do; he just quietly goes ahead and does it. Quite often he accomplishes more than others in this quiet way.

The person born under this sign enjoys helping others. By nature, he is quite a sympathetic individual. He does not like to see others suffer or do without. He is willing to make sacrifices for someone he trusts and cares for. The Cancerian, as was mentioned before, has a maternal streak in him, which is perhaps why he works so well with children. People born under the fourth sign of the Zodiac often make excellent teachers. They understand young people well and do what they can to help them grow up properly.

Cancerians also are fairly intuitive. In business or financial matters, they often make an important strike by playing a strong hunch. In some cases they are able to rely almost entirely on their feelings rather than on reason.

Water attracts the Cancer person. Often they have connections with the sea through their professions. The Cancerian housewife may find herself working with various liquids quite successfully while at home. Trade and commerce often appeal to the person born under this sign.

The average Cancerian has many choices open to him as far as a career is concerned. There are many things that he can do well once he puts his mind to it. In the arts he is quite likely to do well. The Cancer man or woman has a way with beauty, harmony, and creativity. Basically, he is a very capable person in many things; it depends on which of his talents he wants to develop to a professional point. He has a rich imagination and sometimes can make use of it in the area of painting, music, or sculpture.

When working for someone else, the Cancerian can always be depended upon. He makes a loyal and conscientious employee.

It is important for the Cancerian that he select a job that is well suited to his talents and temperament. Although he may feel that earning money is important, the Cancerian eventually comes to the point where he realizes that it is even more important to enjoy the work he is doing. He should have a position which allows him to explore the recesses of his personality and to develop. When placed in the wrong job, the Cancer man or woman is apt to spend a good deal of time wishing he were somewhere else.

Cancerians know the value of money. They are not the sort of people who go throwing money about recklessly. The Cancer person is honest and expects others to be the same. He is quite modest in most things and deplores extravagance and unnecessary display. There are many rich Cancerians. They have a genius for making money and for investing or saving it. Security is important to the person born under this sign. He'll always see to it that he has something put away for that inevitable rainy day. He is also a hard worker and is willing to put in long hours for the money it brings him. Financial success is usually the result of his own perseverance and industry. Through his own need for security, it is often easy for the Cancerian to sympathize with those of like dispositions. He is a helpful person. If he sees someone trying to do his best to get ahead—and still not succeeding—he is quite apt to put aside his own interests temporarily to help the other man. Sometimes the Cancerian worries over money even when he has it. He can never be too secure. It would be better for him to learn how to relax and not to let his worries undermine his health. Financial matters often cause him considerable concern—even when it is not necessary.

Home and Family

People born under this sign are usually great home-lovers. They are very domestic by nature; home for them spells security. The Cancerian is a family person. He respects those who are related to him. He feels a great responsibility toward all the members of his family. There is usually a very strong tie between the Cancer person and his mother that lasts through his whole life. Something a Cancerian will not tolerate is for someone to speak ill of a member of his family. This for him is a painful and deep insult. He has a great respect for his family and family traditions. Quite often the person under this sign is well-acquainted with his family tree. If he happens to have a relative who has been quite successful in life, he is quite proud of the fact. Once he is home for the weekend, he generally stays there. He does not particularly care for moving about. He is a born stay-at-home, in most cases.

The Cancerian is sentimental about old things and habits. He is apt to have many things stored away from years ago. Something that was dear to his parents will probably be dear to him as well.

Some Cancerians do travel about from time to time. But no matter what their destination, they are always glad to be back where they feel they belong.

The home of a person born under this sign is usually quite comfortable and tastefully furnished. The Cancerian is a bit of a romantic and usually this is reflected in the way his house is arranged.

The Cancer child is always attached to his home and family. He may not care to go out and play with other children very much but enjoys it when his friends come to his house.

The maternal nature of the Cancer person comes out when he gives a party. He is a very attentive host and worries over a guest like a mother hen—anxious to see that they are comfortable and lack nothing. He does his best to make others happy and at home, and he is admired and loved for that. People who visit Cancerians are usually deeply impressed by their out-going ways. The Cancer hostess prepares unusual and delicious snacks for her visitors. She is very concerned about them and likes to see to it that they are well-fed while visiting her.

Homebodies that they are, Cancerians generally do what they can to make their home a comfortable and interesting place for themselves as well as for others. They feel very flattered when a visitor pays them a compliment on their home.

Children play a very important part in the lives of people born under this sign. They like to fuss over their offspring and give them the things they feel that they need. They generally like to have large families. They like to see to it that their children are well-provided for and that they have the chances in life that their parents never had. The best mother of the Zodiac is usually someone born under the sign of Cancer. They have a strong protective nature. They usually have a strong sense of duty, and when their children are in difficulty they do everything they can to set matters right. Children, needless to say, are fond of their Cancerian parent, and do what they can to make the parent-child relationship a harmonious one.

Social Relationships

The Cancer person may seem rather retiring and quiet and this gives people the impression that he is not too warm or sympathetic. However, the person born under this sign is very sensitive and loving. His ability to understand and sympathize with others is great. He likes to have close friends—people who love and understand him as well as he tries to love and understand them. He wants to be well-liked—to be noticed by people who he feels should like him. If he does not get the attention and affection he feels he is entitled to, he is apt to become a little sullen and difficult to deal with.

The Cancer man or woman has strong powers of intuition and he can generally sense when he has met a person who is likely to turn into a good friend. The Cancerian suffers greatly if ever he should lose a friend. To him friendships are sacred. Sometimes the Cancerian sets his friends on too high a pedestal; he is apt to feel quite crest-fallen when he discovers that they have feet of clay. He is often romantic in his approach to friendship and is likely to seek people out for sentimental reasons rather than for practical ones.

The Cancerian is a very sensitive person and sometimes this contributes to making a friendship unsatisfactory. He sometimes makes the wrong interpretation of a remark that is made by a friend or acquaintance. He imagines something injurious behind a very innocent remark. He sometimes feels that people who profess to be his friends laugh at him cruelly behind his back. He has to be constantly reassured of a friend's sincerity, especially in the beginning of a relationship. If he wants to have the wide circle of friends he desires, the Cancerian must learn to curb these persecution fantasies.

LOVE AND MARRIAGE

The Cancer man or woman has to have love in his life, otherwise his existence is a dull and humdrum affair. When he loves someone, the Cancerian will do everything in his power to make her happy. He is not afraid to make sacrifices in order to make an important relationship work. To his loved one he is likely to seem uncertain and moody. The Cancer person is usually very influenced by the impression he has of his lover. He may even be content to let his romance partner have her own way in the relationship. He may not make many demands but be willing to follow those of his loved one. At times he may feel that he is not really loved, and draw away somewhat from the relationship. Sometimes it takes a lot of coaxing before he can be won over to the fact that he is indeed loved for himself alone.

The Cancerian is often possessive about people as well as material objects. This often makes the relationship difficult to accept for his partner.

His standards are sometimes impossibly high and because of this he is rather difficult to please. The Cancer man or woman is interested in finding someone with whom he can spend the rest of his life. He or she is not interested in any fly-by-night romance.

Romance and the Cancer Woman

The Cancer woman is usually a very warm and loving person. Her feelings run deep. She is sincere in her approach to love. Still and all, she is rather sensitive when in love and her lover may find her difficult to understand at times. The Cancer woman is quite given to crying and when she has been wronged or imagines she has, she is capable of weeping buckets. It may be quite a while before she comes out of her shell again.

Marriage is a union quite suited to the Cancer woman's temperament. She longs for permanence in a relationship and is not fond of flings or meaningless romantic adventures. Her emotions are usually very deep. She desires a man who is protective and affectionate; someone who can help and guide her through life.

She may be too possessive with her husband and this may cause discord. The demands she is likely to make on her family may be overbearing at times. She often likes to be reassured that she is loved and appreciated.

She makes a devoted and loving wife and mother who will do everything to keep her family life harmonious and affectionate.

Romance and the Cancer Man

Quite often the Cancer man is the reserved type. He may be difficult for some women to understand. Generally speaking, he is a very loving person; but sometimes he has difficulty in letting this appear so. He is a bit afraid of being rejected or hurt, so he is liable to keep his true feelings hidden until he feels that the intended object of his affection is capable of taking him seriously.

Quite often he looks for a woman who has the same qualities as his mother. He is more easily attracted to a woman who has old-fashioned traits than to a modern woman. He likes a woman who is a good cook; someone who does not mind household chores and a quiet life.

When deeply in love, the Cancer man does everything in his power to hold the woman of his choice. He is very warm and affectionate and may be rather extravagant from time to time in entertaining the woman he loves.

Marriage is something in which the Cancer man is seriously interested. He wants to settle down with a warm and loving wife—someone who will mother him to some extent. He makes a good father. He is fond of large families. His love of his children may be too possessive.

Woman—Man

CANCER WOMAN
ARIES MAN

Although it's possible that you could find happiness with a man born under the sign of the Ram, it's uncertain as to how long that happiness would last.

An Arien who has made his mark in the world and is somewhat steadfast in his outlooks and attitudes could be quite a catch for you. On the other hand, men under this sign are often swift-footed and quick-minded; their industrious mannerisms may fail to impress you, especially if you feel that much of their get-up-and-go often leads nowhere.

When it comes to a fine romance, you want someone with a nice, broad shoulder to lean on. You are likely to find a relationship with someone who doesn't like to stay put for too long somewhat upsetting.

The Arien may have a little trouble in understanding you, too . . . at least, in the beginning of the relationship. He may find you a bit too shy and moody. Ariens tend to speak their minds; he's liable to criticize you at the drop of a hat.

You may find a man born under this sign too demanding. He may give you the impression that he expects you to be at his beck-and-call. You have a barrelful of patience at your disposal and he may try every last bit of it. He is apt not to be as thorough as you are in everything that he does. In order to achieve success or a goal quickly, he is liable to overlook small but important details—and regret it when it is far too late.

Being married to an Arien does not mean that you'll have a secure and safe life as far as finances are concerned. Not all Ariens are rash with cash, but they lack that sound head you have for putting away something for that inevitable rainy day. He'll do his best, however, to see that you're adequately provided for—even though his efforts may leave something to be desired as far as you're concerned.

With an Aires man for a mate, you'll find yourself constantly among people. Ariens generally have many friends—and you may not heartily approve of them all. People born under this sign are more interested in "Interesting" people than they are in influential ones. Although there is liable to be a family squabble from time to time, you are stable enough to take it all in your stride. Your love of permanence and a harmonious homelife will help you to take the bitter with the sweet.

Aries men love children. They make wonderful fathers. Kids take to them like ducks to water. Their quick minds and behavior appeal to the young.

CANCER WOMAN
TAURUS MAN

Some Taurus men are strong and silent. They do all they can to protect and provide for the women they love. The Taurus man will never let you down. He's steady, sturdy, and reliable. He's pretty honest and practical, too. He says what he means and means what he says. He never indulges in deceit and will always put his cards on the table.

The Tauren is a very affectionate man. Being loved, appreciated, and understood is very important for his well-being. Like you, he is also looking for peace, harmony, and security in his life. If you both work toward these goals together, you'll find that they are easily attained.

If you should marry a Taurus man, you can be sure that the wolf will never darken your door. They are notoriously good providers and do everything they can to make their families comfortable and happy.

He'll appreciate the way you have of making a home warm and inviting. Slippers and pipe, and the evening papers are essential ingredients in making your Taurus husband happy at the end of the workday. Although he may be a big lug of a guy, you'll find he's pretty fond of gentleness and soft things. If you puff up his pillow and tuck him in at night, he won't complain. He'll eat it up and ask for more.

You probably won't complain about his friends. The Taurean tends to seek out friends who are successful or prominent. You admire people, too, who work hard and achieve what they set out for. It helps to reassure your way of life and the way you look at things.

Like you, the Taurus man doesn't care too much for change. He's a stay-at-home of the first degree. Chances are that the house you move into after you're married will be the house you'll live in for the rest of your life.

You'll find that the man born under this sign is easy to get along with. It's unlikely that you'll have many quarrels or arguments.

Although he'll be gentle and tender with you, your Taurus man is far from being a sensitive type. He's a man's man. Chances are he loves sports like fishing and football. He can be earthy as well as down-to-earth.

Taureans love their children very much but do everything they can not to spoil them. They believe in children staying in their places. They make excellent disciplinarians. Your children will be polite and respectful. They may find their Taurus father a little gruff, but as they grow older they'll learn to understand him.

CANCER WOMAN
GEMINI MAN

Gemini men, in spite of their charm and dashing manner, may make your skin crawl. They may seem to lack the sort of common sense you set so much store in. Their tendency to start something, then—out of boredom—never finish it, may do nothing more than exasperate you.

You may be inclined to interpret a Geminian's jumping around from here to there as childish if not downright neurotic. A man born under this sign will seldom stay put and if you should take it upon yourself to try and make him sit still, he's liable to resent it strongly.

On the other hand, the Gemini man is liable to think you're an old slowpoke—someone far too interested in security and material things. He's attracted to things that sparkle and dazzle; you, with your practical way of looking at things, are likely to seem a little dull and uninteresting to this gadabout. If your're looking for a life of security and permanence—and what Cancerian isn't—then you'd better look elsewhere for your Mr. Right.

Chances are you'll be taken in by his charming ways and facile wit—few women can resist Gemini-magic—but after you've seen through his live-for-today, gossamer facade, you'll most likely be very happy to turn your attention to someone more stable—even if he is not as interesting. You want a man who is there when you need him. You need someone on whom you can fully rely. Keeping track of a Gemini's movements will make you dizzy. Still, you are a patient woman, most of the time, and you are able to put up with something contrary if you feel that in the end it will prove well worth the effort.

A successful and serious Gemini could make you a very happy woman, perhaps, if you gave him half a chance. Although you may think that he has holes in his head, the Gemini man generally has a good brain and can make good use of it when he wants. Some Geminians who have learned the importance of being consequent have risen to great heights, professionally. President Kennedy was a Gemini as was Thomas Mann and William Butler Yeats. Once you can convince yourself that not all people born under the sign of the Twins are witless grasshoppers, you'll find you've come a long way in trying to understand them.

Life with a Gemini man can be more fun than a barrel of clowns. You'll never have a chance to experience a dull moment. He lacks your sense when it comes to money, however. You should see to it that you handle the budgeting and bookkeeping.

In ways, he's like a child himself; perhaps that is why he can get along so well with the younger generation.

CANCER WOMAN
CANCER MAN

You'll find the man born under the same sign as you easy to get along with. You're both sensitive and sensible people; you'll see eye-to-eye on most things. He'll share your interest in security and practicality.

Cancer men are always hard workers. They are very interested in making successes of themselves in business and socially. Like you, he's a conservative person who has a great deal of respect for tradition. He's a man you can depend on come rain or come shine. He'll never shirk his responsibilities as provider and will always see to it that you never want.

The Cancer man is not the type that rushes headlong into romance. Neither are you, for that matter. Courtship between the two of you will be a sensible and thorough affair. It may take months before you even get to that holding-hands stage of romance. One thing you can be sure of: he'll always treat you like a lady. He'll have great respect and consideration for your feelings. Only when he is sure that you approve of him as someone to love, will he reveal the warmer side of his nature. His coolness, like yours, is just a front. Beneath it lies a very affectionate heart.

Although he may seem restless or moody at times, on the whole the Cancer man is a very considerate and kind person. His standards are extremely high. He is looking for a girl who can measure up to his ideals . . . a girl like you.

Marriage means a lot to the Cancer male. He's very interested in settling down with someone who has the same attitudes and outlooks as he has. He's a man who loves being at home. He'll be a faithful husband. Cancerians never pussyfoot around after they've made their marriage vows. They do not take their marriage responsibilities lightly. They see to it that everything in this relationship is just the way it should be. Between the two of you, your home will be well managed; bills will be paid on time, there will be adequate insurance on everything of value, and there will be money in the bank. When retirement time rolls around, you both should be very well off.

The Cancer man has a great respect for family. You'll most likely be seeing a lot of his mother during your marriage, just as he'll probably be seeing a lot of yours. He'll do his best to get along with your relatives; he'll treat them with the kindness and concern you think they deserve. He'll expect you to be just as considerate with his relatives.

The Cancerian makes a very good father. He's very patient and understanding, especially when the children are young and dependent.

CANCER WOMAN
LEO MAN

To know a man born under the sign of the Lion is not necessarily to love him—even though the temptation may be great. When he fixes most girls with his leonine double-whammy, it causes their hearts to pitter-pat and their minds to cloud over.

But with you, the sensible Cancerian, it takes more than a regal strut and a roar to win you over. There is no denying that Leo has a way with women—even practical Cancerians—and that once he's swept a girl off her feet, it may be hard for her to scramble upright again. Still, you are no pushover for romantic charm when you feel there may be no security behind it.

He'll wine you and dine you in the fanciest places. He'll croon to you under the moon and shower you with diamonds if he can get a hold of them. Still, it would be wise to find out just how long that shower is going to last before consenting to be his wife.

Lions in love are hard to ignore, let alone brush off. Once mesmerized by this romantic powerhouse, you will most likely find yourself doing things you never dreamed of. Leos can be like vain pussycats when involved romantically. They like to be cuddled and curried, tickled under the chin and told how wonderful they are. This may not be your cup of tea, exactly, still when you're romantically dealing with a man born under the sign of Leo, you'll find yourself doing all kinds of things to make him purr.

Although he may be big and magnanimous while trying to win you, he'll let out a blood-curdling roar if he thinks he's not getting the tender love and care he feels is his due. If you keep him well supplied with affection, you can be sure his eyes will never stray and his heart will never wander.

Leo men often tend to be authoritarian—they are born to lord it over others in one way or another, it seems. If he is the top banana of his firm, he'll most likely do everything he can to stay on top. If he's not number one, he's most likely working on it and will be sitting on the throne before long. You'll have more security than you can use if he is in a position to support you in the manner to which he feels you should be accustomed. He's apt to be too lavish, though—at least, by your standards.

You'll always have plenty of friends when you have a Leo for a mate. He's a natural born friend-maker and entertainer. He loves to kick up his heels at a party.

As fathers, Leos tend to spoil their children no end.

CANCER WOMAN
VIRGO MAN

The Virgo man is often a quiet, respectable type who sets great store in conservative behavior and level-headedness. He'll admire you for your practicality and tenacity—perhaps even more than for your good looks. The Virgo man is seldom bowled over by glamour pusses. When looking for someone to love, he always turns to a serious, reliable girl.

He'll be far from a Valentino while dating. In fact, you may wind up making all the passes. Once he gets his motor running, however, he can be a warm and wonderful fellow—to the right girl.

The Virgo man is gradual about love. Chances are your romance with him will start out looking like an ordinary friendship. Once he's sure that you are no fly-by-night flirt and have no plans of taking him for a ride, he'll open up and rain sunshine all over your heart.

The Virgo man takes his time about romance. It may be many years before he seriously considers settling down. Virgos are often middle-age when they make their first marriage vows. They hold out as long as they can for that girl who perfectly measures up to their ideals.

He may not have many names in his little black book; in fact, he may not even have a little black book. He's not interested in playing the field; leave that to the more flamboyant signs. The Virgo man is so particular that he may remain romantically inactive for a long period of time. The girl he chooses has to be perfect or it's no go.

With your sure-fire perseverance, you'll most likely be able to make him listen to reason, as far as romance is concerned; before long, you'll find him returning your love. He's no block of ice and will respond to what he considers to be the right feminine flame.

Once your love-life with Virgo starts to bubble, don't give it a chance to die down. The Virgo man will never give a woman a second chance at winning his heart. If there should ever be a falling-out between you: forget about picking up the pieces. By him, it's one strike and you're out.

Once married, he'll stay that way—even if it hurts. He's too conscientious to back out of a legal deal of any sort. He'll always be faithful and considerate. He's as neat as a pin and will expect you to be the same.

If you marry a Virgo man, keep your kids spic-and-span, at least by the time he gets home from work. He likes children to be clean and polite.

CANCER WOMAN
LIBRA MAN

Cancerians are apt to find men born under the sign of Libra too wrapped up in their own private dreams to be romantically interesting. He's a difficult man to bring back down to earth, at times. Although he may be very careful about weighing both sides of an argument, he may never really come to a reasonable decision about anything. Decisons, large and small, are capable of giving a Libran the willies. Don't ask him why. He probably doesn't know, himself.

You are looking for permanence and constancy in a love relationship; you may find him a puzzlement. One moment he comes on hard and strong with declarations of his love; the next moment you find he's left you like yesterday's mashed potatoes. It does no good to wonder "what went wrong." Chances are: nothing, really. It's just one of Libra's strange ways.

On the other hand, you'll probably admire his way with harmony and beauty. If you're all decked out in your fanciest gown, you'll receive a ready compliment and one that's really deserved. Librans don't pass out compliments to all and sundry. If something strikes him as distasteful, he'll remain silent. He's tactful.

He may not seem as ambitious as you would like your lover or husband to be. Where you have a great interest in getting ahead, the Libran is often content just to drift along. It is not that he is lazy or shiftless; material gain generally means little to him. He is more interested in aesthetic matters. If he is in love with you, however, he'll do everything in his power to make you happy.

You may have to give him a good nudge now and again to get him to recognize the light of reality. On the whole, he'll enjoy the company of his artistic dreams when you're not around. If you love your Libran, don't be too harsh or impatient with him. Try to understand him.

Librans are peace-loving people. They hate any kind of confrontation that might lead to an argument. Some of them will do almost anything to keep the peace—even tell a little lie.

If you find yourself involved with a man born under this sign, either temporarily or permanently, you'd better take over the task of managing his money. It's for his own good. Money will never interest a Libran as much as it should; he often has a tendency to be generous when he shouldn't be.

Don't let him see the materialistic side of your nature too often. It's liable to frighten him off.

He makes a gentle and understanding father. He's careful not to spoil children.

CANCER WOMAN
SCORPIO MAN

Some people have a hard time understanding the man born under the sign of Scorpio; few, however, are able to resist his fiery charm. When angered, he can act like an overturned wasps' nest; his sting can leave an almost permanent mark.. If you find yourself interested in a man born under this sign, you'd better learn how to keep on his good side.

The Scorpio man can be quite blunt when he chooses; at times, he'll seem like a brute to you. He's touchy—more so than you—and it is liable to get on your nerves after a while. When you feel like you can't take it anymore, you'd better tiptoe away from the scene rather than chance an explosive confrontation. He's capable of giving you a sounding-out that will make you pack your bags and go back to Mother—for good.

If he finds fault with you, he'll let you know. He's liable to misinterpret your patience and think it a sign of indifference. Still and all, you are the kind of woman who can adapt to almost any sort of relationship or circumstance if you put your heart and mind to it.

Scorpio men are all quite perceptive and intelligent. In some respects, they know how to use their brains more effectively than most. They believe in winning in whatever they do; second-place holds no interest for them. In business, they usually achieve the position they want through drive and use of intellect.

Your interest in home-life is not likely to be shared by him. No matter how comfortable you've managed to make the house, it will have very little influence on him with regards to making him aware of his family responsibilities. He does not like to be tied down, generally, and would rather be out on the battlefield of life, belting away for what he feels is a just and worthy cause. Don't try to keep the homefires burning too brightly while you wait for him to come home from work—you may just run out of firewood.

The Scorpio man is passionate in all things—including love. Most women are easily attracted to him—and the Cancer woman is no exception . . . that is, at least before she knows what she might be getting into. Those who allow themselves to be swept off their feet by a Scorpio man, shortly find that they're dealing with a carton of romantic fireworks. The Scorpio man is passionate with a capital P, make no mistake about that.

Scorpio men are straight to the point. They can be as sharp as a razor blade and just as cutting. Always manage to stay out of his line of fire; if you don't, it could cost you your love-life.

Scorpio men like large families. They love children but they do not always live up to the role of father.

CANCER WOMAN
SAGITTARIUS MAN

Sagittarius men are not easy to catch. They get cold feet whenever visions of the altar enter the romance. You'll most likely be attracted to the Sagittarian because of his sun-shiny nature. He's lots of laughs and easy to get along with, but as soon as the relationship begins to take on a serious hue, you may feel yourself a little let-down.

Sagittarians are full of bounce; perhaps too much bounce to suit you. They are often hard to pin down; they dislike staying put. If he ever has a chance to be on-the-move, he'll latch on to it without so much as a how-do-you-do. Sagittarians are quick people —both in mind and spirit. If ever they do make mistakes, it's because of their zip; they leap before they look.

If you offer him good advice, he's liable not to follow it. Sagittarians like to rely on their own wits and ways whenever possible.

His up-and-at-'em manner about most things is likely to drive you up the wall at times. And your cautious, deliberate manner is likely to make him cluck his tongue occasionally. "Get the lead out of your shoes," he's liable to tease when you're accompanying him on a stroll or jogging through the park with him on a Sunday morning. He can't abide a slowpoke.

At times you'll find him too much like a kid—too breezy. Don't mistake his youthful zest for premature senility. Sagittarians are equipped with first-class brain power and know how to use it well. They are often full of good ideas and drive. Generally, they are very broad-minded people and very much concerned with fair play and equality.

In the romance department, he's quite capable of loving you whole-heartedly while treating you like a good buddy. His hail-fel-low-well-met manner in the arena of love is likely to scare off a dainty damsel. However, a woman who knows that his heart is in the right place, won't mind it too much if, once in a while, he slaps her (lightly) on the back instead of giving her a gentle embrace.

He's not very much of a homebody. He's got ants in his pants and enjoys being on-the-move. Humdrum routine—especially at home—bores him silly. At the drop of a hat, he may ask you to whip off your apron and dine out for a change. He's a past-master in the instant-surprise department. He'll love keeping you guessing. His friendly, candid nature will win him many friends. He'll expect his friends to be yours, and vice-versa.

Sagittarians make good fathers when the children become older; with little shavers, they feel all thumbs.

CANCER WOMAN
CAPRICORN MAN

The Capricorn man is quite often not the romantic kind of lover that attracts most women. Still, with his reserve and calm, he is capable of giving his heart completely once he has found the right girl. The Cancer woman who is thorough and deliberate can appreciate these same qualities in the average Capricorn man. He is slow and sure about most things—love included.

He doesn't believe in flirting and would never lead a heart on a merry chase just for the game of it. If you win his trust, he'll give you his heart on a platter. Quite often, it is the woman who has to take the lead when romance is in the air. As long as he knows you're making the advances in earnest, he won't mind—in fact, he'll probably be grateful. Don't get to thinking he's all cold fish; he isn't. While some Capricorns are indeed quite capable of expressing passion, others often have difficulty in trying to display affection. He should have no trouble in this area, however, once he has found a patient and understanding girl.

The Capricorn man is very interested in getting ahead. He's quite ambitious and usually knows how to apply himself well to whatever task he undertakes. He's far from being a spendthrift. Like you, he knows how to handle money with extreme care. You, with your knack for putting pennies away for that rainy day, should have no difficulty in understanding his way with money. The Capricorn man thinks in terms of future security. He saves to make sure that he and his wife have something to fall back on when they reach retirement age. There's nothing wrong with that; in fact, it's a plus quality.

The Capricorn man will want to handle household matters efficiently. Most Cancerians have no trouble in doing this. If he should check up on you from time to time, don't let it irritate you. Once you assure him that you can handle this area to his liking, he'll leave it all up to you.

Although he's a hard man to catch when it comes to marriage, once he's made that serious step, he's quite likely to become possessive. Capricorns need to know that they have the support of their women in whatever they do, every step of the way.

The Capricorn man likes to be liked. He may seem like a dull, reserved person but underneath it all, he's often got an adventurous nature that has never had the chance to express itself. He may be a real dare-devil in his heart of hearts. The right woman, the affectionate, adoring woman, can bring out that hidden zest in his nature.

Although he may not understand his children fully, he'll be a loving and dutiful father.

CANCER WOMAN
AQUARIUS MAN

You are liable to find the Aquarious man the most broadminded man you have ever met; on the other hand, you are also liable to find him the most impractical. Oftentimes, he's more of a dreamer than a doer. If you don't mind putting up with a man whose heart and mind are as wide as the Missouri but whose head is almost always up in the clouds, then start dating that Aquarian who has somehow captured your fancy. Maybe you, with your good sense, can bring him back down to earth when he gets too starry-eyed.

He's no dumb-bell; make no mistake about that. He can be busy making some very complicated and idealistic plans when he's got that out-to-lunch look in his eyes. But more than likely, he'll never execute them. After he's shared one or two of his progressive ideas with you, you are liable to ask yourself "Who is this nut?" But don't go jumping to conclusions. There's a saying that Aquarians are a half-century ahead of everybody else in the thinking department.

If you decide to say "yes" to his "will you marry me", you'll find out how right his zany whims are on or about your 50th anniversary. Maybe the waiting will be worth it. Could be that you have an Einstein on your hands—and heart.

Life with an Aquarian won't be one of total despair if you can learn to temper his airiness with your down-to-earth practicality. He won't gripe if you do. The Aquarius man always maintains an open mind; he'll entertain the ideas and opinions of everybody. He may not agree with all of them.

Don't go tearing your hair out when you find that it's almost impossible to hold a normal conversation with your Aquarius friend at times. He's capable of answering your how-are-you-feeling with a run-down on the price of Arizona sugar beets. Always try to keep in mind: he means well.

His broadmindedness doesn't stop when it comes to you and your personal freedom. You won't have to give up any of your hobbies or projects after you're married; in fact, he'll encourage you to continue your interests.

He'll be a kind and generous husband. He'll never quibble over petty things. Keep track of the money you both spend. He can't. Money burns a hole in his pocket.

You'll have plenty of chances to put your legendary patience to good use during your relationship with an Aquarian. At times, you may feel like tossing in the towel, but you'll never call it quits.

He's a good family man. He understands children as much as he loves them.

CANCER WOMAN
PISCES MAN

The Pisces man is perhaps the man you've been looking all over for, high and low; the man you almost thought didn't exist.

The Pisces man is very sensitive and very romantic. Still, he is a reasonable person. He may wish on the moon, yet he's got enough good sense to know that it isn't made of green cheese.

He'll be very considerate of your every wish and whim. He will do his best to be a very compatible mate. The Pisces man is great for showering the object of his affection with all kinds of little gifts and tokens of his affection. He's just the right mixture of dreamer and realist that pleases most women.

When it comes to earning bread and butter, the strong Pisces man will do all right in the world. Quite often they are capable of rising to very high positions. Some do very well as writers or psychiatrists. He'll be as patient and understanding with you as you are with him.

One thing a Pisces man dislikes is pettiness. Anyone who delights in running another into the ground is almost immediately crossed off his list of possible mates. If you have any small griev-ances with any of your girl friends, don't tell him about them. He couldn't care less about them and will be quite disappointed in you if you do.

If you fall in love with a weak Pisces man, don't give up your job at the office before you get married. Better still: hang onto it until a good while after the honeymoon; you may need it.

A funny thing about the man born under this sign is that he can be content almost anywhere. This is perhaps because he is quite inner-directed and places little value on some exterior things.

In a shack or a palace, the Pisces man is capable of making the best of all possible adjustments. He won't kick up a fuss if the roof leaks or if the fence is in sad need of repair. He's got more important things on his mind, he'll tell you. Still and all, the Pisces man is not lazy or aimless. It's important to understand that material gain is never a direct goal for him.

Pisces men have a way with the sick and troubled. He'll offer his shoulder to anyone in the mood for a good cry. He can listen to one hard luck story after another without seeming to tire. Quite often he knows what is bothering someone before that person, himself, realizes what it is. It's almost intuitive with Pisceans, it seems.

As a lover, he'll be attentive and faithful. Children are often delighted with Pisces men. As fathers, they are never strict, always permissive.

Man—Woman

CANCER MAN
ARIES WOMAN

The Aires woman may be a little too bossy and busy for you. Generally speaking, Ariens are ambitious creatures. They can become a little impatient with people who are more thorough and deliberate than they are—especially if they feel such people are taking too much time. The Aries woman is a fast worker. Sometimes she's so fast she forgets to look where she's going. When she stumbles or falls, it would be nice if you were there to grab her. Ariens are proud women. They don't like to be told "I told you so" when they err. Tongue-wagging can turn them into blocks of ice. Don't begin to think that the Aires woman frequently gets tripped up in her plans. Quite often they are capable of taking aim and hitting the bull's-eye. You'll be flabbergasted at times by their accuracy as well as by their ambition. On the other hand, because of your interest in being sure and safe, you're apt to spot a flaw in your Arien's plans before she does.

You are somewhat slower than the Arien in attaining what you have your sights set on. Still, you don't make any mistakes along the way; you're almost always well-prepared.

The Aries woman is rather sensitive at times. She likes to be handled with gentleness and respect. Let her know that you love her for her brains as well as for her good looks. Never give her cause to become jealous. When your Aires date sees green, you'd better forget about sharing a rosy future together. Handle her with tender love and care and she's yours.

The Aires woman can be giving if she feels her partner is deserving. She is no iceberg; she responds to the proper flame. She needs a man she can look up to and feel proud of. If the shoe fits, put it on. If not, better put your sneakers back on and quietly tiptoe out of her sight. She can cause you plenty of heart ache if you've made up your mind about her but she hasn't made up hers about you. Aires women are very demanding at times. Some of them are high-strung; they can be difficult if they feel their independence is being hampered.

The cultivated Aires woman makes a wonderful homemaker and hostess. You'll find she's very clever in decorating and color-use. Your house will be tastefully furnished; she'll see to it that it radiates harmony. Friends and acquaintances will love your Aries wife. She knows how to make everyone feel at home and welcome.

Although the Aries woman may not be keen on burdening responsibilities, she is fond of children and the joy they bring.

CANCER MAN
TAURUS WOMAN

A Taurus woman could perhaps understand you better than most women. She is a very considerate and loving kind of person. She is methodical and thorough in whatever she does. She knows how to take her time in doing things; she is anxious to avoid mistakes. Like you, she is a careful person. She never skips over things that may seem unimportant; she goes over everything with a fine-tooth comb.

Home is very important to the Taurus woman. She is an excellent homemaker. Although your home may not be a palace, it will become, under her care, a comfortable and happy abode. She'll love it when friends drop by for the evening. She is a good cook and enjoys feeding people well. No one will ever go away from your house with an empty stomach.

The Taurus woman is serious about love and affection. When she has taken a tumble for someone, she'll stay by him—for good, if possible. She will try to be practical in romance, to some extent. When she sets her cap for a man, she keeps after him until he's won her. Generally, the Taurus woman is a passionate lover, even though she may appear otherwise at first glance. She is on the look-out for someone who can return her affection fully. Taureans are sometimes given to fits of jealousy and possessiveness. They expect fair play in the area of marriage; when it doesn't come about, they can be bitingly sarcastic and mean.

The Taurus woman is generally an easy-going person. She's

fond of keeping peace. She won't argue unless she has to. She'll do her best to keep a love relationship on even keel.

Marriage is generally a one-time thing for Taureans. Once they've made the serious step, they seldom try to back out of it. Marriage is for keeps. They are fond of love and warmth. With the right man, they turn out to be ideal wives.

The Taurus woman will respect you for your steady ways; she'll have confidence in your common sense.

Taurus women seldom put up with nonsense from their children. They are not so much strict as concerned. They like their children to be well-behaved and dutiful. Nothing pleases a Taurus mother more than a compliment from a neighbor or teacher about her child's behavior. Although children may inwardly resent the iron hand of a Taurus woman, in later life they are often quite thankful that they were brought up in such an orderly and conscientious way.

CANCER MAN
GEMINI WOMAN

The Gemini woman may be too much of a flirt ever to take your heart too seriously. Then again, it depends on what kind of mood she's in. Gemini women can change from hot to cold quicker than a cat can wink its eye. Chances are her fluctuations will tire you after a time, and you'll pick up your heart—if it's not already broken into small pieces—and go elsewhere. Women born under the sign of the Twins have the talent of being able to change their moods and attitudes as frequently as they change their party dresses.

Sometimes, Gemini girls like to whoop it up. Some of them are good-time girls who love burning the candle to the wick. You'll always see them at parties and gatherings, surrounded by men of all types, laughing gaily or kicking up their heels at every opportunity. Wallflowers, they're not. The next day you may bump into the same girl at the neighborhood library and you'll hardly recognize her for her "sensible" attire. She'll probably have five or six books under her arm—on five or six different subjects. In fact, she may even work there. If you think you've met the twin sister of Dr. Jekyll and Mr. Hyde, you're most likely right.

You'll probably find her a dazzling and fascinating creature—for a time, at any rate. Most men do. But when it comes to being serious about love you may find that that sparkling Eve leaves quite a bit to be desired. It's not that she has anything against being serious, it's just that she might find it difficult trying to be serious with you.

At one moment, she'll be capable of praising you for your steadfast and patient ways; the next moment she'll tell you in a cutting way that you're an impossible stick in the mud.

Don't even begin to fathom the depths of her mercurial soul—it's full of false bottoms. She'll resent close investigation anyway, and will make you rue the day you ever took it into your head to try to learn more about her than she feels is necessary. Better keep the relationship fancy free and full of fun until she gives you the go-ahead sign. Take as much of her as she is willing to give; don't ask for more. If she does take a serious interest in you, then she'll come across with the goods.

There will come a time when the Gemini girl will realize that she can't spend her entire life at the ball and that the security and warmth you offer is just what she needs to be a happy, fulfilled woman.

She'll be easy-going with her children. She'll probably spoil them silly.

CANCER MAN
CANCER WOMAN

The girl born under Cancer needs to be protected from the cold cruel world. She'll love you for your gentle and kind manner; you are the kind of man who can make her feel safe and secure.

You won't have to pull any he-man or heroic stunts to win her heart; she's not interested in things like that. She's more likely to be impressed by your sure, steady ways—the way you have of putting your arm around her and making her feel that she's the only girl in the world. When she's feeling glum and tears begin to well up in her eyes, you'll know how to calm her fears, no matter how silly some of them may seem.

The girl born under this sign—like you—is inclined to have her ups and downs. Perhaps you can both learn to smooth out the roughed-up spots in each other's life. She'll most likely worship the ground you walk on or place you on a very high pedestal. Don't disappoint her if you can help it. She'll never disappoint you. The Cancer woman is the sort who will take great pleasure in devoting the rest of her natural life to you. She'll darn your socks, mend your overalls, scrub floors, wash windows, shop, cook, and do anything short of murder in order to please you and to let you know that she loves you. Sounds like that legendary good old-fashioned girl, doesn't it? Contrary to popular belief, there are still a good number of them around and the majority of them are Cancerians.

Treat your Cancer mate fairly and she'll treat you like a king.

There is one ohing you should be warned about: never be unkind to your mother-in-law. It will be the only golden rule your Cancerian wife will probably expect you to live up to. Mother is something pretty special for her. You should have no trouble in understanding this, for your mother has a special place in your heart, too. It's always that way with people born under this sign. They have great respect and love for family-ties. It might be a good idea for you both to get to know each other's relatives before tying the marriage knot, because after the wedding bells have rung, you'll be seeing a lot of them.

Of all the signs in the Zodiac, the woman born under Cancer is the most maternal. In caring for and bringing up children, she knows just how to combine tenderness and discipline. A child couldn't ask for a better mother. Cancer women are sympathetic, affectionate, and patient with children. Both of you will make excellent parents—especially when the children are young; when they grow older you'll most likely be reluctant to let them go out into the world.

CANCER MAN
LEO WOMAN

The Leo woman can make most men roar like lions. If any woman in the Zodiac has that indefinable something that can make men lose their heads and find their hearts, it's the Leo woman.

She's got more than a fair share of charm and glamour and she knows how to make the most of her assets, especially when she's in the company of the opposite sex. Jealous men either lose their cool or their sanity when trying to woo a woman born under the sign of the Lion. She likes to kick up her heels quite often and doesn't care who knows it. She often makes heads turn and toungues wag. You don't necessarily have to believe any of what you hear—it's most likely just jealous gossip or wishful thinking. Needless to say, other women in her vicinity turn green with envy and will try anything short of shoving her into the nearest lake in order to put her out of commission.

Although this vamp makes the blood rush to your head and makes you momentarily forget all the things you thought were important and necessary in your life, you may feel differently when you come back down to earth and the stars are out of your eyes. You may feel that although this vivacious creature can make you feel pretty wonderful, she just isn't the kind of girl you planned to bring home to Mother. Not that your mother might disapprove of your choice—but *you might* after the shoes and rice are a thing of the past. Although the Leo woman may do her best to be a good wife for you, chances are she'll fall short of your idea of what a good wife should be.

If you're planning on not going as far as the altar with that Leo woman who has you flipping your lid, you'd better be financially equipped for some very expensive dating. Be prepared to shower her with expensive gifts and to take her dining and dancing to the smartest spots in town. Promise her the moon if you're in a position to go that far. Luxury and glamour are two things that are bound to lower a Leo's resistance. She's got expensive tastes and you'd better cater to them if you expect to get to first base with this femme.

If you've got an important business deal to clinch and you have doubts as to whether you can swing it or not, bring your Leo girl along to the business luncheon. Chances are that with her on your arm, you'll be able to win any business battle with both hands tied. She won't have to say or do anything—just be there at your side. The grouchiest oil magnate can be transformed into a gushing, obediant schoolboy if there's a charming Leo woman in the room.

Leo mothers are blind to the faults of their children. They make very loving and affectionate mothers and tend to spoil their offspring.

CANCER MAN
VIRGO WOMAN

The Virgo woman is pretty particular about choosing her men friends. She's not interested in just going out with anybody; she has her own idea of what a boyfriend or prospective husband should be—and it's quite possible that that image has something of you in it. Generally speaking, she's a quiet girl. She doesn't believe that nonsense has any place in a love affair. She's serious about love and she'll expect you to be. She's looking for a man who has both feet on the ground—someone who can take care of himself as well as her. She knows the value of money and how to get the most out of a dollar. She's far from being a spendthrift. Throwing money around turns her stomach—even when it isn't her money.

She'll most likely be very shy about romancing. Even the simple act of holding hands may make her turn crimson—at least, on the first couple of dates. You'll have to make all the advances—which is as it should be—and you'll have to be careful not to make any wrong moves. She's capable of showing anyone who oversteps the boundaries of common decency the door. It may even take quite a long time before she'll accept that goodnight kiss at the front gate. Don't give up. You are perhaps the kind of man who can bring out the warm woman in her. There is love and tenderness underneath Virgo's seemingly frigid facade. It will take a patient and understanding man to bring it out into the open. She may have the idea that sex is something very naughty, if not unnecessary. The right man could make her put this old-fashioned idea in the trunk up in the attic along with her great grandmother's woolen nighties.

She is a very sensitive girl. You can help her overcome this by treating her with gentleness and affection.

When a Virgo has accepted you as a lover or mate, she won't stint in giving her love in return. With her, it's all or nothing at all. You'll be surprised at the transformation your earnest attention can bring about in this quiet kind of woman. When in love, Virgos only listen to their hearts, not to what the neighbors say.

Virgo women are honest about love once they've come to grips with it. They don't appreciate hypocrisy—particularly in this area of life. They will always be true to their hearts—even if it means tossing you over for a new love. But if you convince her that you are earnest about your interest in her, she'll reciprocate your love and affection and never leave you. Do her wrong once, however, and you can be sure she'll call the whole thing off.

Virgo mothers are tender and loving. They know what's good for their children and will always take great pains in bringing them up correctly.

CANCER MAN
LIBRA WOMAN

The song goes: It's a woman's prerogative to change her mind. The lyricist must have had the Libra woman in his thoughts when he jotted this ditty out. Her changeability, in spite of its undeniable charm (sometimes), could actually drive even a man of your patience up the wall. She's capable of smothering you with love and kisses one day and on the next, avoid you like the plague. If you think you're a man of steel nerves then perhaps you can tolerate her sometimey-ness without suffering too much. However, if you own up to the fact that you're a mere mortal who can only take so much, then you'd better fasten your attention on a girl who's somewhat more constant.

But don't get the wrong idea—a love affair with a Libran is not all bad. In fact, it can have an awful lot of plusses to it. Libra women are soft, very feminine, and warm. She doesn't have to vamp all over the place in order to gain a man's attention. Her delicate presence is enough to warm the cockles of any man's heart. One smile and you're like a piece of putty in the palm of her hand.

She can be fluffy and affectionate—things you like in a girl. On the other hand, her indecision about which dress to wear, what to cook for dinner, or whether or not to redo the rumpusroom could make you tear your hair out. What will perhaps be more exasperating is her flat denial to the accusation that she cannot make even the simplest decision. The trouble is that she wants to be fair or just in all matters; she'll spend hours weighing both sides of an argument or situation. Don't make her rush into a decision; that would only irritate her.

The Libra woman likes to be surrounded by beautiful things. Money is no object when beauty is concerned. There will always be plenty of flowers in her apartment. She'd rather die than do without daisies and such. She'll know how to arrange them tastefully, too. Women under this sign are fond of beautiful clothes and furnishings. They will run up bills without batting an eye—if given the chance.

Once she's cottoned to you, the Libra woman will do everything in her power to make you happy. She'll wait on you hand and foot when you're sick, bring you breakfast in bed on Sundays, and even read you the funny papers if you're too sleepy to open your eyes. She'll be very thoughtful and devoted. If anyone dares suggest you're not the grandest man in the world, your Libra wife will give that person a good sounding-out.

Librans work wonders with children. Gentle persuasion and affection are all she uses in bringing them up. It works.

CANCER MAN
SCORPIO WOMAN

When the Scorpio woman chooses to be sweet, she's apt to give the impression that butter wouldn't melt in her mouth . . . but, of course, it would. When her temper flies, so will everything else that isn't bolted down. She can be as hot as a *tamale* or as cool as a cucumber when she wants. Whatever mood she's in, you can be sure it's for real. She doesn't believe in poses or hypocrisy.

The Scorpio woman is often seductive and sultry. Her femme fatale charm can pierce through the hardest of hearts like a laser ray. She doesn't have to look like Mata Hari (many of them resemble the tomboy next door) but once you've looked into those tantalizing eyes, you're a goner.

The Scorpio woman can be a whirlwind of passion. Life with a girl born under this sign will not be all smiles and smooth-sailing. If you think you can handle a woman who can purr like a pussycat when handled correctly but spit bullets once her fur is ruffled, then try your luck. Your stable and steady nature will most likely have a calming effect on her. You're the kind of man she can trust and rely on. But never cross her—even on the smallest thing; if you do, you'd better tell Fido to make room for you in the doghouse—you'll be his guest for the next couple of days.

Generally, the Scorpio woman will keep family battles within the walls of your home. When company visits, she's apt to give the impression that married life with you is one big joy-ride. It's just her way of expressing her loyalty to you—at least, in front of others. She believes that family matters are and should stay private. She certainly will see to it that others have a high opinion of you both. She'll be right behind you in whatever it is you want to do. Although she's an individualist, after she has married she'll put her own interests aside for those of the man she loves. With a woman like this behind you, you can't help but go far. She'll never try to take over your role as boss of the family. She'll give you all the support you need in order to fulfill that role. She won't complain if the going gets rough. She knows how to take the bitter with the sweet. She is a courageous woman. She's as anxious as you are to find that place in the sun for you both. She's as determined a person as you are.

Although she may love her children, she may not be very affectionate toward them. She'll make a devoted mother, though. She'll be anxious to see them develop their talents. She'll teach the children to be courageous and steadfast.

CANCER MAN
SAGITTARIUS WOMAN

The Sagittarius woman is hard to keep track of: first she's here, then she's there. She's a woman with a severe case of itchy feet. She's got to keep on the move.

People generally like her because of her hail-fellow-well-met manner and her breezy charm. She is constantly good-natured and almost never cross. She is the kind of girl you're likely to strike up a palsy-walsy relationship with; you might not be interested in letting it go any farther. She probably won't sulk if you leave it on a friendly basis, either. Treat her like a kid-sister and she'll eat it up like candy.

She'll probably be attracted to you because of your restful, self-assured manner. She'll need a friend like you to help her over the rough spots in her life; she'll most likely turn to you for advice frequently.

There is nothing malicious about a girl born under this sign. She is full of bounce and good cheer. Her sunshiny dispositon can be relied upon even on the rainiest of days. No matter what she says or does, you'll always know that she means well. Sagittarians are sometimes short on tact. Some of them say anything that comes into their pretty little heads, no matter what the occasion. Sometimes the words that tumble out of their mouths seem downright cutting and cruel; they mean well but often everything they say comes out wrong. She's quite capable of losing her friends—and perhaps even yours—through a careless slip of the lip. Always remember that she is full of good intentions. Stick with her if you like her and try to help her mend her ways.

She's not a girl that you'd most likely be interested in marrying, but she'll certainly be lots of fun to pal around with. Quite often, Sagittarius women are outdoor types. They're crazy about things like fishing, camping, and mountain climbing. They love the wide open spaces. They are fond of all kinds of animals. Make no mistake about it: this busy little lady is no slouch. She's full of pep and vigor.

She's great company most of the time; she's more fun than a three-ring circus when she's in the right company. You'll like her for her candid and direct manner. On the whole, Sagittarians are very kind and sympathetic women.

If you do wind up marrying this girl-next-door type, you'd better see to it that you take care of all financial matters. Sagittarians often let money run through their fingers like sand.

As a mother, she'll smother her children with love and give them all of the freedom they think they need.

CANCER MAN
CAPRICORN WOMAN

The Capricorn woman may not be the most romantic woman of the Zodiac, but she's far from frigid when she meets the right man. She believes in true love; she doesn't appreciate getting involved in flings. To her, they're just a waste of time. She's looking for a man who means "business"—in life as well as in love. Although she can be very affectionate with her boyfriend or mate, she tends to let her head govern her heart. That is not to say that she is a cool, calculating cucumber. On the contrary, she just feels she can be more honest about love if she consults her brains first. She wants to size-up the situation first before throwing her heart in the ring. She wants to make sure it won't get stepped on.

The Capricorn woman is faithful, dependable, and systematic in just about everything that she undertakes. She is quite concerned with security and sees to it that every penny she spends is spent wisely. She is very economical about using her time, too. She does not believe in whittling away her energy on a scheme that is bound not to pay off.

Ambitious themselves, they are quite often attracted to ambitious men—men who are interested in getting somewhere in life. If a man of this sort wins her heart, she'll stick by him and do all she can to help him get to the top.

The Capricorn woman is almost always diplomatic. She makes an excellent hostess. She can be very influential when your business acquaintances come to dinner.

The Capricorn woman is likely to be very concerned, if not downright proud, about her family tree. Relatives are pretty important to her, particularly if they're socially prominent. Never say a cross word about her family members. That can really go against her grain and she'll punish you by not talking for days.

She's generally thorough in whatever she does: cooking, housekeeping, entertaining. Capricorn women are well-mannered and gracious, no matter what their backgrounds. They seem to have it in their natures to always behave properly.

If you should marry a woman born under this sign, you need never worry about her going on a wild shopping spree. They understand the value of money better than most women. If you turn over your paycheck to her at the end of the week, you can be sure that a good hunk of it will go into the bank and that all the bills will be paid on time.

With children, the Capricorn mother is both loving and correct. She'll see to it that they're polite and respectful.

CANCER MAN
AQUARIUS WOMAN

The woman born under the sign of the Water Bearer can be pretty odd and eccentric at times. Some say that this is the source of her mysterious charm. You're liable to think she's just a plain screwball; you may be 50 percent right.

Aquarius women often have their heads full of dreams and stars in their eyes. By nature, they are often unconventional; they have their own ideas about how the world should be run. Sometimes their ideas may seem pretty weird—chances are they're just a little bit too progressive. There is a saying that runs "The way the Aquarian thinks, so will the world in fifty years."

If you find yourself falling in love with a woman born under this sign, you'd better fasten your safety belt. It may take some time before you know what she's like and even then, you may have nothing to go on but a string of vague hunches.

She can be like a rainbow: full of dazzling colors. She's like no other girl you've ever known. There is something about her that is definitely charming—yet elusive, you'll never be able to put your finger on it. She seems to radiate adventure and optimism without even trying. She'll most likely be the most tolerant and open-minded woman you've ever encountered.

If you find that she's too much mystery and charm for you to handle—and being a Cancerian, chances are you might—just talk it out with her and say that you think it would be better if you called it quits. She'll most likely give you a peck on the cheek and say "Okay, but let's still be friends." Aquarius women are like that. Perhaps you'll both find it easier to get along in a friendship than in a romance.

It is not difficult for her to remain buddy-buddy with an ex-lover. For many Aquarians, the line between friendship and romance is a pretty fuzzy one.

She's not a jealous person and while you're romancing her, she won't expect you to be, either. You'll find her a pretty free spirit most of the time. Just when you think you know her inside-out, you'll discover that you don't really know her at all. She's a very sympathetic and warm person; she is often helpful to those in need of assistance and advice.

She'll seldom be suspicious even when she has every right to be. If the man she loves makes a little slip, she's liable to forget it.

She makes a fine mother. Her positive and big-hearted qualities are easily transmitted to her offspring.

CANCER MAN
PISCES WOMAN

The Pisces woman places great value on love and romance. She's gentle, kind, and romantic. Perhaps she's that girl you've been dreaming about all these years. Like you, she has very high ideals, she will only give her heart to a man who she feels can live up to her expectations.

She'll never try to wear the pants in the family. She's a staunch believer in the man being the head of the house. Quite often, Pisces women are soft and cuddly. They have a feminine, domestic charm that can win the heart of just about any man.

Generally, there's a lot more to her than just her pretty face and womanly ways. There's a brain ticking behind that gentle facade. You may not become aware of it—that is, until you've married her. It's no cause for alarm, however; she'll most likely never use it against you. But if she feels you're botching up your married life through careless behavior or if she feels you could be earning more money than you do, she'll tell you about it. But any wife would, really. She will never try to usurp your position as head and bread winner of the family. She'll admire you for your ambition and drive. If anyone says anything against you in her presence, she'll probably break out into tears. Pisces women are usually very sensitive. Their reaction to adversity or frustration is often just a plain good old fashioned cry. They can weep buckets when inclined.

She'll have an extra-special dinner waiting for you when you call up and teil her that you've just landed a new and important contract. Don't bother to go into the details at the dinner table, though; she probably doesn't have much of a head for business matters. She's only too glad to leave those matters up to you.

She's a wizard in decorating a house. She's fond of soft and beautiful things. She's a good housekeeper. She'll always see to it that you have plenty of socks and underwear in the top drawer of your dresser.

Treat her with tenderness and your relationship will be an enjoyable one. Pisces women are generally fond of sweets and flowers. Never forget birthdays, anniversaries, and the like. She won't.

Your talent for patience and gentleness can pay off in your relationship with a Pisces woman. Chances are she'll never make you sorry you placed that band of gold on her finger.

There's a strong bond between a Pisces mother and her children. She'll try to give them all the things she never had as a child. Chances are she'll spoil them a little.

CANCER

YEARLY FORECAST: 1992

Forecast for 1992 Concerning Business and
Financial Matters, Job Prospects,
Travel, Health, Romance and Marriage
for Those Born with the Sun
in the Zodiacal Sign of Cancer,
June 21–July 20.

People born under the influence of the Sun in the zodiacal sign of Cancer can look forward this year to progress in their life's work. They can also expect generally good health, new romances, travel to interesting places, and a relatively stable homelife. They will have enough money to enable them to enjoy many social activities as well as to indulge themselves in hobbies. They will be able to fulfill their generous humanitarian impulses and to interest their friends in joining in charitable efforts. Since health plays such an important role, you Cancer people will be very much aware of it this year. You will want to keep fit. You will seek out books and information that will clue you in on the latest developments. You may even join a fitness course or set up an exercise program on your own. Health food stores will see more of you than usual.

Cancer people may be more gregarious than usual. Family ties will be stronger than ever. You will take extra pleasure in your loved ones, your close friends, and your romantic activities. Having been born under this sign, you will want to spend as much time as possible with your dear ones at home. You will be active in clubs and other organizations. You may seek election to important posts, but during May there can be some conflict with other members. Perhaps you will be frustrated in your ambitions. Throughout the year, you will be in active communication with people at a distance, some of whom you will invite to your home. If expected visitors fail to show up, you are likely to become very angry. You will be annoyed if a letter you had counted on is

123

delayed. There will be times when you will be working under pressure. You will run out of time before you run out of work. This will be especially true as the year draws to its close. If you wait too long to take that exciting trip, work and holiday plans will force you to cancel it. You will have to make do with short trips and visits to people nearer home. Dear ones will sympathize. They will be concerned for your health, and will urge you to avoid any strenuous travel that could cause illness.

Career prospects are good. The most progress can be made in April, but the first three months of the year also will be successful. Study and concentration on the tasks at hand will be very important. Get as much done as you can before May, a month that can be both difficult and disappointing. Those who work in the fields of religion or medicine will make progress in June. During the first half of the year, some useful contacts can be made. These can advance your career. Later months bring some frustration. There can be deception by colleagues. Some associates will try to improve their status in the organization at your expense. Be especially cautious during September and October. Conflicts with superiors can cause worry during the last few weeks of the year. Problems can be resolved without permanent damage if you keep a low profile at this time.

Cancers are ambitious and imaginative, so they will be looking for new avenues to the top. Independent study and organized courses can be helpful. If you can study abroad, you will learn new skills and broaden your horizons. This can be of immediate help and also can be a valuable talking point if you are looking for new work. People in the secretarial and business world will find the latter part of the year especially rewarding. If you are self-employed, you should be quite successful. A tight financial situation for other employees can be eased by taking another job outside of regular work hours.

Cancer people who are not regular members of the work force can have an interesting and productive year. Those of you who have children will find that their activities can take much of your time and attention. A little advance planning will make it possible for you to have some time for your own interests also. Home decoration can be important, since you enjoy being surrounded by beautiful things. But your activities will not be confined to the home. Since Cancers have a real concern for the welfare and happiness of others, you will want to put time and energy into worthy causes. New interests developed this year will be helpful to those starting on new careers or those doing volunteer work outside the home. Levels of energy will be especially high in June, July, and September. Then you will be unusually busy with home and creative work. Gardeners can be quite successful during these three months.

As a Cancer person, you will have your home and enjoy being in the company of family, but you want to see the world as well. So you will welcome any opportunity to travel and to meet new people. Even short trips to visit friends and relatives can be exciting. Business can take you far afield. Children should be included whenever possible; trips can be educational as well as fun. Although Cancers will be on the go during much of December, short trips will be more likely than extended journeys.

Travel, home improvements, charity, social activities, and just plain living call for money. You Cancer people will be happy to learn that, on the whole, financial prospects are just fine for 1992. Jobs will be remunerative, and there will be opportunities to make money on the side. The situation will be especially good in July and August, when you will be having a run of good luck. Problems can arise from time to time this year, during holiday periods for example; but it should be relatively easy to get loans to tide you over the crises. The necessary funds usually will be available for creative projects and entertainment. Some of you will have a windfall in the form of an inheritance or lucky investment.

Even though it will be easier than usual to borrow money this year, be discriminating when it comes to your reasons for doing so. Loans have to be repaid sooner or later, and you will want to shake yourself free from debt as quickly as possible. A few lessons in thrift can be a good idea when you are discussing finances with the family. Your earnings can fluctuate from month to month, and people have a tendency to overspend when the cash is available. You will have to curb your own trend toward extravagance before you can honestly ask others to follow suit. Your earnings will be at their highest in August, so the temptation to spend too much on summer fun can be overwhelming. The best time to apply for loans will be the last several weeks of the year. You should put as much money into savings as you can while the funds are available. If you are wise and lucky, you may not even have to borrow.

All this does not mean that you and your family will have to go on an austerity budget. Even after making regular deposits in your savings account, there should be enough left over for outings with the family, some new furniture, or for taking to dinner that attractive person who catches your roving eye. Cultural events can broaden your horizons and raise your qualifications for the job that you will be seeking eventually. A work of art or a rare book can be a good investment. Tickets for concerts or dance recitals can cement family relationships. Music seems to be your passion, so you and your loved one will enjoy listening to recorded music at home. If children show aptitude for any of the arts, encourage them. Exposure to such activities will be of value to them in the future.

If you are a Cancer who has not yet settled down, you will spend much of your time searching for romance. Music and other cultural activities can provide opportunities to meet prospective partners will similar interests. Drama groups, museum courses, musical groups all should be considered in the light of meeting the ideal partner. Adult education or college courses also can be useful. Do not overlook the possibility of a love affair with someone you meet at work. Conditions vary throughout the year. That summer romance can be exciting but not likely to last too long. April is a much better time. An affair begun then can culminate in wedding bells late in the year. November is tricky for romance. You may be held to any statement you made, however wild, even though you may have changed your mind in the meantime.

You married Cancer people can have a fairly good year. It is a great help to have a family to turn to when the going gets rough. The support of loved ones will get you through troubled times. But remember that dear ones can have their own worries, so be prepared to offer the support and comfort that you would expect from them. Children keep you young, although that may be hard to believe at times when they are driving you up the wall. Get involved with them and their interests. Always be ready to lend a sympathetic ear if they are troubled and seeking help or advice. There will be times toward the end of the year when everyone will be too busy for family fun, but your interest in and suggestions for family projects will be much appreciated.

Probably there will not be any very serious health problems this year. Holidays can be tiring, so watch you health at those times. Many people overdo it in November and December; make sure that you are not one of them. A problem requiring special care can arise in early summer, but avoid hospitalization in July unless it is an emergency. Emotional and physical health are so closely related that you will want to avoid endangering either. There are bound to be upsets, worries, annoying people, and romantic and domestic difficulties from time to time. If you can cultivate a relaxed and detached attitude, you should suffer no real ill effects. Learn to roll with the punches. No year can be perfect, but your sociable nature, concern for others, good friends and family, material success, and a generous helping of good luck promise to make 1992 memorable.

DAILY FORECAST

January–December 1992

JANUARY

1. WEDNESDAY. Enjoyable. If you do not have to go to work on this holiday, plan to spend most of it with friends and relatives. A visitor from a distance will urge you to return the visit later in the year. Get together with people who share your interest in the arts. Since travel and creative projects can be expensive, spare some time for figuring out where you can get the money. A friend may come through with a generous offer. You probably will want to get some rest before returning to your job after all the holiday excitement. Some Cancer people will be starting new jobs, while others can look forward to lucrative promotions. Students returning to school shortly will have a new sense of purpose.

2. THURSDAY. Mixed. Today seems to be made for work and the evening for play, so you have something to look forward to. The hobbyist can produce something useful and beautiful. This cuts the ground out from under family members who have been critical of such talents. A new co-worker seems to be so congenial that you can probably count on forming a new friendship. But keep your personal affairs to yourself when talking with new acquaintances. On the whole, you will be getting along well with those most dear to you. You will undoubtedly want to introduce new friends to your romantic partner. A large family get-together could be the ideal setting. A small local band will set your toes tapping as well as livening up festivities and putting people at ease.

3. FRIDAY. Ordinary. Your reputation for compassion and helpfulness is likely to bring associates to seek your advice or to cry on your shoulder. They will go away comforted, and then you must start thinking of yourself. You perhaps have had a nagging feeling for some time that you can do something to improve your career and to make your personal life more rewarding. A stop at the library or bookstore can yield a book that gives you some answers. You should check your mail and the newspapers for information about courses that can improve your mind and your life. Reply promptly to such advertisements. Someone close to you can be persuaded to accompany you to lectures or classes.

4. SATURDAY. Lucky. Today could be quite exciting for you Cancers, especially if romance is on your mind. A wedding might be the focus of the day. If you are not an active member of the wedding, you can find time for relaxing as well as for some mild outdoor exercise. You are likely to meet someone who will broaden your horizons over the months ahead. And you may want to discuss some of your latest, imaginative ideas with your closest companions. Your intelligence and curiosity will always lead you down new paths. All in all, it appears to be a day both for good luck and professional progress. Do not be afraid to speak up, but at the same time avoid ruffling feelings with too innovative ideas. Spring them in phases over a period of time.

5. SUNDAY. Rewarding. You probably will not be thinking of what is in it for you when you go to the assistance of someone in need. Nor will you when you are offering to share your experience with an outright beginner. However, you are likely to learn that someone in a higher position has been taking note. That person's interest could turn your life around, as well as the lives of those most dear to you. But no matter what might develop, you will have the satisfaction of knowing that you were being helpful. Perhaps you are in need of some advice and even material help yourself; turn to someone older and wiser for guidance. Worries that have been building up steadily will probably diminish if you follow whatever guidelines and suggestions that may be forthcoming.

6. MONDAY. Good. Cancer people are noted for their understanding and helpful natures. These qualities can be turned to good account when dealing with family members. Your sympathetic help can make your family happy this evening. You may be asked to served on a committee, or to work cooperatively with someone on your job simply because others know you can be depended on. Eventually, you will have some time to yourself; you will probably then remember that you have been meaning to reply to that letter from abroad. Do it promptly; it can pave the way for a trip. A physical checkup reveals that there is nothing wrong with your health that a more positive attitude cannot cure. Knowing you are healthy should effect a changed attitude.

7. TUESDAY. Successful. Overall, today can be quite pleasant and entertaining. But you must first make something clear to family members. They cannot saddle you with the expense of hosting family friends who may be visiting. Once that is understood, everyone will settle down and concentrate on having a fine time. It can turn into a musical affair, with the entire assemblage participating. Your romantic partner will be there, and that will make your day. Dining at home will be best, since not everybody might think much of the restaurant you select. Your free time could be taken up with financial and legal matters. These should be attended to promptly, even if you have to spend money for legal advice. Someone should be able to refer you to a lawyer.

8. WEDNESDAY. Unsettling. Watch your step today, and do not let stress and tension get you down. The atmosphere can be hostile at times; there are those who are in an argumentative mood, unwilling to drop the subject. Even simple requests for information can have an edge to them. Try to remain calm, and think of your plans for unwinding this evening in the company of good friends. You probably will be called on during the day to do a lot of work with figures. If mathematics is not your strong point, you may have to do a considerable amount of brushing up. Keep reminding yourself that the mental effort is good for you. You should catch up on those letters that call for prompt replies.

9. THURSDAY. Stressful. If the day seems to be made up of one depressing event after another, remember that you are a Cancer. It means that you may have to try harder to overcome your tendency to become discouraged. Avoid brooding over what cannot be helped, at least by you. Your visit can mean much to someone in the hospital. If your love life is unsatisfactory, do not heap recriminations on your partner; there may be a good explanation. A three-handkerchief movie could upset you unnecessarily. Remember that the plot is not likely to be based on reality. If you take things as they come, you will not be thrown off balance at the idea of a sudden business trip. It is all in the day's work, and there is always the chance that you will meet someone who might be destined to change your life.

10. FRIDAY. Changeable. The chief threat to your security today is overconfidence about your situation. As far as money goes, however, you can afford to indulge yourself in something that you really want. Family members are likely to enjoy a challenging game that has just come on the market. Buy it for them, and you can all have fun together. If unexpected visitors should arrive, they may not be the ones you would have enjoyed most. A somewhat pedantic type goes on and on lecturing to you, and you are likely to learn more than you really wanted to know about a certain subject. But you do not have to give your undivided attention as long as you look alert and interested while allowing your thoughts to wander.

11. SATURDAY. Enjoyable.   Most of today is yours to do with as you like. Weather permitting, it offers a good chance to get some fresh air and exercise, with or without company. Since you as a Cancer are basically a family person, you will undoubtedly make loved ones welcome. They will repect your silence if you are wrapped up in your own thoughts. Visitors can be irritating, but they will be less so if you take the trouble to find out what is motivating them. You are likely to find items in the newspapers that are more cheerful than usual, so reading them should be a pleasant change. You may want to share some particularly interesting stories with family members, and enjoy a good laugh.

12. SUNDAY. Pleasant.   This can be another day for doing what you find the most fun to do as well as the most interesting. Some Cancer people will want to start off by attending religious services. If you are one of them, you may find yourself more deeply involved in church activities than you had meant to be. But you will enjoy it all the same, once you get started. Every time you try to do something, you seem to be interrupted. But that should not bother you, since you have a good sense of humor. In addition to the usual Sunday occupations of reading the papers and watching television, artistic Cancer people may have some sudden inspirations that should be acted on right away. Your creativity and imagination are particularly strong today.

13. MONDAY. Successful.   Those of you who are on the lookout for appliances will find that it pays to shop around. You can save money at a time when that is a most important consideration. Partying and overindulgence in food, drink, or luxuries can be detrimental both to your health as well as your bank account. Visiting with old friends can lead to some stimulating discussions, perhaps based on current events. You will find yourself expressing your ideas eloquently and persuasively. Your work should not be very difficult, even though superiors are not particularly cooperative. Cancer successes depend on your concentrating your drive and not diffusing energy.

14. TUESDAY. Lucky. This can be a rewarding day for you Cancers. A surprise gift may arrive, probably the outcome of some chats you have had with family members at a distance. You may not have seen them recently, but you have proof that you are never far from their thoughts. You will meet someone today with whom you can form a lasting friendship. You might well want to explore some rather unusual ideas that were suggested. Intellectual activities should help assure that you remain sharp and interesting. Keep your feet on the ground, however; a head-in-the-clouds act can lead to impractical actions. Shopping for exotic foods can be a real challenge if you keep your eyes open for new products that have only recently come on the market.

15. WEDNESDAY. Challenging. If you are faced with learning how to operate new equipment such as computers or advanced telephones, you Cancers are likely to become upset. You will have to prod yourself into making the effort; otherwise, you can fall behind in the race to the top. Stop procrastinating about opening that savings account and committing yourself to making regular deposits. Early in the day, some disappointing news reaches you about your club's meeting for this evening being postponed. Another date will be chosen by the committee later. You are curious about some historical mystery, such as an ancient civilization. If you pursue such tantalizing searches, you will probably find someone with similar interests.

16. THURSDAY. Variable. With the Moon soon to enter Cancer, you may already be feeling some uncertainty and indecision about your work. Do not let yourself dwell on your problems, real or imaginary. Instead, seek out old friends who can reassure you that you are on the right track. Finish anything you start, even if you are strongly disinclined to do so. Say little unless you are sure of your ground; people are more impressed by logic than by half-formed theories. You seem to be having some problems with your romantic partner, who is apparently just as unhappy as you are. A heart-to-heart talk, no holds barred, could help.

17. FRIDAY. Happy. Cancers can be feeling very optimistic today. But just keep from becoming unrealistic where money is concerned. If you have been thinking of taking the family on a lavish trip, you will probably come back down to earth with a rush when you learn the cost. Do not abandon the idea entirely; if you check around, you are likely to find that something can be worked out. Ideas come thick and fast, and you will want to exchange them in conversation with visiting relatives and neighbors. The evening is especially good for writing letters to those you love. Your thoughts translate readily into words, so you may prefer to telephone your nearest and dearest.

18. SATURDAY. Sensitive. With the influence of the Moon now at its peak in Cancer, a touch of irritability is distinctly possible. You cannot be bothered to be tactful with those who interrupt you at your work, and your immediate family will probably suffer from your snappishness. But your family may be in the right. This is the weekend, and you should be spending less time on your career and more with them. If you are mulling over a new approach to your work or trying to resolve a problem, you probably will not be very good company. Try to plan an outing that includes family members. Enjoy the fresh air as much as possible and try to get away from your usual haunts.

19. SUNDAY. Depressing. You are likely to be feeling moody and at odds with the world for most of the day. You may not want to have anything to do with your fellow human beings. But that attitude can be the wrong approach. You should climb out of your shell and seek some pleasant company to cheer you. A religious service might bring you into contact with some interesting people. Reading an inspiring book could brighten your mood. Getting out and around can lead to a new relationship with someone who is tuned in on your wavelength. A meeting of the minds can be almost telepathic in nature, and you will certainly benefit from sharing thoughts and emotions. Moreover, you will lose the feeling of being lonely and isolated.

20. MONDAY. Stressful. Your Cancer tendency of wanting to help others can depress you. You read the newspapers and watch television, and you worry about those who are in trouble. In most cases, there is little you can do to help so stop tearing your emotions to pieces. Concentrate on how you can help yourself and the people who are nearer to home. Some worry about money is likely to crop up, but everything should work out for the best. Watch for the mail; it may well deliver the answer to your financial problems, at least for now. Turn your energies toward something that you really enjoy doing. Settle down in the evening with friends for some good conversation. Music can be relaxing.

21. TUESDAY. Happy. You are a new and different person today; the clouds have lifted, and your outlook is bright once more. Yesterday's worries about money have vanished. One of the communications you received may have had something to do with it. You may want to write letters in answer to several that you receive. Speak up when neighbors and friends are discussing something of interest. Indulge your love of art by visiting a museum or art gallery. You may turn a corner and literally bump into someone who is destined to become a new romance. You can further your career ambitions if you devote time, energy and common sense to your goal. The only cloud on the horizon will be legal in nature, but fortunately it should not be too serious.

22. WEDNESDAY. Rewarding. Forget about the weather because, good or bad, the sun will be shining for you! The only clouds above your head will be rosy and romantic. The unattached Cancer may receive a proposal. Your response is likely to be so enthusiastic that wedding bells will soon be ringing. If your recent legal problems have involved a difficult divorce, you may now conclude that it was all for the best and you might even start looking around for your next romantic partner. Legal bills can be worrisome, but some kind and understanding relatives will pitch in with loans to help pay them. The day is not favorable for water sports even if you live in a warm climate, nor for swimming in indoor pools anywhere.

23. THURSDAY. Cautious. Money and family affairs, which are not always inseparable, are much on your mind. Now is the time to be sure that you have not overlooked any current bills. After you have paid them, you should do some accounting to see what remains in your bank account. Check your credit line if you use those plastic cards; it would be not only very embarrassing to exceed your limit but it could also cost you dearly. As for family, arguments over spending can arise between you and your spouse, but a frank talk can put things to rights. Do not be a source of unlimited spending money for family. Go about your own concerns; they will soon face the fact that they will have to earn their way and the sooner they start, the more they'll earn.

24. FRIDAY. Mixed. Your moods can have a profound effect on the people around you. Since you do not seem to be in a very good frame of mind today, you can expect the same from others. Some family conflicts from yesterday can exert a strong influence upon your actions today. Avoid all arguments whatever their origin. People are only trying to give you good advice; on another day you would welcome it. Above all, do not discuss politics unless you can do so in a friendly fashion. Foreign news may be bad, but you can always hope for better times. You will be talking with quite a few people today, from old friends to new acquaintances, so make a real effort to be less grumpy and more outgoing.

25. SATURDAY. Variable. The Cancer person is often lacking in self-confidence and can be very sensitive about slights, real or imagined. This can lead to trouble with a romantic partner who does not understand or perhaps care. If the problem seems serious, try to find help from pamphlets and books or in counseling. With some people, you can engage in a no-holds-barred argument that will clear the air and let you get back on a friendly or loving footing. A business matter can be confusing if you are thinking of striking out for yourself. Since your thinking may be muddy, do a little digging for facts before you leap. Relating to others can be hard for you and thus can be a disadvantage. You should try to overcome this fault for your own sake.

26. SUNDAY. Enjoyable. You can be surprisingly busy this quiet day of rest. Before it is over, you could find yourself, if not head over heels in love, at least highly intrigued by someone you meet. The attraction is likely to grow out of your mutual interest in sports or in some form of entertainment for which you serve on a committee. You will be popular with everyone, but more than popular with one special person. Do not leap into anything; a new relationship needs time to grow. So spend time together at some special event to get to know each other's likes and dislikes, background, and attitudes. Do not become possessive too quickly, or you may frighten this person off, but the day should be fun.

27. MONDAY. Fortunate. This can be a day for reading and mental activity. Your sensitivity for the feelings of others gives you the advantage of understanding and sympathizing with their problems. An article or book on philosophy will provide some answers, but you will have to work on overcoming the natural Cancer diffidence if you want to be really helpful. Use your imagination to get away from any dullness in the work routine. If you need a few hours of pure escape, turn to a mystery novel or a psychological thriller. Some physical or romantic problems can stand in the way of continuing the sports that so interested you yesterday. Someone you meet today is likely to have a strong influence on your future.

28. TUESDAY. Tranquil. The Cancer person's interest in others and genuine concern for their welfare is the most active influence today. You have obligations and duties that involve other people, and it is the time to fulfill them. Your responsibilities have been increased; superiors can now be watching your performance from the background. They will conclude that you have the right stuff for advancement in the organization. Your optimism is not misplaced. Take stock of yourself, and you will be able to form a pattern for the future. People you meet today seem to be destined to play a considerable role in that future. They may be from a foreign land or from a different background, but you will enjoy their friendship all the more.

29. WEDNESDAY. Uncertain. Personal relationships seem to have deteriorated since yesterday. Impatience with associates can lead to difficult situations. You are likely to feel that you are being frustrated at every turn. You will probably have an urge to get away from everything that blocks your path, so you may start out on a long trip. This journey, however, is not likely to turn out as you expect. The employer vs. employee relationship can be strained unless you have unusually understanding superiors who are willing to let you go pretty much your own way. It is not worth making any plans today either immediate ones or for the evening, because they will be subject to change.

30. THURSDAY. Easygoing. Much can be accomplished if you put your mind to it. Advice should be welcomed and seriously considered; whether you follow it or not will be entirely up to you. There is an air of optimism at the place where you work, giving your spirits a decided lift. Do not use the excuse of ill health to get out of doing something that is distasteful to you. Blaming poor health is probably a figment of your imagination. You may well be in a sociable mood and eager to greet newly arrived visitors to your home or office. It is possible to learn a great deal now if you keep your ears open. Give a little more thought to your romantic affair. If it has been faltering, make a real effort to rekindle the flame.

31. FRIDAY. Enjoyable. Your career prospects have been positive throughout the month of January, and they hold a promise of being even better in February. Your romantic prospects are also good. When one love affair seems to be on its way out, another is waiting in the wings. You can help things along by trying to meet as many new people as possible. The financial outlook at work is bright, and you may be celebrating a raise or promotion this evening. A good friend, not necessarily a romantic interest, will be able to join you for dinner, followed by reminiscing as well as serious discussion. Working conditions seem to be improving; it's not the time to make any drastic changes.

FEBRUARY

1. SATURDAY. Happy. Work that you did not have enough time to complete earlier this week could be nudging your conscience. Get it done as early as possible today so that you will have freedom to enjoy the weekend. Exciting new adventures can come your way. There may be an opportunity during the day to try something new, such as a language course or some special dance lessons. If you can rope in a few close friends to join with you for some fun this evening, it should be more enjoyable. Outdoor sports are fine if the weather permits. Romance is likely to be on your mind. Friends may want to talk about their conquests, but there will probably be a predominance of fiction. Keep an eye on spending, even for a romantic evening for two.

2. SUNDAY. Successful. Cancer people are likely to want to attend religious services today. But many other people seem to feel the same way so that you find the church crowded. If you cannot attend, why not direct your interests toward humanitarian efforts? People will welcome you to their committees as they strive to recruit newcomers. Also, you should remember that charity begins at home; spend your spare time in doing little kindnesses for those most dear to you. Sports and games can keep you busy, with card or board games an acceptable substitute for the less energetic. It's possible that you will fall in love quite suddenly. Social activities are highlighted in the evening and you can learn the latest dance steps at an impromptu get-together.

3. MONDAY. Excellent. Dreams can come true today, but they may need a little push from you and your friends. Original ideas come thick and fast to writers and other creative types. You will meet some people whose interests run parallel to yours. Those interests could be either in the fields of politics or of journalism. Eventually, the two subjects might be combined, writing articles about current events for a newspaper or magazine. You might want to become a columnist or a reporter. While you tend to be mild-mannered, you can become persevering when you want something badly. If you meet resistance about a loan, you could become agressive.

4. TUESDAY. Mixed. Your mind is likely to be on romance all day. The affectionate nature of Cancers could cause you to be somewhat disappointed when the object of your affections does not go along with your plans. Perhaps you will even go so far as trying to patch up matters with an old love at some distance. But however the results appear to be today, all will end well in time. Instead of nursing your frustrations, continue to work on a pet project. You seem to have something on your mind about this, so try to resolve whatever the problem is now. Your efforts in this direction can lead to a new job or other enterprise. Do not hesitate to branch out if your ambitions tell you so.

5. WEDNESDAY. Pleasant. Mental capacities should be put to good use. Watch out for deception, and keep your own secrets. Perhaps you will gain some interesting insights into your own character. The day could be fairly quiet, but emotions should not be allowed to run wild. Pregnancy is a definite possibility for those born under the sign of the Crab. It can be a good day for distant travel as long as you are clear in your own mind about your destination and your purpose. Since your time is likely to be limited, you undoubtedly realize that you cannot visit every enticing spot that beckons to your romantic nature. Make a list of priorities, then talk to a travel agent or consult travel guides. Once you have made a decision, you will have to stay with it.

6. THURSDAY. Happy. The kindliness of your nature and your generosity to others will be much appreciated just now. If you are having a good time, you will want to share it with others. You are likely to find many outlets for benevolent impulses. Others will be encouraged by your help or a simple pat on the back. Your own health may require a quick visit to the doctor. With that off your mind, you will be ready to go out and enjoy yourself. You can fall in love at first sight. If that love affair is with someone from another country, you will have to face the problem of your future residence. A night on the town can be on the schedule, especially if your romantic partner likes to dance.

7. FRIDAY. Demanding. You are likely to be very glad that the workweek is ending. Now you can spend some time unwinding. But your mind is still hopping around, and you are inclined to be disturbed by outside events. Violent protests are not your style. The Cancer person usually likes to work slowly and methodically to bring about change. You are probably involved to some extent in organizations that aim to bring peace to our world. But even this still does not seem to be enough when you read about natural disasters and the resultant suffering. You will do all you can to try to raise funds to bring an end to human misery. Do not become

too disturbed, and avoid letting any anger affect your relations
with loved ones. It's easy to transfer blame to others.

8. SATURDAY. Disconcerting. World and national events
continue to be very much on your mind. In conversations with
friends and neighbors, you will be discussing little else. Realism
and idealism can clash over your reaction to these outside events,
and arguments will naturally result. After listening to the view-
points of more realistic people, you Cancers may decide to put
your own idealistic approach on hold. What you learn from discussions can be written down; eventually it might become a publish-
able article. Your idealism can also suffer a setback when money is
an issue. Today is a time for expanding your horizons; you are
likely to spend much of it in conversations and reading, perhaps
even research.

9. SUNDAY. Disturbing. You should be relaxing as much as
possible during this stressful period, but your restless mind will not
allow it. There is work to be done, and you want to settle down to
it. There could be interruptions from close associates, especially
children. Those innovative ideas of yours can be misinterpreted,
and you may have to scrap them for the time being. Some news
from New York can worry you, so it will be best to postpone a trip
there and find another destination. Family members are not likely
to see why you act as you do. You can take your mind off your
troubles by finding something of an artistic nature to occupy your
time, possibly sketching or resuming unfinished needlework.

10. MONDAY. Favorable. The emphasis today is on money
and health, and sometimes they have a direct effect on each other.
Health problems can result from eating the wrong things, such as
junk food, instead of a well-balanced diet. Overeating will do you
no good either. Vague feelings of discomfort can color your attitude toward your current financial position. You probably are
concerned about the future, so do something concrete about planning for it. Do not burden others with your money worries; that
will merely spread the gloom around. Envy of those who are more
secure can only make you unhappy. A close look at your bank
account will show that you can afford to buy something that you
really need and want for your home.

11. TUESDAY. Unsettling. Financial matters continue to be
very much on the Cancer mind. Your own money problems pale
beside those of people you know and others about whom you read.
You can make your own small contribution to bettering the world

by getting involved in charitable efforts. You should first make sure, however, that the organizations to which you donate time and money are legitimate. Ask to see their annual statements if you are in doubt. Cancer business people could encounter some legal or financial setbacks at this time. You may hesitate to make personal purchases. You can do much good close to home by assuring someone in worse shape than you of help.

12. WEDNESDAY. Disconcerting. If you are unattached romantically, all the advertisements for Valentine's Day can get you down. An old friend can come to the rescue with an introduction to someone new, and your spirits will soar. However, you will probably be bothered by paperwork that has been neglected, so you will want to spend some time alone to take care of it. Letters should be answered. Bills should be paid and magazine subscriptions or memberships renewed when due. You tend to be verbose today. Keep that in mind when preparing reports, and act accordingly. You are following the news closely right now, and you may learn of the death of a prominent public figure. Do not stay hidden away too long. You need someone to talk to.

13. THURSDAY. Rewarding. The Moon will enter Cancer early tomorrow, and some people can already be feeling that vague sense of insecurity that the Crab can bring. Otherwise, you feel fit as a fiddle and eager to get out and about. In your enthusiasm, you are likely to talk too much. That might result in a secret becoming public knowledge. Shopping can be quite successful. Not only can you find the perfect gift for the one you love but also it's a great bargain. Then a night on the town can be in order, either alone with your loved one or together with friends. If you go out, choose a good restaurant. But do not neglect your job in your search for romance and excitement.

14. FRIDAY. Enjoyable. Cancer people are now more than ever aware of their ties to home and family. You can be torn between the challenges of your job and your desire to be home. If you are self-employed, it may be possible to combine the two. You will probably have to deal with a money or employment problem. But there is no place like home, even though you may feel hemmed in. Instead of brooding in solitude, take an active part in family life. Much of the conversation can center around improvements to the home. You may be planning an extension to the house, or discussing choices of colors and placement of furniture. Any changes that you make can result in more comfortable living.

15. SATURDAY. Mixed.   Cancer people tend to be edgy to-day; blame it on the Moon. When family members finally get on your nerves, look up some close friends; but whatever you do, don't shut yourself away from life. If a relative is expected as a house guest, your dear ones are undoubtedly in a flurry of prepara-tion and you will have to do your share. Try to avoid emotional upsets even if your romantic life seems to be far from stable. That can be a matter of incompatibility. You may encounter some disruptive elements that put obstacles into the path of what you consider true love. You can either find a way around them or give up and concentrate on doing something out of the ordinary to keep your mind fully occupied.

16. SUNDAY. Unsettling.   Conditions become better for soli-tary activities as the day progresses. It can be easy to be alone if your family and friends are all busy with their own interests and activities. They would not be of very much help to you anyway. Get those necessary chores out of the way quickly before you run out of steam. You see many other jobs around you that need doing, but you are not in the mood. Take a careful look at your financial situation to see what you can do to build up your bank account. There seems to be little on television, so what not play some records or tapes? Music can sometimes wash away that feeling of restlessness. Activities you might consider, away from home, seem depressing, but take positive action.

17. MONDAY. Tricky.   The Cancer employee will have to face some unsettling changes at work today. There are new routines to be mastered and adjustments made to new co-workers. Keep any written work strictly factual and objective. If you go out with companions after work, make sure that you are not stuck with the whole check. You will veer away from wanting company to long-ing to be alone to read or listen to music. This is not a good day for romantic affairs and your family is likely to take a dim view of your partner. You can live with that, but your own relationship with the person can understandably be rocky. If the relationship presents too many problems, forget romance for now.

18. TUESDAY. Changeable.   The afternoon might be your best time today for making any real progress. The morning could be taken up with checking over current finances and finding your-self regretting some recent, large expenditures. But a note of cheer arrives in the mail in the form of a check. Study is always impor-tant, whether for your job or for your own development, and it can sometimes be easier to study with others than alone. As your self-confidence increases, you will be less reluctant to ask someone to fill in for you on the job for a short time. Watch out for some of your co-workers; your new associates can be envious and do their best to block your advancement. Ask some to go out after work for a drink or a snack.

19. WEDNESDAY. Happy. Your decision to be more tolerant of others than you have been in the past works in your favor. You can now see the good side of colleagues and friends. Pressures slowly decrease, especially those job- and financial-connected ones. You can have fun with friends, and you can look forward to a reunion with someone from the past. If you have an interest in flying, you are likely to find someone else who shares it. With worry about your future career somewhat diminished, you are now in the mood to write letters. Love letters will get good results, but phone calls bring quicker action. You are in the mood for love, and you should have little difficulty in finding it. What with job and romance, you lead a busy life, but it's not dull or dreary.

20. THURSDAY. Happy. Much as you Cancers love to spend time with your families, it is not possible for you to stay home all day. Your job requires you to expend your time and efforts in the pursuit of profits and success for your firm. You will find your co-workers are sympathetic to your need to get out among the public. But your romantic interest, as well as other dear ones, are always at the back of your mind. Those of you who are making your daily rounds will find new shops that feature goodies that are crying out to be taken home for dinner. Friends and family get together for a pleasant evening meal and good conversation. If your past actions have puzzled your love, you had better have a good reason.

21. FRIDAY. Disconcerting. If possible, call off your travel plans to an area now considered unsafe. Your work, however, may make this impossible if you are involved in direct contacts there. There is no need to worry too much, but it would be well to be cautious; take no chances with your personal safety and your possessions. If you seem to be too much on edge, slow down and catch your breath; do not risk your health. A good friend offers some take-it-or-leave-it advice. Your mind may be on some un-completed chores at home, or on studying and correspondence. Take it easy, and do not let mischievous people at work get on your nerves. Keep your wits about you when hurrying home this evening. The people you encounter seem rather peculiar.

22. SATURDAY. Mixed. Your world is full of so many things now that you do not know where to start your activities. Clubs are interesting, and are hoping for your services in organizing social affairs. They really need you, so give generously of your efforts. A drama club or studio can be a good place to give vent to your creative bent. Window-shopping is a lot less expensive and tiring than going through those doors. If matters are not going your way, keep your temper in check and your lips sealed. Lashing out is foreign to your nature. Save the explosion until you are alone and by then you won't care. Romance can be frustrating, especially if you fall in love with someone from a distant land who is about to return to his country.

23. SUNDAY. Rewarding. Religion and philosophy occupy your thoughts. You may want to think about exploring some new and different ideas. A friend with similar interests can accompany you on your search for new truths. Together you can have a fine time. Reading something light takes up some of your leisure time. You may even be inspired to write down thoughts about what you are learning. Or you could become involved in a painting group that challenges your talents. Someone who is prominent in government can show up at such a gathering. Do not neglect your need to get some exercise. If the weather is clear and crisp, the outdoors will beckon. Walkers and joggers will be out in numbers.

24. MONDAY. Ordinary. The week begins with some changes at work, and they will be for the best. Your involvement can result in an opportunity to teach new procedures to others, leading to a bonus. Activities at home offer nothing unusual; even the news of the world seems to be rather quiet. But do not let yourself fall into a state of indifference. Try to crank up your appetite for useful work. Look around you, and you will see much that can be done while activity outside is at a low ebb. Use the time profitably to advance your career as well as to develop some new interests that will make you a more successful and self-assured person. An effort at self-improvement will pay off in advancement and improved human relationships as well as pride.

25. TUESDAY. Changeable. You Cancers will be busy, but you may not be able to pick and choose your activities. Get the less appealing jobs out of the way first. If you feel overloaded, bring in someone to give you a hand. Then you should have plenty of time to turn to the artistic endeavors that interest you most. You and your friends will enjoy getting together for some fun, since everyone seems to be in a lighthearted mood. Those who are not feeling energetic can find pleasure in reading something that is not too demanding. Or they can experiment with some talent of which they had been unaware. You may not be in the mood to attend a class or lecture in the evening, or you may simply be unprepared.

26. WEDNESDAY. Mixed. This is a day when your mind is likely to be working overtime, so you will be constantly on the go. It can be especially productive for people in the literary field. Even if there are no immediate signs of success, they will be turning out plays, poems, or other writing that will enjoy eventual fame. Salespeople will enjoy a spurt of inspiration that augurs well for the future. A bonus or pay increase will be a more immediate benefit. Some problem in advertising can arise, however. An error or perhaps a misjudging of the market can lead to embarrassment and the need to publish a correction. Airlines can be experiencing slowdowns at every level; weather could be a factor.

27. THURSDAY. Lucky. You will be busy today and probably will find it most satisfactory to work alone. It can be a productive day, and the results can be socially worthwhile. Put to good use whatever talents you possess; they could make a difference in the world. If you are on a farm or have domestic pets, you are likely to find animals better company than humans right now. Having visitors who have just returned from a trip can bring you out of your self-imposed solitude. The news they bring can spur discussions that range over a wide area. Probably they will have brought you an interesting souvenir of their travels. New enterprises can turn out to be highly successful as they develop even further.

28. FRIDAY. Uncertain. The employment picture can be rather murky today. Companies who have overexpanded may have to retrench, putting the jobs of some employees in danger. Anyone who suspects a job problem should start to look elsewhere. Even if your job seems secure, you might find yourself faced with a mountain of work to be done as soon as possible because of lack of help. Co-workers are sympathetic and willing to take over some tasks. Take a good look at your personal financial situation and make any necessary adjustments. A love affair brightens your day, and you are starting to have some serious thoughts about making it permanent. Something that has been given up for lost can reappear. You're too delighted to care how it was mislaid.

29. SATURDAY. Happy. Much as you Cancers love your home and family, some of you resent being disturbed when you are studying. If an exam is coming up, you will want to be left in solitude for a few hours of preparation. Interruptions can throw you off the track and cause emotional upsets. After you have finished, you will be ready for some socializing with family and friends. Their visits to your home will be welcomed. Since this is Leap Year, and another February 29th will not occur until 1996, you will probably receive a proposal of marriage. Perhaps you will be the one to do the proposing.

MARCH

1. SUNDAY. Rewarding.   There is so much that you can do today that you will wish for more hours. The future looks bright if you are willing to put forth some effort. You get along well with people, so it can be a fine day for you salespeople. Art and music events surround you, making choices difficult. You can find yourself involved in organizing groups for philanthropic purposes, perhaps a club to take children off the streets. Financial support is possible if you approach the right people. A social club to introduce unattached people to each other seems to be on the agenda. Science interests you. A hint of romance hangs over some activities and lends a touch of spice as well as curiosity.

2. MONDAY. Confusing.   Your progress seems to be impeded by someone, and you cannot figure out the reason. Just go your own way and accomplish as much as you can. Study will be helpful. Do not let visitors at work take too much of your time. Friendship and romance can suffer setbacks. An old friend moves away from the vicinity. Another offers you financial advice that may lead to eventual monetary loss. Dreams about your love affair are pleasant, but do not be too let down when reality rears its head. You can take what you read at face value; there may be no hidden meanings. If you are frustrated at work, you will welcome a good job at a higher salary. Such an offer is likely to be made today.

3. TUESDAY. Mixed.   What you do for a living seems to have become rather boring. An offer of a new job will be welcomed, and you can start right away. Some of your fellow Cancers are quite content with their jobs, perhaps because of a hefty bonus. Any job change you make could result in a move to another part of the country. If it involves moving to a foreign land, you will probably not be so happy unless there is a time limit. You love to travel, but you do not want to spend the rest of your life out of your own country. You know its history and geography and understandably feel patriotic. Your family will share your views and join eagerly in attempts to find the perfect home in the area of the country to which you are assigned.

4. WEDNESDAY. Changeable. You natural independence keeps you from committing yourself wholeheartedly to every project that is suggested at the meetings you attend today. You will be looking for pitfalls that others are missing. Clubs will offer a variety of agendas, and you can choose what suits you best. An interest in spiritual matters brings you into contact with some peculiar organizations. There is no shortage of opportunities to engage in health activities and exercise. A trip to compete in a contest will fall short of expectations, and you will bow out. Check your bank statement to prevent overdrawing your account. You are not likely to follow friends into new or unusual jobs.

5. THURSDAY. Stressful. Comings and goings and general confusion will keep you on your toes at work today. Visitors can be helpful, but some of them may be there to scrutinize your work. Do not get caught goofing off, especially in idle chatter. You seem to have run up against an invisible wall; you may have an enemy who is sabotaging your efforts. If your projects are dependent on government funding, be prepared for some frustration. Make it a short lunch hour, and put off that necessary shopping until after work. Dinner with your family can be pleasant, but you may be in the mood to spend the whole evening with them. You need some time to unwind in solitude with a hobby or light reading.

6. FRIDAY. Busy. Today at work seems to be a continuation of yesterday. There will be similar interruptions to your efforts to wind up some important project before the weekend. You have been working hard, and the long hours have tired you out. A sudden need can arise to make a trip connected with your career; it may be to train others in the techniques you have developed. You will meet others doing the same thing, so it can be a learning experience for you. If you are fairly tired, you would do well to avoid the bustle and chatter of the lunch and dinner crowd. You should try to find a quiet place to eat, a place where no one knows you. Meanwhile, your mind is turning over a plan for some family activity this weekend.

7. SATURDAY. Mixed. This can be an interesting and pleasant start to the weekend. With more time to yourself, you are free to indulge your interest in creative projects. The ideas will be both original and plentiful. Probably your thinking has become rather stale under the pressures of work. Stimulate it now with some reading on the subject that is totally new to you. Or enjoy the company of someone who has just arrived from an exotic place; conversation can take an unusual turn. Friends and relatives may join you and show a new interest in an artistic hobby that has been occupying you of late. Watch for a tax refund. Experimenting with a new recipe brings out the gourmet chef in you; now you know what to serve at your next party.

8. SUNDAY. Rewarding. Religious and humanitarian activities give a new direction to your thinking. They refresh your soul and give you the enthusiasm and stamina to face the workweek. Friends will readily join in with you as you do your part to make the world better. Enjoy the time off from the daily grind. A stroll in the open air will blow away the cobwebs, but be sure that you are suitably dressed for the weather. Friends may want to join you for your walk and for lunch. The conversation is likely to turn to religious and philosophical subjects. People may be a bit put off at first by your Cancer reticence, but they will soon come to know and admire the concerned and loving person underneath.

9. MONDAY. Sensitive. Your mind is much on financial matters at the moment. What to do with your extra money? Those Cancers who elect to keep it in a sock or other hideaway at home can be taking a big risk. It would be much better to try to find a way to make it work for you. That way definitely does not mean lending it to friends. If you do, you may never see it or your friends again. You are just as glad that some of it is taken out of your paycheck before it even reaches you. Pensions and health insurance take care of some funds, and taxes held back will mean that you have to come up with less money later. Purchases you make now can increase in value over the years.

10. TUESDAY. Mixed. Your attention for much of the day seems to be centered on employment and money matters. Union members can be agitating for better working conditions. Reports printed in the local papers can help your cause. Avoid gossip at work; what you are told in confidence should be kept under your hat. Personal investments can pay off in the future if you can bear to part with money at the present. Some Cancers have developed an interest in explorers and their travels. If you are one of them, you may be asked to speak in public about what you have learned from your own travels and from your reading. Someone close to you is taking flying lessons, but you decide not to join in that particular pleasure.

11. WEDNESDAY. Changeable. Creative Cancers, especially poets, are very busy today. Original ideas and welcome inspiration pave the way to some unique accomplishments. A visit to the library brings encounters with friends. You Cancers also will probably return home with an armful of poetry books and promptly bury your noses in them. You may even be inspired to write some poetry of your own; if it is written for your loved one, it could get fast results. While reading, remember that you are apt to come across some foreign phrases, so have a dictionary handy. Some hospitalization can become necessary if you are overseas, making you thankful for insurance. Watch out for a secret adversary.

12. THURSDAY. Variable. You Cancers are more prone than usual now to seek out company and find comfort in your family. That is because the Moon is in Cancer, and you are feeling rather forlorn and unwanted. Do not crawl back into your shell; go out and find unusual things to do with those you love best. Friends will not resent being interrupted if you telephone them. Plan a gathering of your dear ones and other relatives, and notify them today. You can start preparations at once. While you are working, you will be anticipating a good time with pleasant reminiscing and a bit of nostalgia. If you win some money that can be kept safe from the tax collector, you may want to spend it on travel.

13. FRIDAY. Satisfactory. The bad luck traditionally associated with this day is not likely to bother you too much. At worst, there can be some friction with dear ones. You may be feeling somewhat insecure in your relationships when the Moon is in this phase. There seems not to be anything that some counseling cannot iron out. It will take more than this to break the ties that you as a Cancer have with your loved ones. In fact, risks you take today can prove profitable. Avoid throwing your weight around at your workplace; people will resent it. Thinking constantly of your work and, worse still, talking about it can put a strain on a romantic relationship. So pay more attention to your loved one.

14. SATURDAY. Sensitive. Yesterday's caution against being a workaholic holds true today if you insist on bringing office work home. There is enough to do at your place of residence. Also, you are due to spend more time with your family, whether at work or at play. Not only that, but you probably are in need of some relaxation and some exercise. If you can be outdoors, so much the better. The day is peaceful, but it would not be a bad idea to prepare for future days that are not. Strengthen those muscles, and consider taking a course in self-defense. You never know when you might have to defend yourself against some of the less desirable elements of the society in which we live.

15. SUNDAY. Mixed. You seem to be rather tense at present. Unnecessary arguments leave you feeling frustrated, and you have a tendency to take your irritation out on those who are your nearest and dearest. No good will come of bullying them. If they seem too refined for your taste, it may be that your taste is at fault. Probably you are in need of a long session with a spiritual adviser or other counselor. You might emerge with a whole new set of values and a clearer picture of yourself and your motives. You can then begin to feel free to express your real emotions and let others know how much you care. You will enjoy being a spectator at a sports event or going to a show.

16. MONDAY. Demanding. Your tendency toward practicality and careful attention to detail stand you in good stead at work, but your domestic relationships can be somewhat confusing. Do not let small disagreements get you down; they will blow over quickly. Food and its preparation are much on your mind, but do not overeat and spoil your trim figure. Shop for gourmet foods for special dishes before inviting friends in to share a meal. Do not attempt anything too exotic unless you are sure what you are doing. If you are thinking of taking an evening class in a subject that fascinates you, investigate possibilities now and enroll before it's too late. Or you may prefer to join an exercise group for its next session; don't delay.

17. TUESDAY. Productive. If you discourage interruptions, you will get quite a lot done today. Find a secluded area to assure solitude. It will be best not to worry too much about details; you could get bogged down and accomplish very little. This can be a good day for shopping for clothing. Look for good quality while you are comparing prices. Romance will flourish if you pick up some flowers and a special dessert. If there is a party or dinner at your place of employment, take along the one you love best. Some shopping can be done on your lunch break, but the time may be short. You are inclined to linger over lunch, exchanging anecdotes and gossip, leaving too little time for running errands. You can always make a detour on your way home.

18. WEDNESDAY. Demanding. Problems seem to be flying at you from all directions, but you have an advantage. You have seen them coming so you are prepared. If you stroll in a lonely place, you could face some personal danger, so you will be glad you took that course in self-defense. Friends can be instrumental in causing legal problems, perhaps financial in nature. But you have had an inkling of them, so it will not be too bad. Those of you who travel overseas today will be glad they had the forethought to study the language and customs of the people you will meet. A knowledge of psychology will also come in handy. Those Cancers who stay at home can be planning a party for someone's birthday tonight.

19. THURSDAY. Mixed. The Cancer person is likely to avoid arguments that seem to be over trivial issues. If a matter of principle is involved, however, other people will be surprised by the outspokenness of the usually reticent Cancer. Otherwise, you will probably be content to drift along today and let others make the decisions. Public activities can make inroads on your working schedule. Your sensitive nature makes you acutely aware of the reactions of an audience. Avoid trips that are lengthy and costly and interfere with your home activities. Unexpected visitors can descend upon you. You are glad to see them, but you may resent their taking up time you would rather spend with your lover.

20. FRIDAY. Enjoyable. Efforts to advance your career can take a backseat to family and social matters today. You will enjoy showing friends some places of interest in your area. Such outings can give you much pleasure as long as you avoid unnecessary spending. You may have to turn a deaf ear to the eccentric comments and actions of someone in the party; that person may be having a bad day. If you have a tendency to overeat, you will find yourself putting on more weight than you need. Those Cancers who have long dreamed of building a home of their own will find this a good day for making plans. You will have to explore sources of financing, but this may be less difficult than anticipated. Loan officers will turn a sympathetic ear toward your project.

21. SATURDAY. Cautious. Concern about finances comes to the fore if you are thinking about taking some advanced courses, or even going on for a degree. You are not sure where to turn to get the funds you need, but do not give up easily. If you take time to explore possible sources, you can come up with some good ideas. Some approaches will have to wait for the workweek, but a friend or relative can be of immediate help. If you do receive the needed money, put it aside for your specific purpose. Some friends come around only when you are in the money, so do not let them con you out of it. Your loyalty to friends is commendable, but your belief in fair play makes you defend what you believe.

22. SUNDAY. Disquieting. Problems arise that can keep you from enjoying what should be the Sunday peace. Some friends can still be smarting over your refusal to share your money. It may be that they need it to repay a debt, but that is their problem. Try to pour as much oil on troubled waters as possible without compromising your principles. Mob actions and protests should be avoided for your own safety. Some efforts should be made to improve your physical condition and keep in trim. Exercising with a congenial person is an effective method and far less expensive than indulging in body-building courses. Your loved one likes you just as you are and is not looking for perfection.

23. MONDAY. Changeable. Your mind can be more occupied by abstractions than by concrete thoughts today. You are interested in what makes people tick, so you may be delving into psychology books and articles. Some phase of religious thought proves interesting. It is possible that you will be questioning some of the tenets of your early training. The Cancer gardener can meditate while exercising his or her green thumb. Probably you will be in a mood for buying something in spite of your preoccupation with lofty thoughts. Be careful not to overspend. You are likely to be let down when you discover that some travel time cannot be reimbursed. Accept the fact, and do not go around complaining about it to everyone.

24. TUESDAY. Successful. All studies are likely to seem easier than expected. Even term papers and reports go fairly fast because they present few problems. Of more concern to you can be learning the ins and outs of a new job; you will have to read up on it in your own time. You have an urge to go to see relatives or friends in another state, but the travel can be too expensive at present. Some of them perhaps can come to visit you, and you can always write letters to the rest. Cancer people involved in advertising or publishing will have a profitable day. Those of you who are having a business lunch or partying later are likely to eat and drink too much. Some vigorous exercise will burn off calories.

25. WEDNESDAY. Ordinary. Study continues to be important. A subject that is new to you can change some of your ideas and will be far from boring. But you will have to devote much of your attention at work to completing tasks on time. This is especially important, since there seems to be an influx of orders from government sources. You may be in on the development of a new line of product. There are no slackers at work today. A possible visit from higher-ups from overseas can keep everyone hopping. Travel is of interest, and on your day off you might be lucky and discover a trip by bus to a place that you have not seen before. Travel books or meeting people from abroad will interest you.

26. THURSDAY. Exciting. Someone new catches your roving eye, someone whose response to you is highly flattering. But if an affair develops, perhaps even a secret one, it probably will not last. Since you are in a romantic mood, you will be content to live for the moment. You can be also flattered by an invitation to visit the head office of the company that employs you. If you are self-employed, you can make considerable progress, thanks to a burst of energy. You are particularly good at expressing your thoughts in speech and writing. You may think that you have avoided overspending this past week, but a glance at your wallet will tell you otherwise. As a result, you may have to forgo some social affair. Stay clear of the shops.

27. FRIDAY. Favorable. Travel and holidays are on your mind, but they are expensive. But if you have recently borrowed money for a specific purpose, that could be the answer; you may know there will be some funds left over. This is to be spent on a trip, and you will still have a chance to start paying it back on time. The trip may not be very long because a traveling companion cannot take enough leave for a really extended holiday. Hard work will enable you to keep up with your repayments when the day of reckoning arrives. People around you may be panicking, so it is up to you to maintain an appearance of calm and reassurance. Are you about to be married? If so, be sure that your only reason is love if you want it to be a lasting union.

28. SATURDAY. Happy. Cancers are likely to be feeling gregarious this weekend. They will enjoy meeting and mixing with a variety of people. You probably will be heavily involved in organizations that sponsor sports events. Also, you are likely to be taking an interest in politics. A woman who is active in such affairs is quite persuasive about getting your cooperation. The unattached Cancer can find a new romance among the people met at organizational activities. This time it can result in a long-lasting relationship. There is little hope of keeping the new romance secret; people may know about it as soon as you do. But if it is all out in the open, things will be easier for you, especially travels together.

29. SUNDAY. Unsettled. Possibly you will have to be just a little bit selfish today. You will prefer not to be tied down by commitments to causes, even those dearest to your heart. Be prepared to accept the ideas of others and view unemotionally any situations that arise. The idealistic Cancers will see some of their more deserving thoughts being adopted. Money presents problems. There can be quarrels over it among friends, and there is a possibility of loss through theft. Although friends can be at odds with you over money, they really do have your best interests at heart. A love affair can worry them, and perhaps you too. Exercise is fine, but keep it moderate. Vigorous and prolonged participation in sports can tire you before the working week even starts.

30. MONDAY. Stressful. Sports teams and other organizations keep you on your toes. If you have any dramatic skills, people who are starting up a little theater group will want your services. Even if you are neither actor nor sports figure, you can help by doing things in the background; selling tickets, preparing programs, carrying scenery around all are very much a part of theater. Frustrations may set in on the domestic front. Something can go very wrong; travel faces obstacles; work hours lead to arguments at your place of employment. You probably will have little time to work on advancing your career. If expectations are too high, you can be disappointed; why not accept matters for what they are?

31. TUESDAY. Excellent. The people who surround you seem to be bursting with energy and ideas. Nonetheless, they will turn to you for advice, approval, and suggestions as to how to carry out their projects. Since you also have a lot of get-up-and-go, you will be happy to oblige. Getting together with family and friends will give you a chance to showcase your culinary talents. The people you see every day can be joined by some visitors from far away. You will all enjoy learning more about exotic places and customs. If you have some free time, you may want to express your artistic inclinations by writing or listening to music or poetry, perhaps both. Do watch for those who would take advantage of you, however, and try to get some rest at the end of this hectic day.

APRIL

1. WEDNESDAY. Enjoyable. For some reason, it may not be necessary for you to work today. A whole day free gives you an opportunity to do some of the things that you really want to do. Go to a museum, a concert, or a literary affair. A social gathering or club meeting will be interesting. The actors among you will be preparing for a performance. Some meetings will be notable for their emphasis on one of your scholarly interests. If work has to be done in setting up these activities, you will be right there with your sleeves rolled up. Do not resent any lack of help; you can work better alone anyway. Busy as you are, set aside a couple of hours to visit someone in the hospital. The person may well be on the mend, so will be ready to have a few good laughs with you.

2. THURSDAY. Successful. This can be an active day as well as a profitable one. If you have been under the weather lately, you will now have nearly recovered. Exercise and a good diet should complete the process, and you will soon be as good as new. Your career is going great guns, with the prospect of a promotion or other recognition dancing before your eyes. Someone who works nearby invades your romantic thoughts. A shopping trip reveals the very items you most want. There is an increased enthusiasm for sports, with the spirit of competition high. A good friend takes unlimited time for a long chat. You can get advice on minor setbacks and talk out your most cherished dreams and plans.

3. FRIDAY. Demanding. There is much to be done at work today, and you will want to do it your own way. Interference from any others will not be welcomed. You are likely to tread on some toes in your eagerness to be left alone. In fact, your tolerance can reach a breaking point if lawyers start prowling around and peering over your shoulder. Those Cancers who are in the real estate business will have to be especially careful not to alienate possible clients. The same applies to salespersons in other areas. If you have recently left school, you may be learning to operate a computer, which can be difficult. You encounter someone who claims to have just seen a UFO or something supernatural.

4. SATURDAY. Confusing. You are somewhat out of sorts in the morning. Since you have some work or studying to do, you will have to depend on other family members to entertain visitors from

153

a distance. You seem to be restless and confused and not sure what you really want to do. After getting necessary work out of the way, you can have fun with the family and your visitors; but do not be surprised if you bore of activities quickly and want to go on to something else. Others may not understand. Your body wants to be active, but your mind tells you that you need rest. Some supplies for this evening and tomorrow will be needed, so allow time to go out and buy them before stores close for the weekend.

5. SUNDAY. Rewarding. You probably need some recreation today and a chance to do your own thing. If your family has ideas of its own, you do not need to fall in with them. Send your loved ones off on their own pursuits while you devote your time to a project that interests you. If you can make enough of a start on it, you could find that others become curious and eventually supportive. When you start feeling more sociable, you might consider an outing with visitors or new friends, possibly including a movie or play. Do not neglect your health by merely snacking. You could be feeling a bit short of money at the moment, but that will be temporary. Look forward to a check arriving next week.

6. MONDAY. Mixed. The weekend seems to have done you good, and you have some bright ideas that you are eager to test. Watch for the most propitious moment to present them to others. Some sort of party at work has to be passed up because of the illness of a relative. But the rest of the day should be productive. Local news events are on everyone's mind, and friends and co-workers will want to discuss them with you. Such discussions could lead to your gaining a whole new perspective. The evening is good for going out to a movie or for staying home to watch television with your family. Invite a new friend or two to share your evening; you may later receive an invitation from them to some event.

7. TUESDAY. Unsettling. Thinking before acting can be very important today. It can be a time when people are in a state of confusion and will be depending on you or some other resourceful person to make everything clear. You will have to overcome any feelings of restlessness that can lead you to jump from one project to another, completing none of them. If you are on edge, you will probably tend to talk too much. But if you play the strong, silent role, you should be able to concentrate on putting some of your better ideas into effect. Decisiveness and the ability to work alone can result in much being accomplished. Avoid committing yourself to any course of action until you are sure where it is heading.

8. WEDNESDAY. Disconcerting. Tread warily where personal relationships are concerned. With the Moon about to enter Cancer, you might be feeling rather unsure of yourself. Furthermore, someone may be deliberately deceiving you. But it is quite possible that you are feeling insecure and very conscious that someone has more formal education than you. In reality, your breadth of knowledge can be far superior to that person's because you read widely and retain more of what you read. Do not broadcast your affairs, especially disagreements with superiors and family. Others are all too willing to translate what you say into common gossip. Any reaching out toward romance will be fruitless because of a lack of interest on the part of the one you love.

9. THURSDAY. Changeable. With the Moon in Cancer, your domestic side probably takes over. You enjoy and seek out the company of your loved ones. If friends want to get together with you, you ask them to come to your home. You can get a great deal of work done without setting foot out the door. Good news arrives in the mail as well as through some phone calls. You have probably asked a family member to screen your calls; in that way, you will avoid hearing from an unwelcome caller, perhaps someone at work. Although your life revolves around your family today, you should not boss any of your dear ones. Late in the day, you will find that a walk around the neighborhood perks you up.

10. FRIDAY. Easygoing. You seem to be experiencing a strong sense of déjà vu. Actually, you have probably dreamed about being in a similar situation and place, and that can explain it. You have tended to dream a great deal lately, but you also tend to forget your dreams as soon as you awaken. It is all a part of being a Cancer during this phase of the Moon. If solving puzzles intrigues you, look through back issues of magazines to find ones that you have not worked. The solution to a mystery novel becomes apparent early in the book. Walking or jogging provides needed exercise, and you may want to take along a family member or romantic partner. You seem to be looking for a young student friend.

11. SATURDAY. Challenging. The world is beating a path to your door, and you seem to have little time for yourself. But you manage to find some, either for tutoring or playing an engagement if your talent is music. But it will not be easy. Do not try to take all the limelight. People will admire you more if you show a bit of modesty about your accomplishments. Some friends will want you to help them with their studies, and this can be time-consuming. Neighbors can also be demanding attention. You need a change of pace in the evening, but restaurants and night spots are likely to be too crowded for your taste. If fatigue is sapping your energy, you should try to get to bed early and get a good night's sleep.

12. SUNDAY. Mixed. A smorgasbord of attractions awaits the Cancer person today. But it is not necessary to sample any or all of them. Some of you may want to loaf around and let the world go by. Others will opt to indulge in some participatory or spectator sports. If you are feeling energetic, but do not like sports, you can join a group of friends at a disco or do some other fun activity. Those who are full of vigor, but studious by nature, will probably try to organize a session to pursue interests with others who enjoy the same subject. Someone from your group with such knowledge will help you. If you have romance on your mind, you can be in for a disappointment. Other diversions are favored today.

13. MONDAY. Rewarding. Your romantic life is showing some improvement, so the day starts out on a high note. Studies that you started yesterday prove successful. Employment or self-employment affairs are favorable. You can accomplish a great deal working by yourself and looking at the overall project rather than allowing yourself to become bogged down in small details. Those of you whose jobs are in hospitals can have an interesting day. Some challenging new cases will keep you on your toes. If you are a person whose handiwork includes clothing, or pottery or textiles, you can produce some interesting, fascinating articles in the course of the day. Start prepating for a baby that is on the way.

14. TUESDAY. Profitable. Those who are looking for first jobs or different ones can be quite successful in their search. Money is easier to come by than usual, making it possible that starting salaries will be good. Cancers who have a creative talent can turn out unusual and beautiful objects, which perhaps will increase in value, given time. Do not get so carried away with any work you do that you endanger your health. Listen to wiser people who caution you to call it a day before you overdo. Nor should you let minor symptoms escalate into major health worries. But when you have them checked, you may find that it is all in your head. You continue to have romance very much on your mind, but choose your romantic partner carefully. This may not be the time to fall in love with a near neighbor; it could lead to problems.

15. WEDNESDAY. Changeable. You can be in a peace-loving mood now. Since you will be mixing with many people, perhaps inviting some of them to your home, you will be particularly anxious to have relationships remain friendly. Train yourself to notice when tempers become short so that you can defuse an all-out fight before it breaks. A bit of indecisiveness on your part leads others to take on responsibility for decisions. Anger and undisguised contempt can make you physically ill. You will not be interested in having a meal at a restaurant, since home cooking will taste much better. Watch out for trouble in your romance. Someone may be cheating, arousing much resentment within you.

16. THURSDAY. Stressful. Storm signals may be flying at home today, and you will have to proceed with extreme caution. You want to be in harmony with your love, but you do tend to be overly possessive and unjustifiably jealous. At work and at home, antagonisms can be bubbling beneath the surface. Do everything you can to keep them from erupting into open hostility. Your job and your family life can be at stake. Burying yourself in your work will help. But all your efforts to maintain a placid atmosphere at home and at work could be in vain if legal problems have everyone on edge. Lawyers are apt to make life difficult. Unless you are absolutely sure of your ground, try to settle a case out of court.

17. FRIDAY. Challenging. The Easter and Passover weekend is about to begin, and you will probably be heavily involved in preparations. Today is favorable for travel if you have made some reservations; otherwise, you might have trouble. You will be happy to strike up new acquaintances. Loyalty to old friends is important and will have no bearing on making new friends. Where a principle is involved, stand your ground against the world. If you do owe anyone money, you should see your way clear to early repayment and a satisfactory conclusion. A casual friendship or date can blossom into something that will last for a long time. The Cancer who has a tendency to talk and talk without much thought risks hurting the feelings of someone dear.

18. SATURDAY. Sensitive. People whom you meet today can possibly have a profound influence on your life, now and in the future. Since you are always interested in people and what makes them tick, you may be studying psychology. This can contribute a broader scope to your understanding. You should use that knowledge of human nature to temper your own actions, and prevent a possible end to a relationship that you value very much. You will be much interested in money and possessions, your own and those belonging to other people. You must overcome that tendency toward jealousy if you want the path of true love to be smooth. A sexual attraction can lead to a romance, but it would be better to keep this new love affair under wraps for the time being.

19. SUNDAY. Tranquil. You Cancers often count on this day of rest to catch up with your studying. But since this is Easter and Passover weekend, you will probably be kept busy with holiday activities. There can be extra chores if you have invited guests for the weekend or even for dinner tonight. If you are dining out, there will still be some flurry of preparation. Conversations can fuel your dreams of travel to exotic places. There is much going on in the world, and it can be the subject of conversation on your own part as well as that of family and friends. But do not just sit around; try to get some outdoor exercise. You're a bit unrealistic, perhaps, maybe the result of old-time religious ideas.

20. MONDAY. Variable. If you do not have to go back to work today, you will find plenty to do. Boredom is not likely to be a problem. You may come to the end of the day with some very different ideas. Some of them can be the result of long and serious talks with new friends who hail from other countries or backgrounds. Some can be the result of your reading, especially if you delve into works about travel or philosophy. You are a little startled by some of the ideas advanced. If you must work, the tasks can be heavier than anticipated. In fact, it may be necessary to put in some overtime, but you will be adequately compensated for it. Spend as much time as possible with your dear ones.

21. TUESDAY. Pleasant. You will be in a very good mood for most of this day. Physically, you are a little tired, but your mental outlook is bright. You are able to see other people as they are, and you are not taken in by any of their attempts to influence you. Hard work can be lucrative. You are likely to be reimbursed for some expenditure you have made recently on behalf of your employer. Your willingness to accept responsibility makes a favorable impression. You should keep in mind the axiom about all work and no play etc., and do something about it. Getting together with friends to discuss all manner of topics is one way. One of these pals can have news of a forthcoming job opening up; you may want to look into it if it seems of interest to you.

22. WEDNESDAY. Uncertain. Try to avoid having illusions about the people you meet or with whom you work. Your tendency to idealize them can suffer a rude setback when you realize that they are human and have human faults, just like you. If you can view others in their true light, you will be more sympathetic to their failings and problems, and they will like you the better for it. Your work or your concern for other people can thrust you into the limelight. This can be gratifying, but it will cut no ice with some co-workers whose help you are seeking. Romance is not at all what you would wish. You are likely to be attracted by someone whom you meet in the course of your work. But remember that love at first sight can be wishful thinking, or worse, an illusion.

23. THURSDAY. Changeable. Today can be a truly creative one for you Cancers. You are very imaginative, and your bright ideas can lead to advancement at work and for your career. Your inventiveness brings in extra money. You would be wise to put any such gains aside for future use; it should be earning interest. If you do not see immediate results, take heart. What you do today will pay off eventually, and your energy will be well spent. Exercise helps you to keep fit for future action. On the debit side, some of you will be going through marital separations, with resultant legal tangles. These can interfere with your ability to work productively, but can also lead to a chance to travel. Trips can be pleasant.

24. FRIDAY. Cautious. Any of you who are unemployed or are looking for a better job can find worthwhile opportunities today if you look around. Some companies are setting up new divisions and new projects, and you can find your niche in one of these. Others learn that skills they already have can be adapted to a changing technology. Inquire about training programs in a computer company. You can find yourself employed now by a large corporation or by civil service if you have made adequate preparation. If you have been rather strapped financially recently, there are those who are willing to help out. Rely on old and trusted friends; do not ask for loans from mere acquaintances. Sell some possessions if necessary.

25. SATURDAY. Happy. The homebody Cancer can take much pleasure from today. Invite a close friend to share part of it with you and your family. Tensions have all but vanished, and you can at last catch up on some reading as well as quiet entertaining. You will be happy to see a young relative who has been away too long. Show your understanding of the problems of others, but do not let yourself get too deeply involved. You do not want to endanger your freedom, which is precious to you. Try to be objective about other people You may decide, after much reflection, that your savings are equal to a trip abroad. Plan carefully; it will be fun and educational to get new outlooks and ideas.

26. SUNDAY. Excellent. Attending religious services gives you a spiritual uplift as well as a chance to meet some pleasant company. It also can give you an outlet for your humanitarian interests. Women figure prominently; one who is active in politics will try to recruit you to the cause. New contacts can mean new friends. If cooking is a major interest, money can be made today by catering an affair sponsored by a women's club. You may hear, rather belatedly, that you have won the office lottery. You will want to spend some of your earnings and winnings on children of your neighborhood or on a group that works toward improving the lot of underprivileged children. Sports interest you, so you might be tempted to lend support to a children's athletic group.

27. MONDAY. Rewarding. As you know, Cancer people are very sensitive to the emotions and needs of others. This is why people flock to your side, seeking reassurance and help. You should be aware, however, that there are those among them who would take advantage of your kindness and generosity. But the majority are legitimate, and you will get much satisfaction from helping them. This is great day for the creative Cancer. Your talents are unleashed by your unusually active imagination, so you can do something important in the line of music or poetry. Those of you who were born when the planets were exactly in the right position can be lucky in monetary matters. Money can come from some quite surprising, not to say mysterious, sources.

28. TUESDAY. Challenging. Your mental and physical energies are so high now that you feel that you could take on the world. Channel some of that energy into self-improvement projects. Acting and other work in the theater will be of unusual interest. Audition for a role that intrigues you. You have enthusiasm both for the mysterious and the occult. Make sure that you can trust the people involved in these activities, and do not fall for the schemes of charlatans. Keep personal papers hidden in a safe place, and do not divulge any secrets. If you are experiencing vague feelings of anxiety, they may be caused by some subconscious fear. By talking your problems over with a friend, you might regain some peace.

29. WEDNESDAY. Productive. Concentrate all your considerable energy on getting ahead. Be tolerant of others, but do not let them tell you what to do. If you follow your own route, you can get a lot accomplished today. Interference from others will always be irritating to you. Still, you are sensitive to people's feelings, and will not want to say anything to hurt them. Keep a tight rein on that temper of yours; speaking hastily will hurt you, as well as offend the person you are addressing. If you yourself have been hurt by the words or actions of others, you may want to be alone. The best cure is to bury yourself in your work. Action is more effective than just planning, so do not waste much time on words.

30. THURSDAY. Difficult. You will have a strong urge to be at home with your family, especially your romantic partner. But work will interfere, and some tasks will be far more difficult than you anticipated. Interruptions by people stopping at your desk for a chat will only increase your difficulties. When word of a forthcoming raise or promotion is confirmed, that will make it all worthwhile. You have some good ideas; write them down before they get away. When you do break away, at last, to go back home, you will find that people are looking to you for reassurance. Usually you are sympathetic, but today this seems harder than usual. If you are subconsciously feeling inadequate, you will probably fudge it by being demanding. Just be yourself.

MAY

1. FRIDAY. Excellent. Women's clothing is featured prominently today. Possibly you take a job in the garment industry; or you might opt for a course in fashion designing. If neither of those, you may start looking for bargains in summer clothing in the stores. You will be surrounded by many people in any of these activities, so you will not lack companions if you want to go sightseeing. While you are in the stores or at tourist attractions, you see just the right gift for someone dear to you. It might be a good idea to choose one or two others, to have on hand, as needed. Money and health present no problems. If you want to have a party or dine out in style, nothing will stand in your way. Friends will be glad to do whatever you like.

2. SATURDAY. Uncertain. Your regular job may run from Monday through Friday, but you now can arrange for a second job for evenings and weekends. It seems to have something unusual about it, possibly involving the manufacture and sale of some novelty items. It can be slow to get off the ground, and your partners will probably have some doubts about its eventual success; they are also worrying about local competition. There will be loans to be paid off as soon as the bottom line starts showing a profit, but you can rest assured that the profit will come. Have confidence in yourself and your ideas, and that confidence will rub off on your friends. You will miss an old friend at a club get-together, but you can make new friends.

3. SUNDAY. Unsettling. If you can manage to spend most of the day at home, you will be quite contented. Surrounded by your loved ones and familiar possessions, you will be more comfortable. It is not wise to become too much attached to one's possessions, however. If they are damaged, or borrowed and not returned, you will feel the loss keenly. Keep in mind while shopping that your money is better spent on something you really need. Impulse buying could include necessities, but otherwise should be avoided. Those of you who are seriously involved with clubs or other organizations may not see eye-to-eye with the committees running them. You want to tell them where they are going wrong, but that would not be advisable at this time.

4. MONDAY. Challenging. Cancer people continue to put their emphasis on family ties. Visits to relatives can be very pleasant, and you may hear some interesting news. You would love to spread it around, but the ability to keep secrets greatly enhances your reputation. Friends can profit from your generous sharing of what you have learned from experience. When you are alone, you have a tendency to be too conscious of your own self and your goals. A successful effort to take a more objective view of current happenings will be to your advantage. Try to relax at the end of the day. Do not brood about past actions and their effect on other people; it will only put you on the defensive.

5. TUESDAY. Mixed. Today is good for your career. You have enough money on hand to go grocery shopping for some special items. Preparing a real feast for some friends is at the back of your mind, so call people up and invite them. They will be impressed by the abundance of your dishes, and you will not be tempted to indulge yourself by overeating. Your money can also be used for some self-improvement activity, perhaps a correspondence course that will augment your chances for getting ahead. Some evidences of antagonism can sour part of the day. Arguments can arise, and certain neighbors may be nursing an old grudge. Call upon a friend to pour oil on troubled waters.

6. WEDNESDAY. Favorable. With the Moon in Cancer, your thoughts turn to the comfort of being with your family. Money is

not an immediate problem, so you will splurge in buying the best
for them. The signs, however, may not be propitious for overspending, and you might therefore experience vague feelings of
guilt. These can mix with your desire to make your home as
attractive as possible. If you are making extensive renovations to
it, inside and out, the cost can prove higher than anticipated,
justifying your feelings of unease. Do as much as you can without
calling in outside help. Your love for your family spreads out to
all, both near and far, old and young. From such sincere feelings
can come a warm, embracing glow in which to bask.

7. THURSDAY. Sensitive. The influence of the Moon in Cancer continues strong today. You feel the most comfortable at home
and enjoy especially close relationships, preferably those with
family members. If they are not forthcoming, there is a possibility
of your feeling rejected and sorry for yourself. You should look a
lot more closely, though, and you will see that you are receiving all
the support from your family you could hope for, even down to
temporary loans. Romance can be another matter, and perhaps
you should avoid your romantic partner today. A telephone call
can iron out some of the major problems, however. Childhood
influences can be strong as well as comforting. There is a possibility of your having to put in an hour or two extra at work.

8. FRIDAY. Difficult. A romantic involvement calls for consideration and tact. Do not be hurt by imagined slights; they may
not have been intended. On the other hand, do not read more into
an affair than is really the case. Your tendency to be possessive
about someone you love can turn the person off. You are perhaps
worrying about money. The dollar no longer buys as much as it
once did. Friends seem to understand inflation better than you do,
and their efforts to convince you can lead to arguments. You can
be somewhat tight-fisted and determined to increase what you
already have. You are not inclined to listen to any others' reasons
why you should part with some of your money. Someone dear to
you will be grateful if you consent to giving driving lessons.

9. SATURDAY. Unsettling. Your financial worries continue
into this weekend. You may want to get away for a while, but feel
that you cannot before you have cleared up your obligations. A
ray of hope is that all such worries are resolved, in time, and that
you will find the necessary funds to pay your bills. Meanwhile, you
are bound to be unhappy when collectors or phone calls remind
you of your overdue debts. If you cannot get away, spend your
time at home in making plans to expand your business or career

activities. Quite possibly you can produce some innovative work or make progress with a creative project if you set your mind to it. Do not neglect your physical welfare; exercise in the fresh air.

10. SUNDAY. Rewarding. If you have to work Sundays, there can be some recompense. Possibly you will be paid at a higher rate than usual. If the job involves outdoor activities or working with animals, you can be laying the groundwork for a new career or a retirement interest. Your green thumb might result in your going into partnership with a friend or a family member to start a nursery. Caring for animals could fuel your interest in farming. Some younger Cancers will discover that they have an aptitude for looking after pets and may think seriously of attending veterinary college. Such young people should try to find work for the summer with an established veterinarian.

11. MONDAY. Variable. Cancers are essentially domestic creatures. You and your loved one are probably thinking seriously about buying your first home. It comes as a blow to learn that interest rates on mortgages are too high at present to make that possible. If you are truly determined, you will decide to go ahead anyway, even though you will have to skimp on something else. Perhaps you are on the outs with some friends, but your love affair leaves nothing to be desired. Word arrives in the mail that you are going to have house guests. You and members of the family start planning and looking forward to some good times. You celebrate a new and challenging task at work by going out with a group.

12. TUESDAY. Frustrating. The mood you are in at present requires all the affection and understanding that people can give you. You are likely to be both emotional and aggressive in your dealings with others. Things may not be going well at work, but your boss takes a dim view of your taking work home, and denies you permission. If you want to preserve a loving relationship with your sweetheart, family and friends, work on changing your attitude, now. Why not go off on a short cruise or visit some national historic site, and give yourself a chance to review past events? If you do not change, and for the better, you will be out in the cold.

13. WEDNESDAY. Changeable. Self-improvement activities and learning are important to your future. So seize every opportunity to put your nose in a book and brush up on your knowledge. Forget the light fiction; sink your teeth into something more substantial. Riding as a passenger on public transportation gives you time to read. The harmony of your home seems to be upset by some friction or by the arrival of some uncongenial strangers. But despite everything, you do enjoy the company of friends and relatives. You soon realize that the best course is to fade out of the picture when an argument starts. Since so many unsettling things have happened, you will be in an indecisive mood.

14. THURSDAY. Cautious.   There is much good in today, and you will enjoy every minute when things are going well. Your romantic life is especially to your liking. Emotions will be deep and strong, and the future looks promising. Your loyalty to friends is intense, and you are distressed when someone lets you down. If that happens, you are likely to hold a grudge for a long time. Your popularity can suffer if you insist on telling people the truth even when it is unpalatable. But you stand up for your principles, regardless of the cost. Daytime is good for sharing activities with young people even if you neglect some pressing tasks. The evening is good for romance and a quiet candlelit dinner.

15. FRIDAY. Mixed.   In some ways, this can be a lucky day for Cancer people. It is good for playing the lottery; you may not become a millionaire, but you should win something. That would help to offset the rising cost of groceries. Showing higher-ups your talents can better your financial position too. This is an especially important day for watching your words. No matter how annoyed you get, guard your tongue if you want to keep your work and your family life harmonious. You have a great interest in other people, but can become tongue-tied with your loved one. Speaking your deepest thoughts comes easier when you are talking to friends. Make sure there is more to an attachment than attraction.

16. SATURDAY. Sensitive.   You are likely to have some problems in relationships if you expect too much of others. They may not have your strong principles and your fierce loyalty. If you tend to be too idealistic about friendships, you can be in for a real disappointment. You start the day full of optimism about your love affair, but it could go downhill quite rapidly. While you usually speak quite bluntly to others when truth is at stake, this may not be the day for saying too much. Hurt feelings can result in damage to friendships and love that is slow to heal. If your plans do not work out as hoped, try to avoid getting too depressed.

17. SUNDAY. Successful.   With seemingly unlimited energy at your disposal, you can accomplish more than you had dreamed possible. Your interest in travel makes you wish to visit all the places which you have ever read about. If that is not practical, you can at least read about them and also keep up with the news. There are usually events of historical importance happening elsewhere in the world and you will certainly want to follow them closely. You can sometimes be a little self-centered and undemonstrative to your sweetheart and friends. If they do not understand, you have only yourself to blame. Spare time can be spent working with your hands; some of you may dream of careers as models.

18. MONDAY. Confusing. Your current restless mood may be caused by boredom. Although you may not have realized it, you need a change. You are tempted to explore new places in your search for the perfect loved one, or even the perfect friend. If you have the opportunity to go to a different country, you will probably meet people whose background and ideas are far different from yours. This can be beneficial. If people at home are too busy to listen to what you have to say, someone you meet elsewhere today can be just the right audience. If you cannot get away, you probably will want to withdraw and read a book. Some of the ideas you come across can shake you up a bit.

19. TUESDAY. Tricky. Cancer salespeople and those in public relations should fare particularly well today. Your work can put you in the limelight. The artistic Cancer is likely to produce a work that raises some controversy. Since your public image and social standing are considerable, no one will dare to refuse to put it on exhibit. It may, however, lead to a disagreement with someone concerned with putting your work on public view. Your popularity is high, probably because of your sympathetic understanding of the needs of the people with whom you come in contact. You are likely to get an offer to help you, but be cautious about accepting it. There can be good reason for turning it down.

20. WEDNESDAY. Profitable. Hard work can bring in increased pay today, and you can use it. Your efforts are likely to be recognized by someone in the background, and this can lead to a lucky break for you. Do not hide your light under a bushel; the more people know about your work, the better. You seem to be a rather reserved person; this leads others to think you are cold and aloof. Do not let that worry you. You may need to be on your dignity. Also, if you can keep your own emotions under control, you will be helpful to those who are too sentimental for their own good. Try not to be taken in by someone who has a smooth manner, but you can still have much in common with that person.

21. THURSDAY. Changeable. The Cancer person needs constant reassurance of the love and high opinion of friends. This can be one of those days when you will round up some of these friends and find new ones through some organizational activity. There is a possibility that you are on the outs with someone whose opinion you value. Money, especially money received off the books, can be the cause. If that is the case, find that person and try to put matters to rights. Among the friends you make today may be someone who will in time become a lover. Anyone interested in politics might encounter a woman who is charismatic and dedicated. That person can have a profound effect on your outlook.

22. FRIDAY. Pleasant. You are sympathetic to the actions of others and tolerant of their differing ideas and philosophies. But it would be a good idea today to be a little standoffish and objective. If you get too deeply involved with others, you may lose some of the freedom of thought and action that you cherish. Someone with whom you share an interest may agree to take an evening course with you or to study a subject together. Read newspapers and magazines, and talk to people from other walks of life. You seem to have been spending too much money lately on entertainment and nonessentials. Take a look at your spending pattern. Put aside enough for emergencies. Taxes and other bills will soon arrive.

23. SATURDAY. Cautious. Although you seem to have Cancer's tendency to worry about money, the problem is not as serious today as it seems. People may have to be cutting back in order to cope with rising costs. So this would be a bad day to ask for loans from family and friends. You should not lend money to them either. It also is not a good day for approaching your boss for a raise. You know that your work and initiative will ensure that someday you will be comfortably off, so do not rock the boat. Some extra money can be made if you want to throw a selling party offering household goods, jewelry, and so on. Some people may seem difficult because they are harboring guilty secrets.

24. SUNDAY. Mixed. You may want to attend religious services in the company of family or good friends. The services are inspiring and encourage you to think about some of the mysteries of life. If you hold somewhat extreme views about religion, this is not the day to try to win others over to them. People who are patients in hospitals, or those who are connected with these facilities, can experience an exceptionally good day. You should think less of your own importance and more about what you can do to raise the morale of others. Ego trips are unnecessary. You may not be in the mood for driving around, so you will hope that you can be in touch with family and friends or have a visit from them.

25. MONDAY. Fortunate.   Those of you who are not at work on this Memorial Day will have no trouble finding things to do. You will want to spend most of the day with family and friends. A picnic can follow watching a parade. Or you may want to visit a cemetery to honor those of your family who have died. There can be other patriotic observances, including concerts. You will want to help others, as Cancers usually do. Your sympathy and material help will be much appreciated by those less fortunate than you. But you expect others to help you, and can feel persecuted if such help is not forthcoming. Take your mind off your troubles by doing some creative work, perhaps music or poetry.

26. TUESDAY. Mixed.   Changes in your family and neighborhood can lead to a great deal of coming and going. New neighbors appear, and you want to get to know them. Someone from your family seems to be about to change residence, and you will be enlisted to help with the moving. Friends can be less guarded in what they say; some secrets can come out. That evening course for which you recently signed up can prove disappointing. It seems to be useless for your purposes and not worth the considerable sum involved. Financially you can do rather well today. If you have any time left over from your hectic activities, you will enjoy visiting and chatting with relatives.

27. WEDNESDAY. Disconcerting.   Make a real effort to view today's happenings objectively. Interruptions that keep you from completing work on time can happen. Try to understand why the interruption is absolutely unavoidable. From the point of view of the person involved, it may be essential. If you show resentment, it might reveal that you were hurrying to get away early for personal reasons. The Cancer sensitivity to the feelings of others is likely to triumph. A call to the one you love will put you in a better frame of mind. You probably will want to retreat into the comfort and safety of your own home when the day's work is over. Do not pull back into your shell; join in family activities.

28. THURSDAY. Useful.   Interference from others is bound to cause resentment on your part. Perhaps you are being a little too independent in hotly resenting others' well-meant efforts to set you straight. Conversely, avoid telling other people what you think they should do. Solitude is the safest course. The work you are doing is rather challenging, so outside interference will not be welcomed. Those of you who like to break ground and do exciting things may enjoy today. But a steady diet of adventure would be a bit too much, so enjoy some more restful activities when you get the chance. Reading and discussing a current book with others can be just what you need.

29. FRIDAY. Happy.   Your income should be quite adequate at present. Even though it varies, it averages out to a good sum. Shopping today, however, should be confined to necessities rather than impulse buying of luxuries. Your possessions mean much to you, and you will be reluctant to part with them, even on temporary loan to a friend or institution. If you are spending the day at home, you will enjoy looking around at all the things you cherish. But there may be little time for that, as telephone calls from relatives come one after another. Do not allow yourself to get upset if the mail includes an anonymous letter; try to ignore it. There will be enough letters with pleasant news to please you.

30. SATURDAY. Manageable.   You are apt to feel rather optimistic today, but desirous of sticking to your regular routine. That should include some outdoor exercise for the sake of your health. Hard work does not bother you, so you can get much accomplished with the help of cooperative associates. Continue to watch your spending when out shopping, even if you are feeling in the money just now. Some short trips can be on the agenda, but you will be glad to get back home. Repairs that are deemed necessary can come to your attention, and you will enjoy making them in a leisurely fashion. Be careful what you say to a valued friend. If you are too demanding, you risk losing a friendship.

31. SUNDAY. Mixed.   Money continues to be very much on your mind. Your income seems to be from various sources and how best to invest it most profitably is the problem. Perhaps someone among all the people who are running in and out all day has an idea that is worth investigating. Make sure of your source. There are those whose idea of a good investment is to spend a night on the town, but that's definitely not yours. You would really prefer to spend the day alone with a good book, but that does not seem to be in the cards. If you drop in at a neighbor's party, it will be pleasant, but you will not stay long; you need your rest. A secret proves impossible to keep.

JUNE

1. MONDAY. Fortunate. As a new month begins, it is time to start thinking about a new project. You will have enough energy to handle the hard work involved. Talking with other people can produce new ideas that can be helpful to your work. But be sure to keep your wits about you and avoid showing impatience or anger at any thoughtless comments. Keep your personal feelings out of business dealings. You probably will want to spend many hours in research. This should be done in relative secrecy to prevent competitors stealing a march on you. New products can come out of that research, and you can have some meaningful dialogues with another person concerned in the project.

2. TUESDAY. Rewarding. Jupiter is likely to bring you good luck today. Working with other people and sharing ideas can be good for the future career. The need for secrecy does not exist at the moment. If the weather is not to your liking, you can find much to do with your family indoors. Since the morning is free from interruptions, you will have plenty of time to complete necessary tasks before joining in family activities. If the weather turns pleasant, you will enjoy gardening. Fruits and vegetables should do well, and relatives will welcome some flowers from your garden. During your free hours, you might even want to take short trips to deliver bouquets to these relatives. They will be overjoyed.

3. WEDNESDAY. Unsettling. You may want to blame the fact that the Moon is in Cancer for the disturbing state of your emotions. You can hardly wait to return to your home and the comforting presence of your loved ones. But there are some neglected or unfinished tasks that must be taken care of before you can enjoy that pleasure. Also, as much as you love your family, you may have some vague feeling that you would like to get away for a while. You naturally crave having some fun on your own. At least the financial picture is fairly bright at present. If you are in selling or promotion of a product, that picture could become even brighter. You may meet a new love through a study group.

4. THURSDAY. Excellent. The communications situation is very good today. If you want to go off by yourself and study, your family will be understanding; or if you want to talk about your plans and dreams, they will encourage you. They agree with you about the need to save more money, but they will not begrudge you a mild flyer on a lottery ticket. Winnings can be small, but at least there are winnings. The mail brings some welcome letters from people with whom you have been out of touch. The news can interest you greatly. More news can come from telephone calls, of which there will be many. Sitting around and carrying on serious discussions can be useful. There is also much merriment.

5. FRIDAY. Easygoing. Romance can be fun today, but do not expect anything permanent to come of it. There will be many other things to occupy your mild. You may attend a play or watch something interesting on television at home. Sports events and night clubs both offer diversion. If you earn some money on the side, do not spend it all on entertainment. Put some away for a rainy day. You are less likely to withdraw into your shell than usual, and you will be welcomed at social get-togethers. You may be feeling insecure, although there is no reason for it. Your reaction, however, is likely to take the form of showing off and bossing others around. It is better just to be yourself.

6. SATURDAY. Tranquil. You seem to have numerous unfinished tasks, so get on with them. Try to see the overall picture rather than one petty detail at a time. People will have second thoughts about interrupting you when they see how hard you are working. You are one of those people who like things to be just so, but do not make a big issue of it. If your surroundings are clean, do not worry too much about whether everything is in its place. Some reading will improve your mind and your prospects at work. Those who are interested in style can have a field day if they know where to go. Your lover probably will not be in the mood for jokes, so avoid teasing. Your health is likely to be better than you think it is.

7. SUNDAY. Slow. You want to be useful today, so spend some of your spare time thinking about how you can improve your working conditions. You could come up with some ideas that will impress superiors. Family members may be away from home, so you will probably feel lonely. Trying to rustle up a date can be fruitless; it might turn out that people whose company you do keep are not those you would ordinarily choose. So you may be better off amusing yourself. Is there a game or other sports activity to which you can go alone? Shopping can be a pleasant way to pass the time, but maybe you should leave your credit cards at home so that you are not tempted to spend needlessly.

8. MONDAY. Inactive. Yesterday you were seeking company, but today you will probably prefer to be alone. Close contacts with relatives can be irritating if they start nagging you about your health or your way of life. An older relative can come to your rescue and tell others to stop bothering you. If you are not feeling very well, it could simply be a case of nerves and worry. Try to distract yourself with an absorbing book; something either on religion or science might do the trick. Those Cancers who are interested in creative work can enjoy today; crafts and textiles are of special interest. The money needed to buy supplies, however, may not be available. If you do not feel like working, take a break.

9. TUESDAY. Happy. Personal relationships play a big role in your life at present. Spouses or partners are more important than ever. You will turn to them for support when the going gets rough. Your emotions can be very important; possessiveness and jealousy can do considerable harm. If you want to be loved, you must be prepared to love in return. Failure to carry out your side of the bargain can mean a less happy domestic life. But if you are in harmony, you will welcome visits from relatives for dinner or overnight. Otherwise, the two of you will be happy dining alone or going out to your favorite restaurant. There may be a museum exhibit that you want to see or a new book that you want to buy.

10. WEDNESDAY. Tricky. This is one of those days that can bring numerous disagreements and upsets at home and at work. Since it is your nature to seek harmony, these can bother you to the point of affecting your health. Make an effort to understand the motives of others, and try to talk out differences of opinion. Do not avoid arguments, however, by telling other people to go ahead and make all the decisions for you. Disagreement is a natural way of life, so don't expect everything to go your way all the time. If arguments escalate into shouting matches, nobody wins. You would prefer, of course, not to have to apologize.

11. THURSDAY. Enjoyable. Cancer people always show a special interest in and caring for their home and family. This is a day when that concern will be especially strong. You have some reason to be thinking about the health of a dear one. Also, you may be a bit worried about someone's emotional problems. You may want to read current articles on health and psychology. The safety of older relatives is on your mind. Their troubles should not be serious enough to keep you from having fun together. It can be a good time to make plans for a vacation trip. But first, you may have to deal with a matter of insurance or taxes. An evening activity can bring a new love or a case of jealousy.

12. FRIDAY. Confusing.   A new romance that may have started yesterday takes much of your time. You cannot get your mind off the object of your affection. This time the affair can become permanent, since there seems to be much in common between the two of you. Your experience and level of education are similar enough to make you the perfect pair. You again are deeply concerned with your various relationships. You expect from your family and friends the same loyalty that they get from you. You also expect them to stand up for what they believe in. You tend to be tactless, so do not say anything even when you feel others need to know the truth. You might just be imagining slights.

13. SATURDAY. Good.   You are inclined to be a little restless and want to get away, off the beaten path. If you can afford to travel, fine. If not, you should start saving for a budget tour. Meanwhile, a book about an interesting and exotic place can whet your appetite. Some of you see little chance of getting away in the near future, so you may want to enroll in a course with the idea of expanding your mind. Since you are feeling gregarious, you will probably postpone any quiet study until you are alone later in the day. Earlier, you can round up some good friends and get together for an outdoor concert or play. Be sure to include your romantic partner; this is a great day for a love affair.

14. SUNDAY. Productive.   This may be a day of rest, but get some checks written. You will be surprised to learn that you have overlooked several bills. While your income is generally adequate for your needs, it should be budgeted carefully. Otherwise you will not have the little extras that you crave. You may be saving for a trip later in the year when you have fewer obligations. Now is the time to explore relative costs of travel, such as by air or sea, or by car or train. You enjoy meeting new people, but soon become impatient with those who do not share your high ideals. Since people are only human, do not expect too much of them. You should have no trouble finding companions for a sports event.

15. MONDAY. Pleasant.   Cancers who have been putting those distasteful jobs aside should get on with them now. Your efforts will not go unnoticed by the people who matter. If you keep your nose to the grindstone early in the day, there is a chance of a pay raise or some public recognition. Co-workers are likely to respond to your consideration by pitching in to help you get some chores out of the way. Some of you will want to go home to loved ones when the work is done. Others will concentrate on getting ahead in the area of romance. You may crave some entertainment in the evening. You and your romantic partner will try to round up any relatives or friends who want to attend a play or movie.

16. TUESDAY. Challenging. The natural reserve of Cancer people is not always understood by their associates. When others are disturbed by unorthodox ideas and eager to discuss them, you will probably want to remain aloof and give no hint of your thoughts and emotions. It can be your way of protecting yourself against sentimentality and heated arguments. It will be just as well if you do not let yourself be distracted from your goals, whether making money or studying. If you are interested in languages, you may look into a course in a foreign tongue. In some, you will find many similarities such as in word roots that will help you to understand your own. Do not shirk new responsibilities at home.

17. WEDNESDAY. Mixed. Work at your place of employment seems rather dull, though it affords you a good chance to relax. If you find yourself nodding over your work do not worry; that is, of course, unless you are working with dangerous tools or machinery. Otherwise, the forty winks you catch can help you store up energy for the tasks you will have tomorrow. People you meet today can turn into friends for life. This evening, you may find yourself in the midst of a crowd in your home. It seems that you decided to invite several family members to dinner, those with whom you are very close. Then suddenly there may be visitors from a distance, even abroad. Improvise, but do not overdo.

18. THURSDAY. Happy. Solving problems intrigues you, so you should be good at puzzles, cryptograms and detective stories. Work on puzzles can turn into a group activity if you have friends with similar interests. Others may just look at you in utter disbelief at your strange tastes. Someone of the opposite sex attracts you, but you find yourself as bashful and tongue-tied as an adolescent. If you try hard enough, you will be able to find something in common with that person, possibly an interest in languages or an unusual organization; you will then be off and running. Your imagination and creativity stand you in good stead. In the evening, you may want to go out with friends to a favorite spot.

19. FRIDAY. Unsettling. You seem to have some big plans for the weekend. Since entertaining or going out on the town can be expensive, be sure that your budget can handle it. After all the buying is done, you may have to stop by the bank for some extra money. The family may be gathering tomorrow to celebrate a new addition, so everyone should be excited and happy. Any of you Cancers who have special talents will probably be asked to provide the entertainment. One or more of the relatives may bring a guest or two. These will be welcome and can prove to be good additions to your circle of friends. You are likely to be confused by the ambivalent attitude of your romantic partner.

20. SATURDAY. Successful. You may want to spend at least a few hours on self-improvement activities. Those of you who are students will have some important homework to be done this weekend. Adults who are considering changing jobs can do some research at home or at the nearest library on requirements and opportunities in their own fields. Such study and research can prove lucrative in the long run. Much as you like your freedom, you like your family more; so you will want to plan some domestic entertainment. The weather may be fine for a picnic. Yesterday you were worried about some problems your partner was having, but they should be cleared up today, to your relief.

21. SUNDAY. Exciting. The Cancer interest in the mystical leads you into some fascinating paths today. You also can indulge your flair for drama. Some subconscious worry can be making your life unhappy. You should talk it out with someone, but choose your confidant with care. Keep your secrets to yourself. Those of you who are on vacation may decide to fly to some exotic place that has long intrigued and attracted you. It could include a tour of historic places and magnificent scenery where few tourists have ever been before. Relatives may want you to stop off to visit them, but your airline does not allow stopovers. Either they can come to you soon or you can visit them later.

22. MONDAY. Enjoyable. Your recent heavy schedule seems to have interfered with your correspondence, so try to catch up on it today. You are in a romantic mood, and your love affair might move ahead rapidly if you were to take the trouble to write to your true love. That person may not be expecting a love letter, but will undoubtedly appreciate the sentiment. If you know someone who has recently suffered a loss or who is ill, at home or in the hospital, a letter would be welcomed. People naturally turn to you for help, but make sure that no one takes advantage of you. Someone is interested in a course you are taking and will be glad to have a chance to talk about it with you. Your imagination soars.

23. TUESDAY. Demanding. Your own affairs occupy most of your time at present. But solitude does not appeal to you so you want the company of those you love most. There should be little friction, since you will be keenly aware of the problems and needs of others. But look after your own interests, even to the point of seeming demanding. Just be sure that you do not expect more of others than you yourself can give. Apply yourself at work; superiors will be watching. Any shirking on your part can become a black mark against your employment record. The people with whom you spend social hours may be so close to you that you get involved in their problems and relationships with others.

24. WEDNESDAY. Fortunate. Keep a tight rein on your temper today, and try not to let your anger dominate your actions. That is not saying you should not say what you think, but try to do so unemotionally. There is no reason why you cannot follow your own inclinations as long as your actions do not hurt others. You are likely to resent interruptions, especially if you are doing something of great importance at work, but keep calm. The languages and attitudes of people from a distance can cause misunderstandings, but goodwill on both sides can resolve the problems. If you have time, go in for some home decorating and improvements. You feel that your financial position warrants it.

25. THURSDAY. Exciting. What starts as a fun excursion with good friends can turn into a love affair. Both of you may be surprised at the depth of your feelings for each other. Those who decide to make a match of it and start a home will be eager to begin buying furnishings. This project should be approached with caution. If your head is in the clouds, you might well choose things that you do not really need now and spend too much for them. Material objects do attract you, and you will probably be unwilling to lend anything to people who ask. Cancer artists find this a favorable time for attempting new ventures. There should be enough money, and there is no lack of enthusiasm on your part. Work out of your home, if possible.

26. FRIDAY. Stressful. You are very conservative at the moment and drag your feet when it comes to starting anything new. But some changes can be for the good. Once you are convinced of a new project's worth, you will probably plunge wholeheartedly into it, making it a success. You will not overlook the fact that a new way of doing things can be lucrative. Those who serve on any committees would try to reach agreements quickly. If it is a large group, keep in mind that too many cooks can spoil the broth.

Personal problems can be uppermost in your mind. These can interfere with your ability to work effectively, so you will want to leave work early.

27. SATURDAY. Inactive. Some Cancers are feeling restless and a little nervous today. You cannot seem to make up your mind about anything. Perhaps you tend to talk too much. Or you may try to keep too many balls in the air at one time. If you can overcome this tendency, you can come up with some good ideas. You will be resourceful enough to make the most of them. Do not be tempted by money to sell secrets; that is not worthy of your high ideals. You can be in a sociable mood and will enjoy getting together with friends. Have fun, but avoid making any commitments. Concentrating on your goals will pay off. Much as you like to hang out with friends, you will be eager to get home.

28. SUNDAY. Mixed. Communications play an important role in your life at present. Your mind may be so much on your own problems that you talk to others without thinking much about what you are saying. If you want to have your conversations accomplish anything, you will have to get hold of yourself. An understanding friend can see the state you are in and help you to gain more control of your own emotions. Automatic, unwise comments can get you into trouble. Do not allow yourself to get to the point where you are constantly on the defense. If others seem to find your life interesting, they may encourage you to write it down, with the idea of eventual publication. Avoid overspending as you go gadding about with friends.

29. MONDAY. Sensitive. Nostalgia and family closeness govern most of your actions today. This is not too surprising, with the Moon in Cancer. Some childhood behavior patterns reemerge. You may seek the comfort of dear ones or simply withdraw to a hideaway with a book that you have been wanting to read. If no one can find you, they cannot hurt you. On the other hand, some favorable publicity can be coming your way, so do not make yourself too inaccessible. Your romantic partner will get a big kick out of seeing your name in the newspapers or your face on television. If your talent lies in cooking and you are feeling adventurous, you can concoct something new and delicious for guests.

30. TUESDAY. Happy. Home and family occupy much of your time today. There seems to be no shortage of money, so you can plan a family outing with a clear conscience. Friends are fun, but today your dear ones, especially parents, will seem more

important. Avoid strangers if at all possible. Efforts to get in touch
with someone may be thwarted when your telephone is discovered
to be out of order. Once that is taken care of, you will be able to
accomplish much while working at home. A friend can give you a
hand if you are starting a new, creative enterprise, and both of you
will profit monetarily. Some young person can be helpful too. If
you have any self-doubts, do not worry; they will soon pass.

JULY

1. WEDNESDAY. Excellent. With the Moon in Cancer, you
are at your happiest when you are at home with your family. Music
will play an important role, calming your thoughts and providing a
pleasant, soothing background for dining. You may be asked to
speak in public, and some lively music could ease your jitters at the
prospect. Good ideas come from many sources, but especially
from relatives today. Put them to use, and your value to the
company will rise in the eyes of superiors. If you are in a gambling
mood, a family card game might fill the bill; gains and losses will
be all in the family. You may even be the lucky winner! Losers will
not mind if you spend your winnings on a treat for the children.

2. THURSDAY. Stressful. All is not quiet on the domestic
front. There can be arguments over money, and some older relatives will be unhappy. They are likely to call you irresponsible.
Friends may go off in a huff if you refuse to get involved in their
financial deals. The romantic picture is bright, however; and a
flirtation could blossom into a genuine love affair. Or you may
meet someone new and be in love before you are aware of what is
happening. A new restaurant proves to be surprisingly romantic;
or is it just that stars are in your eyes? When you are home again
with the family, you will find them eager to plan a special outing or
some entertaining for the long weekend that is coming.

3. FRIDAY. Changeable. You Cancers who are not at your
place of employment now will have more time to think about
world issues. With the state of the world being what it is, you may
become slightly depressed. That is more than enough reason for
casting about to see what you can do to improve conditions.
Remember that every little bit helps. You will also want to spend

as much time as possible with your family. Entertainment is not
hard to find. Those who are crazy over computer games will enjoy
playing them with loved ones. Most people will be excited, outgoing and cheerful, always ready for something new. You are more
than likely to feel vague, romantic longings. But you will have to
wait a while for them to materialize in the form of a new love.

4. SATURDAY. Exciting.   With your energy level high, you
will be eager to throw yourself into whatever patriotic or entertainment activity this holiday has to offer. With parades, picnics and
band concerts, you can enjoy a real old-fashioned Independence
Day. There may be a family reunion and you will be happy to see
relatives who come from far and near. Your contribution to the
day's success will range from presiding over the barbecue to teaching younger members of the group what today means. Your mate
or love will be close at hand, helping where necessary and entertaining relatives. Cancers are nostalgic by nature, so old photo
albums and scrapbooks will help jog memories of times long ago.
The day should be memorable for all.

5. SUNDAY. Difficult.   The holiday spirit remains, but you are
more in the mood for romance. If that new love affair is still in
your future, you have something to look forward to. Meanwhile,
spend some time with your family, and listen, at least, to their
suggestions for improving your home. You are such a perfectionist
that you will be upset to think your home has anything wrong with
it. Don't discuss it with any other family members who come on
the scene. The less said about it, the better. You are as critical of
yourself as you are of others, and that obviously interferes with
any creative ventures you attempt. You must shake off feelings of
inferiority, believing you cannot accomplish anything. Get away
from your familiar haunts and see how others live and play.

6. MONDAY. Demanding.   Your emotional life appears to be
in a state of chaos. Your moodiness lately has led you to antago-
nize people, especially those dearest to you. You are restless and
looking for excitement, yet you want to do something useful.
Although people fall victim to your charm, they become wary of
irritating you. They may resent your hesitancy and decide to leave
you to your own devices. Think about it all. You will have to shape
up if you want this to be a productive day. That may not be too
hard if you are creative by nature. Turn all that suppressed restless
energy into an artistic effort; you might well surprise yourself. But
do not go around talking about how much money you will expect
to make. You will be hounded by those who beg you for some.

7. TUESDAY. Manageable. Your willingness to cooperate with others and to consider their points of view and personal faults makes a good impression. It can lead to advancement in your occupation. Others come to expect your help. At the risk of seeming indecisive, you should weigh all alternatives before taking action. Do not make too many plans for your time after work if you need the rest. Provided social activities are not too strenuous, they can be useful for making new contacts. You will have increased confidence in yourself and be more sure of your goals. When you take a new romantic partner home to meet the family, be prepared for some dismay. It will probably take a little time for everyone to get used to the idea.

8. WEDNESDAY. Buoyant. You are not likely to be bored today. Your emotions are high, and you must remain in full control of them. Otherwise, you will run the risk of becoming too involved in the problems of others. You really should be objective and impersonal in dealing with those around you. Your energy is boundless, and you want to get things done right now. Your self-confidence is now enough for you to prepare some convincing presentations for your superiors. You alone can see to it that your talents are visible enough for all to see. Your income is probably quite good, but do not be tempted to go on a spending spree. Putting something away for a rainy day is a smart move. A feeling of happiness and satisfaction brings the day to a successful close.

9. THURSDAY. Challenging. Your energy level continues to be high, and your competitive spirit keeps you on the go. You take your contacts with others very seriously. Do not expect everyone to be perfect; this is not an ideal world. You find concentration comes easily. Do not let emotional considerations cloud your judgment. Your imagination and inner vision have depths that surprise even you. It may be wise to limit your work and outside activities today to what you can do really well. If you try to sample everything on the smorgasbord of fun, you will be rushing from one thing to another and enjoying none of them. A light flirtation is fine, but do not tie yourself down to anything permanent until you have had fun. Concentrate on friendship instead of love.

10. FRIDAY. Sensitive. This can be a day for philosophical reflection and for questioning your attitudes about life. You are looking for your place in the world's activities. Some new ideas can come out of your work and the people connected with it. You gradually realize that the past and the future are blended with the present and that you are part of the whole. Human nature, you conclude, is much the same the world over. The likenesses and differences intrigue you. You may want to read and reflect in solitude, but you also want to spend time in discussion with kindred spirits. The problems faced by people in other countries will come home to you through your reading. You may decide to travel and see for yourself what is going on.

11. SATURDAY. Satisfactory. Your main problems now can arise from your tendency to say exactly what you think. It is nice to be honest, but you must try to be tactful and avoid hurting people's feelings. At the moment, you seem to have enough money to indulge yourself and good friends for company. Do not set your sights too high. Ambition can lead you down many roads, but success can elude you if you expect too much. You seem to have a grasshopper mind at present and find it hard to stick to any one activity for a long time. When you see too many roads to explore, you tend to drift from one to another and do not complete anything you start. Travel intrigues you, but you may have to settle for dreams of faraway places and for reading about them.

12. SUNDAY. Inactive. To you Cancers, life is an adventure today. You are energetic, but more relaxed than usual. So you are ready to take life as it comes and to enjoy whatever is put on your plate. You do not fret unduly about small mishaps and changes of plan because you are sure it will come out all right in the end. You can adapt readily to changes. A philosophical outlook helps you to deal with strained relationships. You go out of your way to avoid violent confrontations. Your generous nature makes you want to share any good fortune you have with others. At times you have the feeling that you are in the hands of fate. Since there is so little you can do about it, you decide not to worry but just enjoy life.

13. MONDAY. Rewarding. Physical and mental energy are at a high peak today. You have one useful idea after another, and want to act on all of them. You will probably prefer to work on your own, but some projects require teamwork. You favor your own ideas over those of others, but your occupation can require that you take some sort of course. You will thus have to pay some attention to the words of other people. Your relationships with others are good, and you will not try to rock the boat if you are involved in an activity that demands cooperation. You could become interested in some type of course in drama if your tastes run that way. The more practical Cancers may enroll at once in a course in investment.

14. TUESDAY. Demanding. Your work today can keep you too busy for friendship activities. Much responsibility may rest on your shoulders, so you will demand a great deal not only of yourself but also of those working under you. You are absorbed in what you are doing, and monetary gain will take a backseat to recognition of your ability. You have goals in mind and are headed unswervingly in their direction. It is possible that this attitude can irritate others, but make every effort to avoid confrontations. At the end of the day, you will feel satisfaction in work well done. Now you will be ready for recreation with friends or even for some further study at the library or light reading at home.

15. WEDNESDAY. Uncertain. Music may dominate the day for Cancers who are so inclined. If you teach voice or an instrument, it is possible you will have visitors, perhaps several young girls. But some of your own friends and you plan to work on original pieces with the idea of taking part in a recital some time. Unfortunately, influential friends who had earlier promised support for your group now appear to be bowing out. There's no need to mention that now. Be careful where money is concerned today. Rely on your own judgment when it comes to an important decision in that regard. A self-assured business associate may feel secure about a financial deal, but remember it's your money! Keep in good physical shape with regular checkups.

16. THURSDAY. Difficult. Money is very much on your mind. The apparent lack of it can cause you some worry. Check back over your budget to see where you have miscalculated. If you have been spreading your money around too lavishly, you may need some professional advice about savings and investments. You hate to have your fast pace slowed down by a shortage of funds. A new project involving sales or promotions can put you back in the black. Then you can pay those bills for entertainment and study. You appear to have leadership talents; do not let them go to waste. It may not be possible at the moment to fulfill your humanitarian hopes and dreams, so you will just have to wait until they can be made to come true.

17. FRIDAY. Frustrating. When it comes to channeling all the energy you have today, you can be torn in several directions. Some active participation in sports can burn up part of the energy while pursuing a love affair can use up some more. Going out with friends in search of entertainment is still another way to tax your energy. Perhaps the best way of all is to follow your humanitarian instincts. You are appalled by the hunger in the world, and you

will be canvassing friends and relatives in search of funds to help
the situation. You may hop from one interest to another, since you
are easily bored. The plight of the poor all over the world worries
you, but there is little you can do at the present.

18. SATURDAY. Tricky.   You are continuously fretting about
what is going on around you and wish you could change it. But do
not get involved in humanitarian efforts unless you are truly dedicated. An immediate, personal problem is likely to be finding
money for education. You will be trying to find ways to raise
enough to continue your education. If your savings are not adequate, a loan may be the answer. Some relative may come
through, or you can be planning to try to get a bank loan. You
Cancers with artistic leanings should try to find a few hours to
spend in solitude to develop some bright ideas that have been at
the back of your minds. Your intuition and determination to
succeed should take you far.

19. SUNDAY. Rewarding.   Your recent spurt of energy serves
you well today. There is much you can do on a local level to
improve the quality of other people's lives. Sports and other
physical fitness activities prove to be unexpectedly lucrative.
Coaching or teaching can bring in some extra money. Or perhaps
you will win a prize at an athletic event. You want money, but you
do not want to work too hard for it. Family differences can arise
over this. If you are involved in a town drama group, you will be
keen to participate actively. Some of your excess energy can go
toward raising funds to continue the group's programs. Being so
much on the go will give you a good appetite, which is beneficial.

20. MONDAY. Successful.   Family affection helps you to relax
after a hard day's work. There is so much for you to do that you
will have to choose your activities and projects carefully. For those
who are artistic by nature, there is an opportunity to make something useful and beneficial. If there are no telephone calls at all
today, be glad for the chance to work without interruption. The
mail will contain little of interest, so you can discard most of it.
Financially, you will not make a killing, but there seems to be a
small, steady income to keep the wolf from the door. Some of the
income will be connected with food. A book you start can grab
your attention, and you will not be able to put it down.

21. TUESDAY. Changeable.   Your expertise and willingness to
pitch in will be much in demand at your place of work today. You
have some skill at fixing minor problems with office or factory

machinery. This can save the company the cost and delay of calling in a repairman. You also have a talent for writing and can produce some snappy advertisements for your employer. The extra work will make you late in getting home, but it will be well worth it financially. There is some possibility of delays in the mail, or a telephone call may not go through promptly. Misunderstandings with clients can result. Do not carry too much money. You can be entertaining friends in the evening or out attending a class.

22. WEDNESDAY. Uncertain. If your income has dropped, it will be necessary to work out a new budget. Perhaps you have been spending too much on entertainment. Look ahead to the future; you should surely have enough money on hand for a holiday. It may not be you who is responsible for overspending; it could be a family member. You should remind that person that money does not grow on trees, and that college expenses lie in the future. The purchase of things that you do not really need can lead to family arguments. Do not be a soft touch for someone who comes to you with a tale of woe. Paying current bills is most important, and should take precedence over other expenditures. You may start thinking about raising a family.

23. THURSDAY. Difficult. Money continues to influence many of your actions. You are by nature cautious about your spending, but you can get carried away when you are out with friends. Be sure that you are not stuck with the bill for club activities. Possibly you will be able to make up for extravagant spending by working harder and putting in some overtime; but do not count on it. Perhaps your friends have more money or a different attitude toward it than you do. Someone older and wiser can step in and steer you in the right direction. Your best bet is to concentrate on your work, even if it does not suit you to do so. Leave the expensive social times for another day.

24. FRIDAY. Inactive. Your budget is beginning to show some progress now. But there is always the tendency to forget it momentarily, especially when you see something that you really want. So you will still have to watch your spending. You do have the tendency to buy things on the spur of the moment and then pack them away and forget them. There seems to be a risk of unknowingly buying illegal or stolen goods, so be careful. Club activities absorb much of your attention. No one can miss your leadership qualities, so you are a natural for an important position on a committee. Do not accept unless you are willing to spend much time and energy, but do not sink your own money into it.

25. SATURDAY. Fair. You are usually not inclined to waste time when there is a job to be done. Right now, however, you may be a bit lazy. You soon will find that your laziness makes it harder to get back into the swing of things. Routine seems dull to you today, and you will have to work on your concentration. A little discipline will enable you to get your thoughts in order and to express yourself clearly and forcibly. Your extravagance of the past week may have caught up with you. You find that you really do not have enough money available to go out on the town with your friends. You can still have a good time with them, however, if you attend an organization's meeting; the cost can be negligible.

26. SUNDAY. Slow. Last week appears to have been rather wearing, and now you are ready for some rest. Put the children to work on an interesting creative project, and they will not interrupt your nap. Letters to relatives should be written today. You could be disappointed when someone sends you a message instead of coming to see you. Someone else may be a house guest, but whoever it is wants to catch up with family visits, so you find yourself left to your own devices. You can augment your income today by doing some typing. The job will not last very long, but it will not be too demanding either. If you do a good job, you probably will be asked to work again evenings or weekends.

27. MONDAY. Enjoyable. Your family almost always comes first with you. Now, when the Moon is in Cancer, the desire to spend time at home is stronger than ever. You may not get much backing for your plan to go shopping for items for the home or for your suggestions to get out into the fresh air. Your dear ones seem to prefer to stay inside and play board games. This is all right with you, up to a point. You page through your books, trying to find something to interest you later; or you may decide to try out a new recipe. The enticing smell will bring people running, even the laziest of them. So be sure to prepare enough for your family and anyone who drops in, possibly a neighbor.

28. TUESDAY. Tricky. Your spirits can be lifted when you receive an unexpected gift. It can be just in time to fit in with your plans for vacation. But do not plan to spend that vacation at a casino, where the gambling is for much higher stakes than your friendly games at home. The lunar aspect of Cancer makes you more vulnerable than ever to imagined slights or put-downs. You will naturally turn to your family for comfort. Be wary of anyone who tries to sell you something you do not really want. When you catch on later to the fact that you have been deceived, it can be very hard to cancel your contract or get your money back. Romance is on your mind. Do not believe what people tell you about friends, unless it is highly complimentary.

29. WEDNESDAY. Excellent. Today is just fine for fresh starts, whether in careers, romance, or travel. If you are not changing jobs, you can be finding new ways to use your talents and spare time to make more money. You have an urge to write so take advantage of a pleasant trip to further that ambition. Your experiences will be worth writing about, and some study or visits to cultural landmarks will broaden your mind. A bonus could come from meeting someone with whom you will want to share your life one day soon. Do not expect love at first sight. A permanent relationship will take time to grow. You need not be on the go all the time. A rest at a resort can do you much good.

30. THURSDAY. Happy. This continues to be a good time for romance. Do not spend too much money on a romantic outing, or you will be in trouble in the future. A small and inexpensive foreign restaurant can be just as romantic as something more lavish if you are accompanied by your loved one. You will enjoy listening to music together. Those Cancers who are unattached can show off their culinary skills by inviting some young relatives to dinner. Their company can make you have some vague yearning for a child of your own eventually. Realizing the cost of raising one, you must start more regular saving than heretofore. Whatever you decide to do, go home early and get your rest.

31. FRIDAY. Sensitive. You have now developed some depths of understanding. But you will still be rather quick on the trigger today. Family arguments can develop over your spending habits or theirs. Young people can irritate you to the shouting point, and even the people with whom you work can upset you. In any case, it will all blow over quickly. Your fondness for books can result in your buying another bookcase. Now you must decide where you are going to put it. Today is good for turning your hand to making something useful for the home. The results may not satisfy you as a perfectionist, but the family will think that it is just fine. Do not brood about failures; seek out the company of congenial friends, and plan some interesting weekend activities.

AUGUST

1. SATURDAY. Enjoyable. Most of you Cancers will be brimming over with energy at the start of this weekend. But those of you who are slightly under the weather should not force yourselves. Nor should you put a damper on other people's fun. Cancer people who have too much energy to sit around without purpose should look into the possibility of a self-improvement course. Others may want to join a crafts group and learn how to make something from scratch. You will catch on quickly and might be very proud of what you create. Whatever you do, try to look your best. Personal hygiene and good grooming are important; also devote thought to how you dress if you hope to make a good impression. Reorganize your home and workroom.

2. SUNDAY. Pleasant. Cancer people who expect to be home today can earn extra income by caring for a child at your residence. Family members who are home with you will be working in harmony, so the atmosphere should be peaceful. Perhaps your romantic partner is out of town, so you decide to plan an outing with other family members. Some friends may also want to join you. You have an interest in the arts, so you might decide to join an art group or little theater society. Everyone left at home will enjoy reading, watching television, or just lazing around. For the unattached Cancer, this will be a good day for developing new relationships. Some may want to get married this weekend.

3. MONDAY. Variable. Emotional conflicts with other people can be avoided if you are willing to be tolerant of their shortcomings. But these may exist only in your mind. You can have some rewarding discussions with associates who have similar tastes. You will probably be feeling friendly and cooperative, although you can be harboring some jealousy about your one and only. The weather can be suitable for a picnic, so take advantage of it. A legal battle resolved in your favor can bring in a large amount of money. The family decides to throw a dinner to celebrate, and you will strive to look your best for the occasion. Keep in mind, however, that overindulgence can be harmful to your health.

4. TUESDAY. Stressful. You are inclined to be emotional and moody, which will not sit well with family members. It will be hard to get them to make what you regard as necessary sacrifices. They are likely to be very touchy if you try ordering them around and rearranging their lives. You have little to complain about regarding your own love life, but there may be some problem areas that would benefit from a frank talk. You mean to economize, but you also are in the mood to buy some new clothes. Dressing up and going out with your love will make you feel like a new person. Do not overdo the purchases, however, since other family members are likely to resent it. Writing necessary letters can be a chore.

5. WEDNESDAY. Mixed. Property and other financial affairs are on your mind. You are apt to be frustrated in some of your efforts to manage your concerns. Investigations into your finances can run up against a stone wall. But other people note that you are doing a good job on some matters and will ask you to help them. Property is important to you, and you are extremely unwilling to part with some things that you have had for a long time. They have a strong, sentimental attachment. Conflicts over joint ownership can be resolved by selling a few carefully chosen items. At some point, you find yourself involved with intellectual types. Take notes of the conversation; you can develop a whole new outlook.

6. THURSDAY. Disconcerting. The money that is available for fun can be limited today, so you will have to budget your entertaining. In spite of that, you are likely to buy too much in the way of party snacks, and you will be stuck with an overstocked refrigerator. Perhaps some neighbors and relatives will take some of the excess goodies off your hands. On the whole, people want to keep the peace and have a harmonious relationship. If you come on too strong, they will resent it. It will be up to you to try to understand their attitudes and motivations, and thus avoid a break in relations. You can suddenly realize how important these friends and relatives are to you, and will hasten to mend fences.

7. FRIDAY. Changeable. You yearn to understand people better and to broaden your outlook. But you have neither the time nor the money for long trips. However, you can take a short trip to the library or a bookstore and pick up some books and magazines. They will have to do until you can make the trip of your dreams. Remember that your income depends on your job, so do not take time off from work. Money does come rolling in today, but it can also roll out equally fast. If you have been brought up in a frugal home, you will view this phenomenon with dismay. But the bills are there, and taxes must be paid soon. You will also decide to spend money on your family and perhaps have a little fun yourself.

8. SATURDAY. Favorable. Today holds promise for those Cancers who seek a career in teaching or in creating writing. Your writing talent can be put to good use in composing a long letter to your love. There seems to be a fundamental difference over life-styles and the seriousness of the relationship. By putting your thoughts on paper, you may be able to convince your sweetheart or change your own way of thinking. You will need solitude for writing, and family members are willing to leave you alone. If you are out in a crowd, you can pick up a summer cold or one of the viruses that are going around. This, of course, would make you a poor companion for either your love or for friends and family.

9. SUNDAY. Rewarding. The Cancer person who is at work today is going to find that conditions are much to his or her liking. You may be moved to a larger office and given more authority, so your prestige will be increased and some of your ambitious urges satisfied. You are prepared to work hard, and superiors will sense this. You can be very much on your dignity and not too responsive to the needs of others. Your attitude is that your personal career comes first. You should be faced with no major problems at work. At home, you are likely to have a visit from some missionaries. Their beliefs are different enough from yours to form the basis for a good argument.

10. MONDAY. Challenging. Good health and lots of energy are of particular importance to your career. Throw yourself into your work, and learn all the ins and outs. Your ambition shows you where the ladder to success is, and your reputation for being an honest and hard worker starts you on the upward climb. Your aims must be clearly defined, or you may waste precious time. Employers are conservative, so this is no time for you to propose procedures that are too innovative. Since you seem to be on your way to success, you are inclined to start thinking of having a home and family of your own, if you are still single. Your earnings will help pay for that, as will the proceeds from a legal action.

11. TUESDAY. Demanding. You realize that you will have to work hard to overcome the problem of your being unable to express yourself lucidly and tactfully. An unfortunate tendency to speak without thinking is offputting and distracting for your lis-teners. If you are talking to important superiors or sensitive friends and family members, the results can be disastrous. And you will of course be deeply hurt by any sharp answers, although you have merited them. If you really want to progress, both on the office front and with friends, you must understand how large a part good communications play in winning promotions and gaining social acceptance. Avoid debt, even if you pass up bargains.

12. WEDNESDAY. Sensitive. Your mood is rather contrary today. You are picky and ready to criticize everything, to the confusion of your romantic partner and friends. You may storm out of a conversation with your loved one, announcing that you do not want to be tied down. Then you will go out on your own or with friends in search of entertainment. You may then become unpleasant, finding fault with everything from the movie to the restaurant. People whom you insult will probably not realize that your mood is sour because you are worried about money. Your best move would be to do everything possible to pay those bills; after that, you can relax and forget them.

13. THURSDAY. Useful. Money worries continue, so try to pay those bills as quickly as you can. You may have to work extra hours if you are connected with a hospital or either a police or fire department. Perhaps you will have to miss an important meeting because of this. Your alertness and the quickness of your mind can be real assets. Try to take time to go home for a good, balanced meal with your family. If you are like most people, you probably have neglected some interesting sights and historic spots in your area. Your free time would be well spent if you take a bus tour of what you have missed. You are in a gregarious mood, so you can meet new people and form new friendships.

14. FRIDAY. Enjoyable. The financial situation is better now, thanks to increased income and your ability to negotiate a loan. You may be given additional responsibilities at work as well as cooperative people to help you. Avoid overconfidence, however. A new worry can surface in regard to health if you have been disregarding your family's advice to see a doctor. Once that is taken care of, you will enjoy family activities. Games and dancing can be pleasant after a home-cooked dinner. Your spouse or partner and young relatives will enter into the fun. If you are attached at present, you may enjoy playing your favorite records or tapes or taking in a good movie on television.

15. SATURDAY. Uncertain. Some Cancer people are at critical times in their lives because of the breaking up of a relationship. Legalities can be confusing. If you are one of these, you will be seeking avenues of escape from problems. Do not draw back into your shell and brood; it could have a bad effect on your health. It would be better to throw yourself into your work and to try to meet people who can advance your career. Or it might be a good idea to take a late-summer vacation. A guided tour, although it may be crowded, will be cheaper and offer opportunities to meet new people. It can be hard to concentrate if you are worried, but give it a try. Progress can be made in the field of music.

16. SUNDAY. Fortunate. If you have withdrawn from society lately, this is the day for coming out of your shell. Plan an outing or a trip. Since Cancer is a water sign, you will gravitate naturally toward the seashore or a lake. Fishing will be good. If you are not a sportsman, you can still enjoy a seafood dinner, or you may find some good buys in shellfish to take home. You will meet new acquaintances, and some of them can direct your attention to areas where your help is needed. The fresh air and exercise will whet your appetite for a good dinner with friends, and the conversation will be equally as good as the food. You may find, in time, that you met someone who will become a friend for life.

17. MONDAY. Difficult. It becomes increasingly necessary to get to that small repair job. Do not forge ahead without preparation. You need help from household members, but you will have to be ready to direct them. So study the problem; consult a manual if you have to. Then you will feel confident enough to go ahead and get the job done quickly, even if others desert you and you are on your own. You can console yourself with the knowledge that you needed the exercise anyway. Travel is too tiring for you today. Also, your regular job will keep you too busy for many trips. No matter how hard you work, you find that no one is happy with the result. At least you are bringing home some money.

18. TUESDAY. Enjoyable. Take time out today to look after your health. The chances are that the problem lies in your grabbing quick meals without regard for proper nutrition. Once you are feeling better, you will be ready for some fun. Visiting relatives will be eager to see where you work and also the various attractions of the area. You are elected to give them a guided tour. If you have no visitors, you can become interested in a secret home project to surprise your loved one. The unattached can be sidetracked by a new and exciting person at work. Do not make a heavy emotional investment; the affair is unlikely to last. This is a time when you are subject to flashes of temper, but they will soon cool down.

19. WEDNESDAY. Rewarding. Money matters claim much of your attention. You handle your own problems very well. So you cannot be expected to be sympathetic when others come to you with tales of woe about having lost money. They have no right to expect you to make it up. You have a strong sense of property, but the less said about it, the better. The subject of your own possessions interests you, but other people do not really care. Do not be surprised if they show their boredom. Your leadership abilities are self-evident. Co-workers are eager to help you and to stand by your side; they would back you up without question. If a problem arises that calls for a quick bit of research, you are equal to it.

20. THURSDAY. Successful.   You are always looking for new ways to make money. Investigating an area in the arts for which you have a talent can prove worthwhile. You are not, however, a person who likes to take a chance on unproved schemes, since you are not a gambler at heart. You are interested in the welfare of other people. You take the time to study your firm's health and hospitalization plan to see whether it can be improved to benefit you and your fellow employees. You like to see others get ahead and may drop a tactful word in the right ears toward that end. Those whom you help will be grateful and will let you know later how much they appreciate your interest.

21. FRIDAY. Productive.   There are so many activities that interest you today that you hardly know where to start. You are conscious that your occupation should be given the most time, but you do tend to become tired quickly. In that case, you should find some undemanding chores and leave the more important ones for a time when you are feeling better. Although you worry about it, your health is fairly good. Perhaps you are just a little run-down. Some solitude will enable you to get your thoughts in order and decide on your priorities. It will also give you a chance to rest. A pleasant diversion while you are resting can be created by some phone calls. Family and friends are waiting to hear from you.

22. SATURDAY. Mixed.   Art and creative work, as well as social contacts, can take much of your time. It is a good day for money matters; a check may arrive, and you seem to be quite comfortably off at present. However, a visit to relatives makes you aware of their need for money, and you want to help. It can be very depressing. You are less concerned about your health, but you should continue to be cautious about overindulging. You may be engaged in an artistic effort. Do not be too disappointed if the finished product is not up to your expectations. Some other hobbies can be more successful. Do not depend on others to do the work that you should be doing yourself. Pitch right in with them.

23. SUNDAY. Good. It is not surprising that you are more than usually family-oriented now. The Moon in Cancer has something to do with it. You will not feel like wandering far from home. If you do decide to visit the local botanical garden or museum, you will doubtless include your dear ones. But you would probably be happier if you just stay at home. Your love of music expresses itself in some impromptu sessions, playing instruments with family and friends. Or all of you could be content to listen to recorded music. You may also decide to organize a group to read certain books and later discuss them. Relatives and family members will urge you on to some genealogical research, and you can have fun trying to puzzle out a family tree of sorts.

24. MONDAY. Fortunate. You are not really in the mood for studying, but it is necessary. Learning is not so hard if you apply yourself. Your humanitarian interests come to the fore. What you do to better the lot of the poor and sick enhances your personal reputation. All these activities will not leave you much time for social plans. Even background music can prove distracting. The person on whom you cast a romantic eye seems to show little interest. You have no complaints about your work, so there should be no worries to carry home with you. It is likely that you will meet someone who seems very eccentric. If you can get beneath the surface of that person's thinking, you will find some good ideas among the oddities.

25. TUESDAY. Buoyant. Your thoughts continue to gravitate toward family and old friends in the early part of the day. That is natural at this time of month for Cancers. You will be looking for fun and companionship. Plan to go to a show with a good friend or your loved one; you can afford it. You are on the lookout for new worlds to conquer. You have no complaints about your health. On the contrary, energy is abundant. On your lunch break, you may want to take a brisk walk in the park with a friend. It seems that your writing ability offers a chance to make some extra money. Keep your journal or diary up to date; you may want to refer to it later. Your affectionate mood makes you write a love letter.

26. WEDNESDAY. Rewarding. You may have the ability now to project your goals for the future and will have some bright ideas about how to achieve them. Having a goal spurs you on to do great things at work. In fact, you may become so absorbed that you are unaware of interruptions. This will not go unnoticed by superiors. You will be kept in mind for important future assignments. Possibly there will be some extra pay for overtime. If you have time for some study or reading, turn your attention to a book on economics. What you will learn will help you to make money. It will also help you to avoid pitfalls that result in losing it. You should have time for fun later, perhaps with a child or romantic partner.

27. THURSDAY. Challenging. Your career dominates all else today. Efficiency is important, but it accomplishes more if there is a strong drive toward success behind it. You have plenty of new and innovative ideas that can speed your work and push you forward into new fields of endeavor. It would be well to keep these under your hat for the time being. You will have to depend on yourself to solve any problems that arise. No one else will have the foggiest notion how to deal with them. This can be a good time to start on a new project, perhaps even on a new job. Your talent for organization will stand you in good stead. Do not let a vaguely restless feeling hamper your efforts to do the very best possible.

28. FRIDAY. Useful. You have been looking forward to a chance to get in some physical exercise. But you may not be feeling at your best physically, so you will have to postpone it. It would not be much fun exercising if you were wondering whether you were doing yourself any harm. A little mild exercise for the sake of your weight should do no harm, however. But you will find this a better day for mental activities. Do not worry if people don't understand some of your ideas and consider you eccentric. Make use of that imagination. Read about career matters, and store up knowledge for future use. The time when you can use what you learn can approach more quickly than you think. Lifetime benefits can come out of your study today.

29. SATURDAY. Excellent. This seems to be a day for domestic activities, although you may decide to include some friends. You are aware of some minor repairs, and want to finish them today. If the job is more complicated, you will probably call in some help from family and neighbors. One such project can be painting the house or perhaps just one room. You may opt to reward your helpers by grilling some culinary specialties on your backyard barbeque. In fact, you will have to if there is a problem with the kitchen range. Ideas that come to you today should be jotted down before they fade away. They might well become the basis for a later article or story. You have some relatives who would appreciate a letter from you.

30. SUNDAY. Happy. The urge to be with loved ones and close friends continues. It can be a romantic day for you and your partner, getting away from it all and finding happiness in an outing to a favorite spot. You will have to face the fact that not everyone among your many relatives and friends approves of the relationship. It is not really their business, except for any effect it may have on such items as occupational insurance or pension. Standards change, and attitudes and the law do not always keep up with them. Possibly you will want to throw a party at home. Be careful in making up your list of guests if you want a happy gathering. You may also have to watch out for gate-crashers who could spoil it all by just being boorish.

31. MONDAY. Productive. Your family life continues to be important to you. The unattached Cancer dwells on romance. The day seems to be rather uneventful as long as you are conscious of the need for security. There may be some burglaries in your neighborhood, so you must be sure to be on your guard. You should consider installing a home alarm system. Make certain that everyone in the family knows how to operate it. Another possibility is an alert dog with a loud bark. You may find just what you want at the local shelter. It can become a member of the family in no time at all. You are giving some thought to how to make your life even more useful. You could start by encouraging young people to stay in school and study hard.

SEPTEMBER

1. TUESDAY. Cautious. You can accomplish a considerable amount today; just how much depends on you. You are learning to keep your emotions under control. Although you may normally be impulsive, you should not give way to this trait at present. Your strength of character and determination to get ahead work in your favor. You will feel that your career is heading in the right direction. You have been reading a good deal about using psychology to get ahead; now you can use it to get others to stand behind you in your efforts. You will enjoy a short trip with business colleagues, but it could be expensive. Perhaps your expense account will cover at least some of the bill. Try to make time for physical exercise for health's sake.

2. WEDNESDAY. Demanding. In your pursuit of the great god success, do not sacrifice your physical and emotional health. You see the necessity to work hard to reach your goals, but you must take time to relax and evaluate your progress. Remember that you are dealing with other human beings. They have their faults, but they can also contribute to your happiness. Strong emotional feelings can involve you in a new love affair. If the person is not responding, try a little drama and flamboyance. You will want to spend some time talking about your ideas with co-workers. Money, or the lack of it, can play its usual role. You need to go out and have some fun, but remember that having fun does not always entail lavish spending.

3. THURSDAY. Changeable. You seem to be too busy trying to get ahead to have time for anything else. You may have to figure out some shortcuts. Instead of going to a class or out to do research at a library, having a tutor come to your home can save time. Do not let the laughter of colleagues deter you. The pointers you pick up from the tutor, and the direction in which he or she points you, can eventually lead to a degree. Your colleagues will replace their jokes with respect for you then. Meanwhile, you are bringing in income. If you are wise, you are banking as much as possible. It will be a good idea to knock off your work and study every couple of hours. Take a walk, and come back refreshed.

4. FRIDAY. Frustrating. This is one of those days when you feel blocked at every turn. Your surplus of energy needs an outlet. This is a time when you can accomplish much once you find your way around the obstacles. Studies can be completed. Your job assignments can be interesting, and you will want to dig deeper into them. If anyone else needs some help on the job, be generous with your time and skills. You will have to slow your pace down if you want to do a good job on anything; this is no time for impulsive action. Control your temper if you are frustrated, because the only person to be really hurt by your rage is yourself. If you must do something physical, try some strenuous exercise. You have a wide range of choices.

5. SATURDAY. Uncertain. You cannot make up your mind how you want to spend the weekend. There are so many things to do and, it seems, so little time. Some Cancers will be content with doing things that require mechanical skill. But you are still feeling rather restless and dependent on others to plan your fun for you. Romance is important, and your partner may want you to get out of the house and have fun doing different things. Since you are feeling quite affectionate, you will go along with whatever the decision is. While you are at home, you can be thinking about a special project on which you want to embark. Or you can be struck by an idea that will make work easier next week. Dining out at a neighbor's home can be both pleasant and unusual.

6. SUNDAY. Excellent. Cancers continue to be in a romantic mood today. They also show a special devotion to family and friends. There may be some kind of anniversary which some want to commemorate with dear ones. Your thoughts will probably turn to the accomplishments of those who lived before you. While some of you will observe the occasion at church, others will be happier doing so at home. The occasion can call for some rejoicing as well as remembrance, and a special dinner is likely to be prepared. Music will play an outstanding role today, wherever you are and whatever the kinds. Someone different from the average person can be a visitor, and the heart of the unattached Cancer starts behaving strangely. Can it be love?

7. MONDAY. Enjoyable. Some Cancer people may be having a day off from work, and they will try hard to make the most of it. Some of you will join in community activities while you have the time; others may try to see more of friends and relatives. While the summer warmth continues outdoors, a trip to a park or beach can be fun. If you have a backyard, you have perhaps planned a picnic and asked a large number of people. You should keep hoping that the weather will be good, because you have asked too many to fit comfortably into the house. You are not a demonstrative person, but you do have deep sympathy for others. If any guests overindulge, they will turn first to you for help and remedies.

8. TUESDAY. Challenging. Be prepared to put in a long day. A lot of work has piled up since last Friday. The sooner you get to it, the sooner you will be free to do other things. Your best work is done in solitude, so discourage interruptions. Your intelligence and common sense of how to accomplish your goal will be assets. A study of art history can be useful. If you have an art book that is due at the library, make haste to finish it; otherwise, renew it if necessary. Cancer students should catch up on their homework so they have the time necessary for research later. You may be feeling somewhat nostalgic about family members who have done so much to make working conditions better for your generation.

9. WEDNESDAY. Confusing. Your current emotional state can cause you some anxious moments. Some mistakes that you have made in the past will return to haunt you. You cannot help feeling that your financial situation would be better today if dear ones had not spent so much money in the past. It is too late for reproaches. You have an uneasy feeling that you should be handling current matters more efficiently than you are. Your love life is not all that you wish, and it can affect you psychologically. You have an idea, perhaps based on a dream, that you can win the lottery. In other words, you seem to be a rather mixed-up person at the moment. A possible cure is to seek out companionship and go out for an evening of all-out fun.

10. THURSDAY. Favorable. Although you may think you would prefer to be alone now, you should try to get out and find companionship, plus new things to do. The company of long-time friends can be a real tonic for you. They urge you to participate in group activities and even do some traveling. Some study that has interested you lately may require you to visit a museum or library at some distance from your home. There is much that will be new to you to see along the way, and you can probably charge part of the trip off to business expenses. Other people are interested in you and want to help you overcome your sensitivity and mental hangups. If someone entrusts you with a secret, it is in your own interest to honor that person's trust.

11. FRIDAY. Changeable. Your emotional reactions are very strong at present, but they may not be right on target. You tend to feel unsure of yourself, and this can make you shy with other people. Relationships can be rather confused, as your thoughts dwell on the past. If you think too much about bygone romances, you can scarcely expect much sympathy from your current partner. You grow impatient with anyone who continues to chatter on and on about unimportant matters. A preoccupation with the past makes you moody and a bit intolerant of companions. You hear of a group of psychic researchers, and you decide to join. Possibly it may help you to clarify your own feelings. A woman offers you an opportunity for advancement.

12. SATURDAY. Frustrating. People will be sympathetic to your problems if you respond to theirs in a similar way. This is no time to be intolerant of the views of others. You will be especially sympathetic to those who have to put in some overtime at work because you may be one of them. A trip will probably have to be postponed. Resentment of this and of any other interference in your life can lead to an eating binge. It is scarcely a mature reaction and health problems could develop as a result. You have a good supply of energy, so do not waste it on anger at what cannot be changed. Use it instead to further your career or to improve your home. There can be some difficulty about taxes. Try to get out into the fresh air for exercise, a change of scene and fun.

13. SUNDAY. Mixed. Cooperation for your plans will not be lacking if you put on a show of authority. This is no day for being wishy-washy. People are likely to take advantage of any indication of sensitivity. They will figure that you can be easily fooled. The tendency to plod along without showing much initiative can drive a romantic partner away, at least for the time being. Your home is very important to you, even though it seems to be in a state of disrepair, or at least of untidiness, at present. Latch on to an unexpected spurt of energy and get rid of unwanted items; then reorganize what is left. You can come up with bright ideas. Visitors may interrupt your work, but you can cut their visits short.

14. MONDAY. Productive. You are back to work and in a far better mood than you were yesterday. A task can come your way that calls for careful planning and attention to detail. You will be equal to the job, and your boss will be pleased. Health can be something of a problem if neglected. Take good care of yourself, and encourage co-workers or family to seek medical advice if necessary. Some of those around you seem to be on edge and worrying about things that will never happen. Try to calm their fears, then apply your own good sense to any fears you yourself may be harboring. Take time out for some reading to relax you or to inform you. You will hear from many people. You can find some kindred souls with whom to pass a pleasant evening.

15. TUESDAY. Rewarding. Your courage and self-reliance make you want to take the initiative in everything. You are prepared to back up your opinions with strong arguments. This gains the respect of others, even though they may think that you are wrong. It does not always lead to successful cooperation, however. So there are times when you should sit back and pay close attention to what others have to say. Whether you work with others or alone, you can have some successes today. Cancer people usually are interested in the arts, especially drama and music. You may want to take a course in acting or some other aspect of the theater. Check comparative costs to find something in your price range.

16. WEDNESDAY. Changeable. Your emotions play a large role in your actions now. People are not likely to realize the depths of your feelings, and can unwittingly tread on your toes. Your mental and emotional state can affect the quality of your work if you are not careful. But if you can keep cool and collected, you will end the day well satisfied with what little you did get done. Some domestic changes may take place unexpectedly. You are inclined to daydream, though you seem to have little interest in a new romance at the moment. Someone out of your usual sphere gives you a lead to a better job opportunity; any change can be for the better. A friend introduces you to someone who is likely to set your heart pounding.

17. THURSDAY. Lucky.   The ambitious Cancer person is in a good position to get ahead now. Your contacts will produce some excellent opportunities. There is not likely to be any communications gap to stand in the way of career advancement. Delving into tomes on psychology or other areas related to your areas of interest can prove rewarding. Your creativity yields some interesting work. Personal communications can take up much of your free time. Letters from friends will contain interesting news. Someone forwards information about your earliest years or your family's background, making you want to dig deeper into family research. Phone calls can be helpful, but personal visits can be far more productive, and also more interesting.

18. FRIDAY. Fortunate.   You come to grips with the realities of life today, and place less reliance on emotional reactions. You are also feeling more confident of your own strength than you have been lately. You appreciate the company of others, but you can do very well without it if necessary. Your domestic situation is neither worrisome nor hectic. Something that puzzles you can take up some of your time, but you can soon get to the root of it. When you go home, you will be pleased to find an unexpected but welcome visitor. The mail can be interesting if it brings letters from old friends. You can find some practical solutions to problems that do arise by talking with an older person with the common sense attributable to years of experience.

19. SATURDAY. Uncertain.   Try to avoid controversy, since you may be sensitive to rebuffs. Someone connected with your occupation is likely to challenge you on some point. Do not bother to argue; it will do no good. The encounter, however, can leave you with a sense of dissatisfaction. Since the Moon will be in Cancer by evening, this is only natural. You should put practical matters aside, and concentrate on something on a mystical or intellectual level; but do not spend too much time alone. Round up some dear ones and friends for a pleasant evening together. If you all feel like going out, someone will be sure to recommend a new restaurant. Those who prefer to stay home can enjoy the company of kindred spirits.

20. SUNDAY. Disquieting. The position of the Moon in Cancer today causes you to have vague feelings of guilt or inferiority. Do not take any real or imagined snubs too seriously. People may have criticized you unfairly, but you can shrug that off. Avoid taking any decisive actions at the present; you are too emotionally unstable. There are some matters related to your residence that require settling, but you should have already made tentative decisions. So all that remains is to put them into action. People who come to the door or telephone you to sell you something can be quite annoying. Do not commit yourself, either verbally or by written contract, without checking out their credentials. An even better idea is to refuse to listen to them.

21. MONDAY. Variable. It is not surprising that you are feeling nostalgic today. Blame it on the Moon. Scrapbooks and photograph albums stir memories. If you have inherited some family furniture or ornaments, you will probably put them out in plain sight so you can admire them whenever you go into a room. But do not let memories of the past eclipse the realities of the present. Attack your tasks with enthusiasm, and they will soon be done. Get together with other people for company and do something exciting. If you suspect that there will be slim pickings at home for dinner, invite yourself to a good friend's house for an impromptu barbecue. Group projects with work associates can be satisfying. In the evening, find something to do with loved ones.

22. TUESDAY. Sensitive. You are probably rather hard to get along with now. It seems to be impossible to find someone on the same wavelength, so communication is difficult. No matter what anyone says, you immediately contradict it. If you continue, people may give up the effort to talk to you at all. You become a little depressed when older people with more knowledge of the world thwart your plans for entertainment. The situation is not helped by your introducing a new love into the family circle. While they are courteous, their manner is disapproving. The Cancer person who lives alone should stop at a general store for miscellaneous items to save time. You may have forgotten that one or two important purchases are a must. But don't keep that date waiting long.

23. WEDNESDAY. Variable. Your romance is coming along very nicely at present, and you are well content with the world.

But this is a day when it may be necessary to put some constraints on your emotions and your activities. Sudden impulses can get the better of you and lead you into unwise actions. Self-indulgence often spoils a perfectly good love affair. You have a compulsive streak that pushes you into doing something that should be more carefully thought out. Tension might have built up in you over a lengthy period, then been dissolved suddenly, leaving you feeling as free as a bird. People around you often reflect your moods, so try to keep a checkrein on your free spirits you as you progress through the day. Your private life is strictly your own.

24. THURSDAY. Exciting. That tendency toward impulsiveness that clouded your life yesterday can give you a feeling of vitality and excitement today. You are in an adventurous mood and willing to try anything new. The main idea is to get away from whatever makes everyday life so boring. A surprise can come your way sometime during the afternoon. Routine shopping can be dull, but today you are looking for something different, something exotic perhaps. You will probably be spending much of the day away from your home, perhaps doing charity work helping others. But a surprise of a different kind lies at home if you had forgotten to lock up. A burglary is a real possibility.

25. FRIDAY. Excellent. Your patience is remarkable today, and certain people and happenings will try it to the utmost. But you must keep your good humor. You are sensitive to the feelings of others, so you will be on guard to avoid hurting them. You are in a mood to delve deeply into philosophies and new experiences, and are unwilling to bother with the superficial. Puzzles and mysteries intrigue you. You are even considering becoming involved in a group that investigates psychic phenomena. If you are less serious, you will settle for a mystery novel or a ghost story. Or perhaps you will be content to do the newspaper cryptogram. Excitement runs through the family when told of the pregnancy of a relative.

26. SATURDAY. Cautious. Keeping your emotions under control helps you to take a realistic view of life without indulging in negativism. The day can bring arguments at home, some of them quite heated, and you may have to act as judge and jury. Try not to be angered or hurt by thoughtless comments; there probably will have been no intention of hurting your feelings. How you react to the atmosphere around you will depend on your romantic partner who can be a steadying influence. By evening, the domestic scene can be all roses. Take advantage of the pleasant conditions to have a party. Members of the family will be invited, and some may bring guests. It will certainly get loud, so why not invite your nearest neighbors for the sake of keeping the peace?

27. SUNDAY. Changeable.   You are full of energy and ideas today. Since you are feeling rather exhilarated, you attempt new projects that you would not dare to do under usual circumstances. You think you see several needs for change in your life and home. The reluctance that would normally hold you back has vanished. So you will blithely proceed, ignoring any roadblocks that are thrown up in your path. Meeting new people is part of your life at present. These can be helpful or quite demanding. Some things you want to do are best handled in peace and quiet, so you decide to spend most of the day at home. This can be a mistake. Merry-makers will pursue you at home and urge you to paint the town with them. It is hard to refuse.

28. MONDAY. Mixed.   Your mood of confidence continues to-day. It makes you sure that you can tackle anything. Those who are feeling a little lonely can be looking around for romantic contacts. While you will doubtless find someone, you will also note that a love affair can be expensive. It can be hard to communicate, since your thinking may not be in tune. You could even become quite confused. Deception shows that your trust is misplaced. It is hard to save money. All of these problems can escalate until you are feeling quite uncharitable toward other people. You might lose some friends, at least temporarily. The good news is that the day is fine for making improvements on your residence.

29. TUESDAY. Profitable.   Love for your fellow human beings guides you at present, although there are some that even you cannot love. Your feelings can be so intense that they threaten to wipe out your common sense and perspective. It can be a strange day, intensely practical in matters of money and somewhat mysti-cal when it comes to deeper feelings. You may have to divide your time between your accountant and some books on psychic matters that provide basis for your research. A session with an analyst, or some group therapy, can provide both answers and new insights into your state of mind. Other group activities will be of interest, perhaps a union meeting. Don't hesitate to speak your mind.

30. WEDNESDAY. Lucky.   Get out and around; mix with peo-ple. If you have been having problems, some fresh air, exercise, and contact with interesting people can give you a whole new outlook. Rest is important, and so is a healthy diet. Get home jobs done as quickly as possible so that you have more time for outside activities. Round up your buddies to help with a major project. Those who participate from the very beginning will have a right to expect to share in the fruits of the group effort. People from other neighborhoods can be involved. This can be your lucky day as a result of some totally unforeseen happening. If you are tired in the evening, you will still be up to some reading or study.

OCTOBER

1. THURSDAY. Excellent. Foreign lands, peoples and cultures have a fascination for you. Travel does not appear to be on the books, but you can have a lot of contact with those from other lands or races right at home. You are not daunted by having to study for part of the day. You will learn from books and from the people you meet that there is a whole world out there with ideas that are quite different from what you have grown up to believe. Your horizons will be broadened and you will become more tolerant of those from different cultures. Learning a foreign language can be helpful. Watch the mail for letters from abroad. For once, you will not resent telephone interruptions at work. Go to a concert or sports event or get some exercise.

2. FRIDAY. Changeable. Cancers who have been burning the midnight oil with their studies will not be at their sharpest now. Try to space out studying by alternating it with work. The urge to travel still nags at you. You may get as far as making plans for a trip before you start to count the cost. If you are not willing to scale it down a bit, you will have to work harder and save more. Or you may decide that it is not worth the expense. The trouble involved is still another matter. Your favorite traveling companion cannot get away at this time; or you will encounter a snag with someone who usually takes care of your house. If you can swing it, though, you will learn a lot and be healthier for the trip.

3. SATURDAY. Uncertain. You seem to have a lot on your mind, and it can hinder your progress. Insecurity can be bothering you, but news that your application for a loan is accepted can help. You tend to worry too much about other people and their attitudes toward you. Visitors can distract you from what you are doing. This interferes with your ability to keep some commitments that you have made. Your romantic partner will resent it if you give too much of your time and yourself to your work, and may become jealous of your career ambitions. Other people will demand a slice of your time too. Family members will not appreciate it if they have to make the home repairs and do the chores that they consider rightfully yours.

4. SUNDAY. Demanding. After yesterday, you are in sore need of tranquillity and solitude. However, it is doubtful that you will get much of either. Some spiritual reflection helps to prepare you for the day, but you may have to take care of someone else's children for a while. This can be strenuous, but at least you will be doing someone a favor. A romantic afternoon or a visit to old friends can help to restore your balance. The people you visit may be on a talking streak, so all you will have to do is to nod occasionally. Do not doze off, however; you might miss something important. Since you are not feeling talkative, you will be glad that you do not have to uphold your end. You prefer to be at some distance from your family.

5. MONDAY. Challenging. You appear to be a little pessimistic at the beginning of the day. Something in your past gives rise to a feeling of guilt, but it may be all in your imagination. You should use all your resources to figure out how you can best serve humanity. The need to feel useful can be coupled with your intuition to suggest new approaches to old problems. Do not let symptoms of illness hold you back; get medical advice, and you will be okay. You are particularly good at study and investigation. Financial problems seem to evaporate when you put your mind to them. Reading can broaden your horizons. A meeting at your home proves inconclusive. The support that you so urgently need from loved ones can be lacking.

6. TUESDAY. Unsettling. You are oversupplied with energy, but are unable to find suitable outlets for it. If you look around, you will discover numerous organizations that welcome your skills and talents for helping others. Things are moving rather fast, so it is hard for you to keep up. A money worry can resurface; your accounting system may not be as good as you had thought. Friends who usually are glad to help you seem reluctant to loan money now. The attached Cancer can run into flak from his or her partner who resents the time spent away from home. Some compromise may be needed. Act on it, because your partner or spouse will probably seem to be the only friend you have in the world today.

7. WEDNESDAY. Enjoyable. Travel is much on your mind. If you can arrange to get away for a week or so, you will delight in planning a trip. You will probably not want to talk much about it, but you will enjoy reading travel books and poring over maps. You may even want to learn a little of the language. The homebodies among you can find much to do, too. There will be some tasks that require peace and quiet, but do not let yourself pull back into your shell. Instead, look for activities that appeal to your intellectual nature. Those who belong to a drama group will not suffer from boredom as there is probably a play in production. Others may keep a journal, or join a literary discussion group.

8. THURSDAY. Favorable. Try to be a little more gregarious than you have been lately. There are lots of interesting people out there in the world, so you will have no lack of companions, romantic or otherwise. Do not forget those who may be counting on a visit from you to brighten their day. Household members can be more than unhappy if you are away from home too much. You can mollify them by telling them that you can now afford to have some improvements made on the home, so there is not too much need for you to work around the house. Having been bitten by the travel bug, you will welcome an invitation to take a trip with someone you know. If you can include family members, it will further boost your stock at home.

9. FRIDAY. Uncertain. Your interest in the occult or other mysteries of life is strong at present; you could perhaps be having some unusual dreams. Try to remember them long enough to record them. News about an unusual happening somewhere in the world prompts you to do some reading or other research. A domestic crisis can arise if you insist on bringing your romantic partner home for a visit. There seems to be a mutual dislike and you will be forced to take sides. You have a tendency to tire easily today, so it would be wise to avoid going in for strenuous exercise. Cancer is a water sign, so you probably love most water sports. But right now you should rest or get mild exercise safely on land.

10. SATURDAY. Pleasant. The chances are that you are feeling quite sociable, so there is no thought of drawing back into your shell. A new organization comes to your attention and you can hardly wait to join. You had probably forgotten that organizations are always on the lookout for people to help with their projects. Now is the time to remember before you plunge feet first into every activity the club has to offer. Don't forget that you have some interests of your own to which you are committed. Your

temper matches your energy today; both are high. Do not work
out your frustrations on your loved one. It may be true that you
have become quite selfish. Turn to sympathetic friends or older
people for some sage advice.

11. SUNDAY. Variable. During the day you seem to encounter many people who are either dreamers or drinkers. Both kinds
are trying to forget their troubles. You may sympathize, but you,
too, have troubles of your own. You can be worried about your
place in the scheme of things, or your health can be troublesome.
You and your romantic partner dream of a bright future; but it is
hard, if not impossible, to see far ahead. Your mind is alert, but
not quite enough to deal satisfactorily with the legal problems that
are plaguing you. You can imagine the heavy legal costs not too far
down the road. Court cases have a chance of being settled in your
favor, though, so do not borrow trouble. Your family should be
the most important part of your life.

12. MONDAY. Rewarding. Financial and romantic matters
both are on your mind, and it may be hard to keep them separate.
A lack of funds is not the problem; your income can be up or
down, but it is adequate. If you are tempted to take the day off,
your awareness that the income will stop is all the reminder you
need. The married Cancer may grow especially fond of his or her
family when a partner receives an inheritance. If you are thinking
about getting a new job, social work can be especially appealing. It
will offer real rewards to you in the form of opportunities to help
people who are less fortunate than most or in need of sympathy
and concern. It can also involve children who crave love.

13. TUESDAY. Productive. Your home and family remain the
real foundations of your life. Numerous distractions today reflect
all the changes going on around you, and you will meet some
unusual people. You can steer a friend who needs help in the
direction of some of these people. You have an extra degree of
sensitivity at present. A creative venture comes to your attention,
and you will rush over to become involved. A surprise gift comes
your way and is especially welcome because there seems to be a
lack of ready money. People tend to speak their minds, so you are
never unaware of how you stand with them. Although you may
have a lot of energy, you cannot afford to neglect your diet and
exercise routine.

14. WEDNESDAY. Variable. Continue to watch your diet for
the sake of your health. You would do better to spend your food

allowance on simple, nutritious foods than those that are exotic and perhaps harmful to your health. If you are embarking on a new romantic affair, you will want to dress up. You should remember, however, that marriage and setting up a new home are going to stretch your financial resources to the limit. Surely you can dress well on what is already in your closet. Along with your thoughts of romance, you become interested in the world around you. You find that you are in a position to help others. The people around you are warm and friendly; they share your happiness and concern for the well-being and progress of others.

15. THURSDAY. Successful. Your body may need rest, but your mind is going full speed ahead. You are in a serious mood and you want to know more about the problems of the world as well as of your own community. Read the newspapers and listen to the radio or watch television. You will gain background knowledge, but what you hear and read will raise new questions in your mind. You want a meaningful discussion, and you probably can find it with an older friend. This friend can have the experience and insight into the affairs of the world that you lack. Even though you are resting, your mental stamina will be considerable. Neither reading letters nor telephone conversations with good friends will tax your physical strength.

16. FRIDAY. Happy. Things are going well as the working week draws to a close. You are energetic enough, but you do not get much work done. Probably that is because there is little of importance that needs doing. The people around you seem to be in good moods; some of them may ask for some advice, which you give willingly. You are in a position to do a favor for someone. Your family life is harmonious, with no one bearing a grudge against another. Since you do not have to exert yourself very much today, you will not be tired after work. This can be a good time to go visiting. Perhaps you and a friend or romantic partner can go out for the evening; you are free to go where your fancy dictates.

17. SATURDAY. Challenging. Cancer people who are involved in occult or mystical matters find this a good day. Because of the lunar aspect, you can be somewhat moody, but intuition and psychic talent are foremost in your activities. You fear being alone and so are inclined to seek the company of dear ones or other companions. Someone you meet may come to be your next love. You are somewhat introspective and turn your thoughts toward self-discovery. You begin to understand how the past can influence the present; you cling to possessions, and have an almost obsessive fear of losing personal and family mementos. If you try to relax a little, you will learn how to loosen your grip on what you cherish.

18. SUNDAY. Cautious. You may not want to venture far from home, but that is no problem. There are so many things crying for your attention that you can be kept busy for most of the day. Visitors, especially unwelcome relatives, can prove irritating if you are trying to get something done. You will accomplish more if you do not allow your thoughts to wander. Above all, do not try to put what are merely dreams into practice; someone could get hurt. You may hear that extra money is coming your way. If you have been studying a foreign language, try it out on family and friends. If you do go out, stick to the beaten path, and do not trust what strangers tell you. Control your emotions and temper.

19. MONDAY. Enjoyable. Your home seems to be even more important to you than usual. It can be the center of your life today. You may go to extremes in protecting your family members, especially children. In fact, you stand up for them even when you suspect that they may be in the wrong. Improvements can be made in your residence. Perhaps you are on the verge of marriage, and you want things to be harmonious. You are feeling generous and eager to help others in your locality. Set up a group activity to benefit your favorite cause. New friends include some professional people as well as those from foreign countries. Your popularity is very high. If you want something, you need only ask; wishes will be granted.

20. TUESDAY. Uncertain. Handle the people with whom you are in contact with kid gloves. Not everyone understands your sense of humor. You cannot seem to help yourself when you react unfavorably to the actions and words of others. It is not necessary to give in to the desires of someone, but you can at least try to compromise. Avoid emotional confrontations; you are not thinking clearly. You may narrowly avert a robbery. Money can be a problem, although credit can be obtained for major home projects. You know what you want and how to go after it. If what you want is a good time, you can get it, but you will have to pay the piper when the bills arrive. A family member may be willing to loan you enough to tide you over the crisis.

21. WEDNESDAY. Changeable. The Cancer love of art and music gains full expression today. Take in an art exhibit or a concert. You like being surrounded by beauty, so you will be doing all you can to make your home luxurious, perhaps going on a buying spree to find required items. If you have time, get involved in a creative activity. It should not be hard to find crafts groups or art leagues in your locality. Do not smother your dear ones with affection; you can show your love without overdoing it. An interest in someone with an unusual or foreign background is quite possible. If you go on a short trip with someone dear to you, be careful what you eat. When dining out, avoid overindulgence in food as well as drink.

22. THURSDAY. Rewarding. Some of you Cancers appear to be going through a phase in which you are very critical of everyone. You expect every detail to be just right; your tolerance of sloppiness is nonexistent. Snap out of it; people are not perfect. You may even discover some flaws in yourself. This search for perfection can be triggered by your efforts to redecorate and improve your home. Watch the spending on any such projects; you do not like to be under obligation to anyone who lends you money. You think a lot about your romance and ways to improve it. A study of psychology and learning more about other people can be helpful. Even reading some romantic fiction can give you ideas. A strong imagination helps, too.

23. FRIDAY. Enjoyable. Romance continues to benefit from your efforts yesterday. You do have to be on guard against showing too much possessiveness, which could wreck a love affair. Perhaps some counseling will help. Insights can come out of such action. When you are feeling good about yourself and your relationships, you become less hesitant about inviting old-time friends out to dinner or to a play or concert. Keep moving in order to meet new people and form new relationships. You will want to invite a few kindred souls home for an evening of stimulating talk and soothing music. Those of you who are planning a big social affair at home will spend much of the day working to make it a success.

24. SATURDAY. Sensitive. All is not quiet on the home front today. The fault probably lies in your own emotional state; everything irritates you. You can be sure of this if you are at work and are having similar problems. That work may not be what your family would prefer you do, so there could be some heated exchanges. It gets worse if your spouse or romantic partner becomes involved. Visitors can be annoying; you would like to be diplomatic, but you seem to have forgotten how. Maybe a good blowup would clear the air enough for you to go on doing your thing, not feeling so frustrated. Do not let yourself be put on the defensive; it will add to your despair and prevent your solving the problems.

25. SUNDAY. Rewarding. This is a good day for beginning something new. It is also good for making changes in your domestic situation and even your personal life. Any project on which you embark is likely to be quite successful. Your activities can bring you into contact with some of the most influential people around. There may be some worries about finances; taxes can be higher than you were anticipating. Some hitch seems to have developed in the matter of a joint trust from which you would inherit some money. You may be starting a marriage, parenthood, or simply a new romance. Students will be embarking on new courses. You come to realize that possessions are not really so important to you.

26. MONDAY. Changeable. It seems that you have been letting your emotions take over your life. You cannot achieve real happiness or success while you are building a wall of negative thinking against your dear ones, your work, your friends and romances. Stick to the practical if you want to get ahead. You have some good ideas that should be used to further your career. Work toward changes that you can make in your own life. Your financial situation will benefit from your industry. If you have been looking on the dark side of life, start peering around for that silver lining. It is there if you search for it. Even the world news may not be as gloomy as you think. Concentrate on the needs of other people.

27. TUESDAY. Challenging. There have been times when you wished you could express your emotions better. Communication has been difficult, but this is not one of those times. It is now easy to say what is in your heart. As you open up with others, so will they open up with you. You can learn a lot of new things. Information you gather can be used to make decisions in the future. You keep wishing for an opportunity to visit new lands and experience new cultures and customs. That may not be possible now, but you will make some contacts with people from other cultures and enjoy chatting with them. Meanwhile, you can read about foreign countries and start learning one of their languages.

28. WEDNESDAY. Fortunate. At some point, you will probably want to be alone with your thoughts. You have ideas that can be developed. You are not really being unsociable but just want to reflect on your life. You will tolerate the presence of those who are serious and intellectual, but you are not feeling frivolous. That mood can change, however, and your gregarious nature take over. You will welcome friends who bring their children. The warmth of your personality draws people to you. An invitation to a party will be accepted with alacrity. Long-lost relatives and friends will be greeted with open arms. Your work is not too demanding and may be quite interesting. But guard against a tendency toward laziness when the going gets easy.

29. THURSDAY. Excellent. You now have good reason for optimism. Your financial situation appears to be secure. You can look forward to enjoying a pleasant life-style during the foreseeable future. Your work is both lucrative and interesting and you are being given challenging assignments to test your mettle; you prove equal to them all. All this can translate into more security and comfortable living for your loved ones, and this pleases you. Your relationships with family and romantic partner are stable. If you take good care of your health with exercise and good food, you can go ahead with some plans. Now is the time to start thinking about a winter vacation, perhaps some extended travel. See your travel agent.

30. FRIDAY. Exciting. Many of your activities take place in public today, so make sure they are above reproach. You surely will not enjoy having a shouting match with your spouse or lover take place in the glare of the spotlight. You should hope that you have no forgotten, dark secrets in your private life, because they might come out in the open. Those who are not yet committed should not consider marrying for money or power. Your life has been moving along quite fast, so try to find a few hours to stop and reflect. If a loan is needed to cover some unexpected expense, such as a home improvement, you will find your banker sympathetic and helpful. Be sure you have the facts at your fingertips before making an appointment.

31. SATURDAY. Variable. Boredom with the normal routine of your life, coupled with irritability and bad temper, can be an explosive mixture. If you take it out on loved ones, your relationships with them can become badly strained. Try instead to learn all you can about their feelings and motivations. If they are not speaking to you, you can write to them at length to try to patch things up. You could also get into acrimonious discussions with strangers. Keep your cool, if possible, although such arguments do start the adrenalin racing. Problems that are serious enough can be talked over with older and wiser friends. Solutions can and will be found. Your good reputation seems to survive many conflicts.

NOVEMBER

1. SUNDAY. Enjoyable. You are bound to come into contact with people from all walks of life and with a diversity of ideas. This can broaden your horizons if you allow it to. You avoid close associations, but like lots of company. Despite your intelligence and understanding, a weak spot manifests itself. You are so wrapped up in your own concerns and your desire to maintain personal freedom that you can be insensitive at times. Your moodiness can put people off. A carefully chosen companion can help you to shake off this attitude. Intellectual conversations bring you abreast of some unusual and perhaps unpopular ideas. A self-improvement course by mail can advance your career and bring monetary rewards in the long run.

2. MONDAY. Rewarding. Current and past history challenges your mind. You want to know more about the peoples of the world, ancient and modern. Since you probably cannot travel at present, read about them. Better still, get in touch with foreign visitors or write to someone overseas. If the atmosphere around you is a little depressed, school yourself to ignore it and look on the bright side. You can learn much from old friends. Look for romance with someone from a distance. Artists can develop an interest in drafting. An excursion to an art museum can open up new worlds for you to explore. A surprise visit from someone from the past brings you joy. Now you know that you have not been forgotten.

3. TUESDAY. Mixed. It is hard to get much work done at home when your mind is in a turmoil. Put aside everything that you can. Go out somewhere with a friend; you will feel more like working when you return. An optimistic attitude, and the conviction that you are equal to any task will be helpful. You are more and more curious about what is going on in the world and wholly receptive to new ideas. Study, reading and travel help to slake that thirst for knowledge. Learning about other ideas and cultures requires a high degree of tolerance. If these were not different from ones you know, they would not be likely to interest you. Be tactful when you are dealing with strangers; avoid offending them.

4. WEDNESDAY. Frustrating. You can become rather depressed when matters do not work out as you would like. You feel

213

that your luck has run out and the world is against you. Since emotions affect physical health, you can be feeling tired and uninterested in doing much of anything. Personal relationships are unsatisfactory. It can take only one bit of bad news to trigger a scene. Try to stop short and analyze what is bothering you. If you are having a problem, it would be best to talk it out and clear the air. You do not have to sit passively by while someone is doing something you do not like. Tell the person, but in a calm and rational way. An emotional outburst will accomplish nothing, and can do a great deal of harm.

5. THURSDAY. Changeable. Leadership qualities come to the fore. Others follow your lead when you present your case forcefully. Cooperation for new projects is likely, but you have enough energy to do everything on your own. Some undertakings cannot be completed in one day, but you will have made a good start. An intense attitude, along with a show of confidence, will result in remarkable progress. A serious and positive outlook can lead to important changes in relationships. The Cancer quality of love for home and family is very evident, but do not smother dear ones with your affection. You are inclined to be somewhat nostalgic. Old photos and scrapbooks can bring tears to your eyes. Do not relax your diet; you are on target.

6. FRIDAY. Mixed. You feel up to anything now; challenges are welcomed. You will brook no interference with your forward progress. Other people will not be able to budge you when you think you are right. This can lead to some friction with a dear one, probably a romantic partner. You are feeling witty, but be sure that wit is not sharp enough to hurt others. You write amusing letters at this time. You may want to do some research into philosophy or religion. Your energy seems to be boundless, and your ideas are sound. Romance seems to be just right; someone new can appear. It promises to be an extremely busy day. If you need more money, you can earn some extra tutoring at home.

7. SATURDAY. Tricky. You are restless and looking for some excitement. But your serious mood of yesterday is still with you. The company of friends and older relatives appeals to you, and you enjoy discussions on serious topics. You get along well with most people as long as they do not try to boss you around. You do not take kindly to criticism; it can spur you to do the exact opposite of what people want you to do. Avoid jumping to conclusions. You may be in a reflective mood and just a little bit sorry for yourself. Friends welcome your company, but do not provide the sympathy you are seeking. They may give you a stirring pep talk instead. This is not a good time for attempting to borrow money.

8. SUNDAY. Stressful.   Your health is adequate, but you are not feeling particularly energetic. This can affect your ability to make the right decisions and to get along well with others. It seems that a period of rest and avoidance of tensions is just what you need. Otherwise, you can find yourself at odds with family and associates. Do not bottle up your anger, but have your say; it can help to clear the air. If you are lucky, people will understand that you are under stress and will make allowances. If someone is working with you on a creative venture, you can become discouraged over that person's failure to grasp your ideas. Be careful about voicing criticism, though you know the fault is not yours.

9. MONDAY. Uncertain.   If you are finding it difficult to deal with life today, look forward to late afternoon and evening. Things will look much brighter then. Meanwhile, muddle through your problems as best you can. It is not true that nobody loves you. Conflict in your relationships can be the result of your own state of mind. If you seem insensitive and cold, people take it at its face value. They will steer clear of you until the mood passes. Financial problems can be worrying you. If you cannot bear to throw anything away, your home will reflect it. A cluttered atmosphere can make you edgy and irritate the other occupants of the home. Save domestic changes and social affairs for the evening.

10. TUESDAY. Rewarding.   This can be a day for taking stock of your life. You will see some need for changes, especially where you are falling short. There are some tense moments, especially if you think you can take control of other people's lives. Your worst qualities can surface. Take an opportunity to scrutinize them and to figure out how you can improve relationships. You are overflowing with ambition, so seize on all chances to improve your own life and to do some good for others. Get enough exercise for the sake of your health. When some financial clouds appear on the horizon, you will have to deal with them. You may lose a good friend, making you more appreciative of those left.

11. WEDNESDAY. Variable.   You are a bit on edge, but you cannot figure out why. Stick to routine tasks that do not involve making any decisions. Avoid serious discussions about your business affairs, since your thinking is not as logical as usual. Try to complete necessary work and get home as soon as possible. Rest and settle down with a book that has some connection with your work. You may have been letting past attitudes color your thinking and impair your ability to reason. Later in the day, you get along well with the people around you. As you become more dependable, they will come to rely on you. Any earlier sense of alienation will vanish once you are rested and feeling like yourself.

12. THURSDAY. Slow. The early hours again find you with your thinking in wild disorder. Make every effort to come to grips with your emotions. Possibly you still are a slave to the attitudes of your upbringing. Instead of retreating into your shell, get out and do something about it. Instinctive action causes bad first impressions, so make sure everything you do is well thought out. A sister or aunt can straighten you out; either one probably knows you better than you know yourself. As you begin to relax, your thoughts turn to an artistic project on which you have been working. A visitor offers valuable suggestions. You feel an urge to travel, but probably have to settle for the armchair variety now.

13. FRIDAY. Unsettling. You are harboring some doubts about your abilities and some uncertainty about the future. They are not caused by this supposedly unlucky day, but by the fact that the Moon is now in Cancer. Hang in there, and do the best you can; the feeling will pass before very long. You feel the need for a strong emotional relationship. Such could exact a stiff price, as the other person may be so different that upsets are bound to occur. Uncertain, you think you can buy friendships if you spend enough money and in this you are mistaken. Generous impulses are fine, but extravagant spending only makes you look foolish. And when you find that it was wasted, that's how you will feel.

14. SATURDAY. Changeable. You begin the day in a rather confused state of mind, filled with vague forebodings. You seem to be out of touch with reality. Do not worry; the mood will pass as the day grows older. Your thinking will become clearer and objective. Your feelings will intensify, and a serious romantic relationship will become even more so. You are in the mood for some excitement, but may get more than you bargained for. A struggle for power between you and someone in a superior position can be quite exhausting. A journey undertaken for pleasure can turn into an emotional experience that you will remember all your life. When you talk to an interesting person, don't try to show off.

15. SUNDAY. Rewarding. Your interaction with other people is very important now. You have a lot of energy, but it should be directed into useful channels. Your curiosity about and interest in some of the larger issues of life lead you into some discussions that help you to clarify your thinking. The discussions can be reinforced by some study on your own or with a group of kindred souls. Do not let your mind dwell on your own troubles, real or imagined. Instead, you should talk to those who have more problems than you can imagine. You will be humbled, and you will feel eager to do what you can to make their lives easier. If you are feeling very emotional and just have to let off steam, do it at home where your loved ones will understand your tensions.

16. MONDAY. Unsettling. You seem to be going about carrying your own little dark cloud above your head. Yesterday was so active that a letdown today is almost inevitable. The situation is not improved by a personal financial worry. This will affect your mood all day. Fate seems to be conspiring against you; minor failures seem like disasters. You have a feeling that no one cares and that you are on your own. This attitude could actually drive away the very people who would like to help you. If you can get rid of that black cloud, you will see that there is plenty you could do toward finding entertainment and pleasure. Music can do a lot to lighten your mood, and a wise friend encourages you to relax by listening to your favorite records or tapes.

17. TUESDAY. Difficult. Remnants of earlier tensions and emotional upsets could spoil your day if you let them. You will have to take a positive and optimistic stance if you want to avoid trouble. Stick to your guns if anyone disagrees with you. A constant change of position to blow with the prevailing winds will earn you a reputation for not knowing your own mind. You often feel emotionally upset over the problems of others. Your general disgruntlement adversely affects your relations with a person of the opposite sex. Lighten your mood, and you will find your romantic life will be vastly improved. By evening, you will be ready for some social activity, perhaps a get-together at home.

18. WEDNESDAY. Excellent. Inventiveness and imagination lead you into some new field of creativity. Stimulating activities are just what you need now. Your energy is high, even though you are a bit of a hypochondriac. Put that energy to work in reorganizing your workplace and home. You will find new projects, perhaps even a new job. Your horizons have expanded, and no one can question your spirit of enterprise. Get away from humdrum routine by taking some visiting relatives on a tour of your area. They will enjoy going through a television station, a factory outlet, or a winery if there are any of these nearby. Varying your daily routine is most important. There is a strong possibility that a surprise is headed your way, and it will be not only unexpected but fabulous.

19. THURSDAY. Pleasant.   A sense of satisfaction comes from your efforts to bring comfort and care to someone who is ill or troubled. Your own health may need attention, but the problem should not be serious. It is not always easy to visit someone in a hospital or a hospice, but your presence would bring cheer and make the person feel wanted. Get involved also with a local humane society group or the nearest shelter for animals. You will doubtless find a dog or cat that needs a home. If you adopt it, it might give you years of pleasure. You and your loved one will enjoy a short trip together; you both may need the change of scene. But do not offer to pay your romantic partner's share.

20. FRIDAY. Unsettling.   You are tempted to give a superior a piece of your mind and this can lead to some complications. If your boss is an understanding type, the results may not be too serious. After all, you are a valuable employee. It might even turn out that any blame for the confusing situation can be equally attributable to all those concerned. So you will get off lightly, fortunately. You may be taken out to dinner by someone who is visiting you. If you think this is a reflection on your cooking, you are probably right. An old friend invites you to take a trip. You know it is a generous offer, and are as delighted as you are appreciative. A visit to a romantic interest can be both pleasant and rewarding. It might be the preview of a wedding.

21. SATURDAY. Mixed.   You usually enjoy the company of relatives and friends. Today, however, they seem to fill every nook and cranny of your home. Differences of opinion can arise. While you feel your experience entitles you to have your ideas accepted, others do not share those feelings; you are facing some obstinate people. Your nearest and dearest will understand if you withdraw from the fray in favor of peace and solitude. Settle down in private and read something that you have been longing to for past weeks. It will have brought home to you the consequences of being too jealous and possessive of loved ones. As soon as the company has gone, rejoin your loved one and show how much you care. Do not let money matters come between you.

22. SUNDAY. Rewarding.   Money can be the cause of strained relationships early in the day. Misunderstandings occur when you and others fail to make yourselves clear in conversations. A romantic relationship may suffer from various hangups or stubborn attitudes. All these difficulties can keep you from starting out with an optimistic air and may even cause you to fall prey to negative thinking. Take your mind off your troubles by getting in touch with someone overseas. Any such contacts you make today should be filed away for future reference. As the day goes on, skies will start to clear; take deep breaths and relax for a while. Relationships will improve visibly and a desire for adventure will lead to exciting and pleasant times.

23. MONDAY. Fortunate. You are not easily discouraged today. A romantic relationship will blossom if you both speak unreservedly about your deepest feelings. The good sense to speak out about everything will advance your cause. Your confidence enhances and reveals your leadership qualities to others. People will choose you for picking up pointers about how they should handle difficult situations. You may even have a visit from some organization's delegation asking for your opinions. Your energy is high so this is the day for taking on some tricky job around the house that has defeated you thus far. Gamblers who think they have a system for beating the odds should do more research before heading out to the nearest casino or card game.

24. TUESDAY. Enjoyable. Concentrate now on improving your mind and increasing your knowledge of the world. Pull one of those dusty classics from your shelf and find out what good reading can do for you. Bypass the light fiction in the library, and head for the philosophy, the history or the travel section. You will be amazed at the extent of the library's collection. Your relationships with other people are fine at this time. Have serious discussions with knowledgeable people; do not forget to include someone older and wiser than all of you. If you run a business out of your home, it will become increasingly successful. Salespeople find that they can easily sell almost anything. Have a romantic evening with your loved one.

25. WEDNESDAY. Easygoing. Keep your mind on your work, which should prove easier than usual. Much can be accomplished, but do take a break occasionally, and get out into the fresh air. The travel bug appears to have bitten you, but you may not be able to do much about it at present. Short trips are possible, but the long, exotic journeys for which you yearn can still be in the future. You should keep in touch with friends and business associates from overseas. Word from foreign contacts indicates that some new business may be coming your way. A meeting with someone from another country whets your appetite for more information about that person's homeland and its people. Meantime, why not study the arts and crafts of the Orient, for instance?

26. THURSDAY. Exciting.   It will be an enjoyable Thanksgiving Day, if you are celebrating. It could also be an exhausting one for you. A houseful of guests keeps you hopping if you are chief cook and bartender. Between music and talk, the noise level will reach new heights. The neighbors are not likely to object if they are also entertaining, but possibly they are away for the day. The only cloud on your horizon may be your worry as to how much this is costing you. Late in the day things will quiet down, and you will have time to get the house back in order. You may want to go out for a while, though, with your romantic partner. Romance seems to have blossomed in the holiday atmosphere and you discover new depths of feeling for each other.

27. FRIDAY. Encouraging.   People who learn languages easily will make considerable progress today. If you think your family would be interested, persuade some members to take a course with you. You will have to guard against having unrealistic expectations. Your emotions, quite high at this time, can carry you away. The realities of life and love and work can come as a shock. A romantic encounter comes about so suddenly that you have little time to explore the person's background and attitudes. You should make an effort to remedy this before you get too deeply involved. You meet a valuable contact at a social function. After talking with you, the person is so impressed that your career can take a giant step forward.

28. SATURDAY. Frustrating.   Today you may wish that the telephone had never been invented. If you are at your workplace, you will have constant interruptions from the people at home asking you how to deal with their problems. If you work at home, calls from outside can be equally irritating. Others do not understand that you do work that must be completed and get angry if you do not rush to their rescue. You, in turn, are likely to blow your stack. Simmer down; more can be accomplished if you keep your cool. Your income is good, but the money does not stay in your hands very long. Your frustration puts you in an angry mood which you the take out on family, neighbors and even your loved one. Many good romances go down the drain that way.

29. SUNDAY. Successful.   This is no day for withdrawing from the world; too many things are happening. You have an opportunity to do some traveling with a teacher friend. An organization with high goals welcomes you as a new member. Your energy and positive outlook are needed to combat some negative feelings among old-time members, but you can help put the group back on the right track. You will be able to persuade others to join whose experience can help present members develop new skills and broaden their horizons. Your personal financial situation appears to have improved. Now you can carry out some cherished plans for your home. There is enough money to embark on a new business venture, but keep it small.

30. MONDAY. Worrisome. The financial outlook is not so bright after all. Checking your accounts reveals that there is less money in your savings than you had thought. Perhaps you have forgotten some recent heavy expenses? Someone may even have withdrawn money without your knowledge; check that with your bank manager. Personal relationships will deteriorate if you persist in pushing one idea that seems to obsess you. People do not take kindly to pressure. A major difference of opinion arises between you and an associate. Each of you feels sure that you have all the answers, and neither is willing to give in. If you start drawing back into your shall, you may miss some important changes in your resources that could affect your future.

DECEMBER

1. TUESDAY. Enjoyable. Cancers who happen to be starting a honeymoon have picked a good day for it. Others may just be following their routines, using their energy in the normal course of their daily activities. Since money is not a problem at the moment, there may be a choice of tempting social activities available which keep you going from one to another. New acquaintances will doubtless be made, perhaps new friendships formed. You might meet someone from out of state and as you are in a friendly, helpful mood, you will be free with advice and assistance, if asked. You are also conscious of the plight of those less fortunate than you. When alone, you will be thinking of what you can do to alleviate poverty, homelessness and hunger where you live.

2. WEDNESDAY. Changeable. Artistic talents come to the fore. Study can be a source of pleasure as well as a possible step up the ladder to success. Something will make you conscious of a talent that has remained hidden up to this point, but if success does not come immediately, you are likely to become discouraged. You may feel that you are going nowhere, so you should be easy prey for those who sell self-help courses or books. If these do not help, you might then decide to quit your job and start on some new totally different tack. Such a risk may be too great to take at this time; consider all angles. Some of you may turn to new beliefs, possibly religious, mystical or occult, in your search for the road to personal improvement and occupational success.

3. THURSDAY. Unsettling. Your Cancer curiosity about the occult and the mysterious is foremost, but still you try to avoid getting too deeply involved in any such activity. You will probably be able to express some of your feelings in drama, music or poetry. You like other people and are often inclined to place too much trust in them; but you then worry about the people you do trust. You also wonder whether they are talking about you behind your back. You expect to receive the same help that you are willing to give to others; and you can become almost neurotic about other people's actions. Take a brisk walk in the fresh air and let the cold winds blow away your fears. If you think someone is taking advantage of you, confront the person and find out.

4. FRIDAY. Variable. Do not let your hot temper and impulsive actions put a damper on otherwise good relationships. Be open with others about your thoughts and opinions, and make it clear that you expect the same of them. Objectivity should be your rule. You will want to be independent of course, and do things your own way so that anyone who tries to interfere will automatically be your enemy. Do not take everything so personally, but try to see other points of view. Since you are a homebody at heart, and put your family above everything else, you will not wander very far from home. Perhaps the type of work you do can be set up so that it can be done out of your home. That will be a plus for both your homelife and your peace of mind.

5. SATURDAY. Misleading. Romantic feelings about a long-time friend surface unexpectedly; after some discussion, the two of you decide to take a trip. It will be a choice between a short cruise or tour by car of some scenic grandeur. Do not assume, however, that your companion's emotions necessarily match your own. While your friend may be openly affectionate, it does not follow that marriage is the goal. If this happens to be an office romance, you should be glad to call it off; they are often subject to malicious gossip. Be aware of any flu warnings for the coming season, and take shots if recommended. Illness, even if only a brief one, could ruin plans for parties and similar festivities. If you send Christmas cards overseas, now is the time for mailing them.

6. SUNDAY. Demanding. Some friends you see today are artistic and during a conversation with one of them, you get an idea about using your abilities to make some extra money. It will come in handy if there is something you especially want to buy. Utilize whatever talents you possess. Your income, although it may fluctuate, is adequate for your everyday needs, but extra funds are always a welcome bonus. If there are clashes with family members over spending it remind them you earned it. There are fewer than three weeks till Christmas, so any extra money will be welcome. If you are planning a cruise this winter, check rates and transport costs early, or you may be disappointed. Also, check as to proof of citizenship requirements or if you will need shots.

7. MONDAY. Difficult. Cancer people are especially attached to the past and to family heirlooms. They are unwilling to part with anything that has a sentimental meaning for them. This could present problems with home redecorating. The family will opt for getting rid of anything that does not suit the décor. If you expect to travel during the holidays, you may need to check your closet to be sure you don't have to buy clothes or gear. The stores will be extra busy and frantic. Try shopping after work; it may be less hectic. This is not a particularly good day for spending, however. A love affair seems to be on the way out, but do not worry because another seems to be waiting in the wings. One fly in the ointment might be the appearance of a romantic partner out of the past, causing an intensely emotional scene.

8. TUESDAY. Easygoing. A love affair can make you happy for the moment, but do not count on its lasting very long. Secrecy lends a touch of excitement, but sooner or later the secret is out and the suspense dispelled. You would undoubtedly prefer getting together with friends than sticking to your routine work, but laziness will not advance your career. Do not trust acquaintances fully until they have proven their worth. You are inclined to get quite involved in serious conversations with people you meet and if you are at a party, you will probably go off in a corner to talk, ignoring festivities and other guests. Unfortunate past experiences can make you react with haste to others' actions; simmer down and try to be tactful.

9. WEDNESDAY. Variable. Your health comes first, since all of your other activities depend on it. When the weather is not suitable for a brisk walk, you can do some exercising at home. You may be able to get someone else to join you, which would be more fun. Family affairs predominate while some worrisome news from a parent who is overseas at present is upsetting, but not critical. On the plus side, you notice a thawing of relations between your romantic partner and your family. Receiving unexpected payment for some recent research, perhaps of a genealogical nature, gives your morale a boost. Your relationships with people in general are very good, thanks to your tact and diplomacy.

10. THURSDAY. Happy. Today is good for catching up on your rest, although you will have to be out and about at times. When you are at home, play some music or relax with a good book. If you have been smart, you kept a notebook of the many original ideas you have had lately so you can expand them into a short story or poem. If you did not record them, they could vanish completely. You may become interested in taking an art course in the evenings. A short trip might mean new friends, but relatives or neighbors would be entertaining if you stay around home. You feel an overwhelming urge to put your thoughts on paper in a letter to someone who lives at a distance. People you meet help you put your ideas to good use, whether commercial or personal.

11. FRIDAY. Unsettling. When the Moon is in its present phase, you generally turn to home and family, but do not carry it too far. You can become so wrapped up in a home project that you see no harm in trying to put visiting relatives to work, too. Some will be delighted to help you, but others will turn you down flat. If you overreact, you will only appear spoiled and bossy. Try to satisfy their interests, either in sightseeing or going to museums they prefer, or just tour nearby places of historic interest. A concert or musical might fill the bill. Carefully chosen music can usually change your mood for the better. With only two weekends left before Christmas, you may need to stock up on food and drinks, especially if you will be entertaining.

12. SATURDAY. Enjoyable. If you are waxing nostalgic, it is not too surprising at this time, with the Moon in Cancer. You will be searching through records and tapes to find the favorite melodies of your youth which you enjoy most if others are with you. Those of you who are feeling more active may be interested in a health or self-defense program. These can be beneficial, although the results will probably seem slow to appear. You begin to take more notice of the outside world only later on in the day. A party at home can be fun if you keep it informal and invite some young people who will perhaps be classmates or relatives. If you go out with your loved one, it will probably not be expensive, so there will be no need to borrow money.

13. SUNDAY. Mixed. Today you Cancers will be in a gregarious mood. Anything that smacks of fun and sociability will have your enthusiastic support. You shine as host or hostess, and you need have no worry about your invitations being accepted. A picnic for the children can be a good idea for those living in a warm climate, while others will have to stage an informal one indoors. You are hoping to be surrounded by friends, plus new and congenial acquaintances. A shadow falls over the gathering when an old friend says no to your invitation, but that is the only one. You may be concerned about some business problem of a financial nature; but at least it does not touch your home. Travel does not work out. In your spare time, develop interest in some creative activity.

14. MONDAY. Changeable. Routine occupational chores bore you; your mind is too active to want to put up with the humdrum. You can find outlets for your intellectual interests in studying legal matters, putting down on paper your original ideas, or doing some research into mysticism. You should develop a new hobby that might fascinate you for a long time. Some financial accounting is necessary, but it will be less boring than many similar tasks. Someone from a foreign country, or with just a different background, may be visiting you or someone close to you. You look forward to having long talks with the person in your effort to learn more about customs and cultures other than your own. This is a good day for those in advertising and publishing.

15. TUESDAY. Slow. Those ideas that were incubating only yesterday may be hatching today. Making the most of them will keep you busy. Solitude is desirable if you want to get your best work done. You are in no mood to seek sympathy, regardless of what is worrying you. This will only make others feel more guilty when they learn that you have been bearing some burden alone. Groundless worries about your health can drive you to making an issue about the care of your home since you feel partially responsible for cleaning it. You want to help others who do it, but forget it; everyone has his or her ways of doing things. Your well-meant interference may be resented. You will be spending much time studying today.

16. WEDNESDAY. Sensitive. You will do your best work in solitude today and much can be accomplished. You will have to speak up if you want people to know that you are serious; frankness and sincerity are important. There are, however, some tensions below the surface, either at work or at home, and they can manifest themselves with startling suddenness. Even though you should not hesitate to say what you are thinking, you should do it diplomatically. Money can be the source of the trouble; do nothing to endanger joint savings accounts that involve your spouse. In dealing with any tensions, be prepared to compromise. Relax with friends after work. A sports event or a walk will ease tensions.

17. THURSDAY. Excellent. Everything seems to be right with the world today. But if you are feeling a little down, round up some friends to lift your spirits. Actually, you have no excuse for being grumpy. The future looks bright for one of your talents, with due recognition on the way. While visiting an old friend, you might meet someone interesting, and in time, strike up a long-lasting correspondence. Something good is waiting for you at home; it could be a gift for you or an invitation to some future social event. Someone in a profession appears to be taking an interest both in you and your accomplishments. The unattached Cancer can do very well romantically. An unexpected, but much desired, proposal could be coming your way.

18. FRIDAY. Tricky. There is a possibility that a storm is brewing over your love affair. If tempers flare at home over your choice of romantic partner, you and your partner should get away for a week or so; you would avoid much of the criticism. Eventually, people will cool down and feel rather foolish about some of the things they may have said to you. There may even be a conciliatory letter, urging you to return home. Your resentment will die hard, nevertheless, and you will have to think it over. With Christmas just a week away, there are many diverse things to be attended to, and too little time, by your standards. But you pitch in and will undoubtedly do a good and thorough job. Don't overtire yourself; you want to be at your best at parties.

19. SATURDAY. Enjoyable. Most of today will probably be spent with your love; you are really not much interested in the company of others. You may share an interest in some of the mysteries of life or possibly in the occult. The local library should offer enough variety to be rewarding. You should find new books on these subjects that both answer questions and raise others. As a result, you want to get involved in some psychological experiments or with an occult group. A meal for which you pool your culinary skills with others' is a pleasant feature of the day. Altogether, it can be rather an emotional period that leads to some changes in your attitudes. Tensions that might arise could be attributable to many and varied problems, depending on the immediate circumstances. Given time, they will be resolved.

20. SUNDAY. Successful. This romance is the right one; you are convinced of it. You view life as a great adventure through which you go hand in hand. As you feel psychic about most things today, you will tell yourself that you knew all along this love is the right one for you. You are quite sensitive and intuitive, so people may begin to thing you can look into the future. Or they may view your powers of prediction in less kindly terms. You seem to know instinctively what moves to make. Rivals who ridicule you lack your sense of logic and inner security. Because they are not as tuned in to the world and current trends, they take the easy way out, saying you think you have magic powers or make lucky guesses. Just go your own way and follow your hunches.

21. MONDAY. Challenging. Your career is taking off. Routine work is no problem; your successful attempts to overcome new challenges is rewarded with a bonus. A better job with increased benefits is lurking in the background; you will soon be made aware of it. Your self-confidence is high and your ambition drives you toward new goals. A letter from overseas makes your day. Interest in other countries and cultures prods you into making plans for a trip abroad. Your homelife can be as pleasant as your relationships with friends. You will want to make the best use of a newly discovered talent. It might enrich your life as well as advance your career. A marriage can improve your position by moving you into a new circle of society.

22. TUESDAY. Excellent. Domestic and social relationships should be very good at present. Working together with family members on household tasks creates harmony. Besides getting on well with individual family members and friends, working in groups is equally favorable; new friendships can be made, some of them with older people. Your job is going well and it is likely that you will be involved in the buying and selling end of the operation. Your artistic talents are an asset and your imagination can take you far. Follow your hunches because your subconscious mind seems to be guiding the pattern of your conscious thinking. You can be quite emotional, so your feelings may dominate your reasoning far more than even you realize.

23. WEDNESDAY. Enjoyable. The holiday spirit colors everything you do at present. You overlook the shortcomings of others at home and at work and hope they will reciprocate. People involved in retail selling know this is the busiest time of the year. But some others, with office or factory jobs, could find themselves with extra time on their hands. Messages are flying back and forth between your home and loved ones at a distance. You get an idea for a new project, and want to start on it right away. The arrival of house guests for the holiday keeps the family busy, but you do welcome visitors. This is usually the time when bonuses are distributed and promotions announced. You naturally hope you will be among the lucky ones.

24. THURSDAY. Satisfactory. Family members are caught up in last-minute preparations, as usual. You will be free to slip away for a small celebration of your own, bringing cheer to a shut-in or helping to prepare some holiday treat for the homeless. Today can be quite difficult if you intend to bring home a new romantic partner. The family may not be ready to approve your choice, especially if your friend is a bit unconventional. The gap between family and a new love can be wide indeed. Little will be accomplished at your workplace today. Someone will have to be there to answer the phones, but otherwise it may be one long office party. If you expect to drive home, you should avoid alcohol entirely, if not for yourself, for others' sakes.

25. FRIDAY. MERRY CHRISTMAS! This will be a busy day for any Cancers who are entertaining a large group of relatives. It is not unknown for family disagreements to break out when everyone gets together and you may play the role of peacemaker. If you are wise enough to see a storm brewing, take action at once. Another helping of something especially tasty at dinner or another drink might distract the people involved; and they will doubtless mellow as the day progresses. Christmas is happiest for the very young; there will be tremendous excitement as they open presents. The delighted surprise of many of the adults as they open their gifts will be equally exciting.

26. SATURDAY. Easygoing. Do not expect to get much work done today. Everyone will probably be tired, especially the adults. If you observe Boxing Day, you will probably distribute gifts to those who have served you or have been helpful to you in some way throughout the year. Your charitable impulses may also take you out for a while, as you pitch in to assist a group that is dedicated to helping those in need. When you return home, either visiting family members or your house guests who are staying overnight may be eager to go out for some fresh air and exercise. But if the weather is too bad, why not try to see a show or some similar kind of entertainment? Sitting around the house can become boring and tempers could flare up. Don't spoil a nice Christmas with such an unhappy ending.

27. SUNDAY. Pleasant.   You may be feeling a little more energetic after some rest last night. Everyone appears to be pleasant and cheerful. Relatives and visitors who have long trips ahead of them will probably want to make an early start for home. The house can seem almost empty if there are no children playing with their new toys. Those of you who have children at home find that the excitement has died down enough for real appreciation of their gifts. They may need help in putting together some construction toys or puzzles or perhaps with reading new books. Some Cancer people will not want to miss religious services, especially during these festive days. Or their humanitarian instincts may be demanding an outlet for truly needed work.

28. MONDAY. Useful.   This can be a rather quiet day for employed Cancer people. Even those going back to work will find little to challenge them. It can be a good time to complete small, neglected tasks. Some will be taking winter vacations now. Since schools are not in session, a family outing will be easy to arrange. Those people who like to escape for a change of climate may go south or for a cruise. And those who crave winter sports and snowy scenery will be heading north. Some Cancers will be content just to hang around their favorite place, their home. It might be a perfect day for others who want to review the current year and make plans for the future, however tentative. Or you can always catch up on some reading and research.

29. TUESDAY. Productive.   For those Cancers who have overspent during the past few weeks, this can be a day of reckoning. While payment is not yet due on holiday expenditures, it would be well to do some estimating to determine how much you may owe when the bills arrive early next year. Those who do not have a budget should set one up before the end of this year. Overseas matters figure prominently in the day. Possibly a romantic partner is abroad at this time, so you may be writing more letters than usual. There will also be thank-you notes for gifts received from afar. But your main concern will be the person who is your one and only. If your new budget looks promising, you can spend a few hours planning a trip for next year.

30. WEDNESDAY. Demanding. There is no lack of work for those of you who are on the job. But the problem is that you do not really feel like doing it. There are too many things going on at home, and you want to be there to participate. You hear with dismay that more visitors are coming, so everyone has to pitch in to clear away the débris from the weekend's festivities and get ready for newcomers. Worries arise when you fail to get word from overseas or some other distant place. The family seems to be planning a surprise for you; do not spoil it by letting them know that you are wise to them. Superiors will understand if you do not get much done at work during this busy week.

31. THURSDAY. Changeable. On this last day of the year, you remember some work that must be finished before 1993 begins. Get it out of the way quickly so you can enjoy the revelry tonight with a clear conscience. You are depending on superiors coming through with your paycheck before the banks close for the weekend. New Year's Eve can be expensive if you are not careful. If you do go out, especially with someone who is a new love, you will find plenty to do. But if you opt to stay home, perhaps with a group of long-time friends, you should have an equally good time. Whatever you decide, look forward to a new year with hope and optimism, and a world at peace!

OCTOBER–DECEMBER 1991

OCTOBER

1. TUESDAY. Variable. You will probably know exactly what you want now and how best to attain it. Cancer people can find themselves blessed with a formidable sense of purpose and direction. Very little will be able to stand in the way of or distract such single-mindedness. Knowing that mundane tasks and chores are just a means to a more important end will allow you to fly through them effortlessly. There's not much chance of finding the peace and quiet you so much need at home. There may be a fair amount of turmoil and chaos in your domestic surroundings. You may have to bail other family or household members out of trouble. Do what you can to respond to any cries for help.

2. WEDNESDAY. Disquieting. Try to get by without borrowing money or asking for favors. Having to carry debts at this time can create problems of their own. It is only if you are right up against it that you should resort to borrowing. Don't indulge the weaknesses or laziness of others. Misplaced generosity may just be encouraging people to take the easy way out. If you give an inch, friends or acquaintances are more than capable of taking a mile. Be wary of getting laden down with other people's work and responsibilities. Taxation demands may be higher than anticipated, creaming off extra earnings and bonuses. Money should be spent only on items that are strictly necessary.

3. THURSDAY. Frustrating. You can glean valuable help and advice from real estate agents concerning property and real-estate affairs. Influential people are likely to be in a more amenable and cooperative mood. It's a good day for making special requests of them or for lodging complaints. They are likely to respond in a constructive manner. But it may not be easy to clear legal problems out of the way. So it's best to keep your thoughts and ideas unpretentious and down to earth. Anything that smacks too much of the new, original and untried will tend to frighten off colleagues or other key people. Be prepared for forgetfulness and unreliability in others, especially when it comes to appointments.

4. FRIDAY. Good. Both Cancer men and women are apt to be feeling much more at one with themselves and with the people and affairs closest to them. Events and activities are likely to run very much according to plan. There is more chance of seeing eye-to-eye with partners and colleagues. For once, everybody is likely to be working toward the same goal at the same time. It's a good day for letting loved ones know just how much you appreciate and care for them. It's favorable, too, for taking mates, spouses or romantic partners on a special treat or outing. It's not a day for staying cooped up indoors. Cancer people can become broody and introspective if they stay in one place too long.

5. SATURDAY. Deceptive. Cancer people may have to go to unusual lengths to win public attention for their goods or services. Dramatic or theatrical publicity stunts will bring your company name or personal image to the forefront. And it will do so in a way that more restrained and conventional advertising could not. Now is the time to make the most of inside contacts within important companies or institutions. You can now lay hands on vital information before it is officially released. Today is good for dating romantic partners for the first time. But it won't be so easy to get on the same wavelength as mates or spouses. Minor misunderstandings can cause a disproportionate amount of friction.

6. SUNDAY. Fortunate. You will only feel uneasy and guilty if you leave household or other jobs and chores undone. Get the mundane things out of the way first and then you can relax and enjoy yourself. Once you have got going on minor tasks, you may find that you have the energy and enthusiasm for getting the home into better shape. Today is good for putting on a fresh coat of paint or changing around the order and function of rooms. Cancer men and women will be at their happiest in the bosom of the family. You will enjoy get-togethers with parents and other family members. You will also enjoy a visit to Sunday stores or markets and may pick up useful items at knockdown prices.

7. MONDAY. Demanding. Thoughts and feelings about the past are likely to troop through your mind in a long procession. Cancer men and women may not be able to get out of their heads some of the people and places they have known. You may feel a strong urge to revisit childhood acquaintances or places. But there is a danger. Nostalgic musings can become an escape or diversion from current problems and responsibilities. Influential people will require your full attention and will not have much use for over-emotionalism. This is not a day for putting blind faith in people in authority. They can fall far short of their responsibilities. By the same token it is not wise to disclose confidences to strangers, at least until you know exactly who they are.

8. TUESDAY. Changeable. Keep your nose to the grindstone in routine occupational affairs. You will only have to catch up later, at a less convenient time, if you slip behind now. Try to stay ahead of the clock. Employers may insist that you stay behind if deadlines are not met. Do not jump to hasty conclusions, especially where family and household members are concerned. Wait until all the facts are in your possession before making any accusations or being critical. It's a good day for affairs of the heart. Time spent with romantic partners can have a magical quality. You probably won't need to make elaborate arrangements to enjoy your time with loved ones.

9. WEDNESDAY. Challenging. This can be a most successful and productive day for people working in the theatrical and entertainment business. It's good for attending interviews and auditions. Cancer actors and actresses can be chosen from among a host of other candidates for interesting and well-paid roles. Writers, designers and artists are also likely to have a lucky break. New commissions or contracts can be won. Let the more adventurous and inventive side of your nature come to the fore, especially where creative and imaginative work is concerned. New frontiers can be opened up in media handling and self-expression. This is likely to be a happy and stimulating day.

10. THURSDAY. Difficult. Children may be feeling left out on a limb and under pressure. Cancer parents must be more sensitive to the needs of their offspring. More guidance, affection and support can encourage a flowering of more self-confidence in youngsters. You seem to be a little stiff and unbending in your relations with others. Be more alive to the fact that people may be pulling your leg. Be wary of taking insult where none was intended. People probably have your best interests at heart now, so don't look for malicious intent. Tempers can flare in romantic affairs. Cancer people may feel they are being maneuvered into untenable positions by loved ones.

11. FRIDAY. Confusing. Loved ones may be closer to the end of their tether than they realize. Cancer people should encourage their partners to ease up a bit. If they go on at the present rate, they can become seriously run down. Try to give them a break from routine or household affairs, however dreary you may find these if you have to do them yourself. Occupational activities can entail something of an uphill struggle. Don't expect much in the way of cooperation from co-workers. Money spent on films, theater or other forms of entertainment and distraction may simply be wasted. It won't be easy to find the kind of escape you seem to be seeking just now.

12. SATURDAY. Profitable.   Cancer people will make excellent hosts and hostesses today. Guests invited to your home will thoroughly appreciate your hospitality and surroundings. Home entertaining can be a particularly good way of cementing closer contacts with influential people. Professional decisions can be made over a good meal and a glass of wine. Access to people occupying positions of power and prestige can be made all the easier through the good offices and contacts of parents or other family members. Keep your nose to the grindstone at work. You will get into the boss's good books if work can be finished on schedule or even ahead of deadline.

13. SUNDAY. Good.   You will probably be feeling in a constructive and energetic mood right now. The day is favorable for having a really good cleaning and tidying session. Now is the time to bring some extra order into your surroundings and affairs. With an additional push it should be possible to terminate matters that have overrun the time allotted to them. It's a good day for throwing spontaneous parties or just inviting a few friends around without prearrangement. There is probably plenty that needs doing in the garden. Cancer gardeners can derive enjoyment and satisfaction from working with the soil. You can also turn your hand successfully to home-repair and maintenance jobs.

14. MONDAY. Disconcerting.   You will have to be more than normally discerning in business and professional affairs if you are not to go barking up the wrong tree. Once you have settled on a course of action and a definite direction, stick to it. Partners and colleagues can come up with imaginative and original ideas and proposals. But on closer inspection, you will probably see that these are merely a distraction from your main aim. It is important that all members of working teams pull together in harmony. Cancer men and women may be the victims of an injustice. People may find legal loopholes or even shadier dodges that allow them to get away with murder.

15. TUESDAY. Fair.   You are unlikely to receive the help or blessing of influential people. In fact, such folk may seem to be doing all they can to disrupt your plans and prospects. You may lose the valuable support of other people because those who hold the reins of power are not prepared to stand behind you. And though worries and anxieties can build up in the light of these events, the outcome may not be nearly so disastrous as you might expect. The best thing now is to forget your problems and negative thoughts. Turn your full attention to happier and more light-hearted affairs. Romantic partners should be in a warm and affectionate mood and will help you to forget your cares.

16. WEDNESDAY. Disturbing. You may again be the victim of a misruling or miscarriage of justice. You have to take the blame for other people's mistakes or shortcomings. Cancer people should try to travel as lightly as possible. If it is possible to avoid taking on new responsibilities, especially concerning other people's property and possessions, then do so. Youngsters can be in a particularly rebellious or mischievous mood. Parents may have to take a firm stand or try to find out what is behind this behavior. This is not a day for taking financial risks. Losses can be heavy and embarrassing. Keep closer tabs on joint funds. They can all too easily go astray.

17. THURSDAY. Disquieting. Cancer people should decide early on whether to devote the day to business or pleasure pursuits. Attempts to combine the two can result in confusion for you and for others. Get your priorities right. Economic factors cannot be ignored. Don't let children maneuver or blackmail you into doing their bidding. Stand back and see just what your relationship to your children is. It is important to stick to your principles, especially if there is a desire to inculcate some moral values and character into your offspring. You may not be eligible for insurance payments after all. There may be some disappointments in your love life.

18. FRIDAY. Successful. Your ability to absorb and understand facts and information should be better than ever. Excellent progress can be made with study and academic pursuits. Teachers and instructors can provide that extra boost and incentive that makes you want to work all the harder. A real love for your subject can now develop. It would be best not to delegate communications with distant people. The best results will be attained if you handle such matters directly. Your spouse's parents are likely to be in a generous and cooperative mood. They may well help you out of a tight corner.

19. SATURDAY. Pleasant. This is not a day for putting your trust in strangers. Contacts in distant towns may fail to pass along vital information. If they do convey messages, the contents can be hopelessly muddled. It is not advisable today to lean too heavily on people from overseas. They can prove unreliable just when you most need their help or support. The promises issued by publishers can prove to be nothing more than empty words. Family members will find it difficult to stick to the plain facts. They can embellish their memories, descriptions or exploits just for effect. There may be some exciting developments in your love life.

20. SUNDAY. Excellent. You probably need a change of surroundings and scenery. A journey, however long or short, will help you to forget your cares and problems. Put occupational and professional matters aside for the time being. You will be able to take care of such things all the better after a refreshing break in your usual routine. Today is good for getting absorbed in a favorite subject of interest or a hobby. Cancer people will be able to concentrate on reading, study or writing activities once a start has been made. Keep on your toes. You can find potential and exciting possibilities in situations that seem totally unpromising to others.

21. MONDAY. Manageable. People who matter will not take too readily to unconventional ideas or behavior. You are best advised to stick to known, tried and traditional ways in business and professional affairs. It's not a day for taking risks. Any such risks are more likely to backfire than to succeed. You should certainly not be placing business funds on the line. The people working alongside you may act erratically. Don't expect too much in the way of cooperation from them. In teamwork and partnership affairs, the secret of success will lie in closer liaison and communication. Keep all members of working teams fully informed of new developments and any changes in plans.

22. TUESDAY. Quiet. It seems that the time has come for Cancer business people to make up their minds and let others know exactly where they stand. You cannot go on hedging your bets forever. It is highly probable that the situation facing you still seems confused. However, you no doubt have enough information at your disposal, and have given current problems enough thought, to be able to make the right decision. You are probably throwing away your chances of success if you attempt to implement major plans today. But it's a good day for preparing the ground and making last-minute arrangements and alterations.

23. WEDNESDAY. Misleading. It is in your own best interest to keep any flippant or off-the-cuff remarks to yourself when you are in the vicinity of influential people. Such people will be expecting a serious and mature attitude from you. Any jokiness or lack of concentration can rub them the wrong way. It is best to check the legal position before getting involved in speculative or gambling activities. Earnings from such endeavors may prove to be illegal. Youngsters may be in a more mischievous and boisterous mood than usual. Their high spirits can lead them into direct trouble with the authorities. Friends can come knocking at your door asking for financial favors.

24. THURSDAY. Variable. Try to avoid crossing swords with influential people. They probably have the heavy guns on their side and you will come off worst if you get involved in power struggles. You'd do best to show a certain respect and reserve with people who carry the clout. Any complaints should be couched in terms that are clearly not an affront to the authority of those in charge. Holiday or weekend plans may have to be revised in light of new instructions or requests issued by employers. You may have to be a little devious if you are to protect the time you have put aside to spend with loved ones.

25. FRIDAY. Good. High ideals are more easily translated into practical and effective action. Cancer people probably have a key role to play in humanitarian and charitable activities or organizations. New doors can open for you on the basis of your reputation and past achievements. People who matter can accord you a respect that you are far from anticipating. But it should be easier to win the confidence and support even of people who know nothing of your past. You can now impress others with the seriousness of your approach and with your honesty and integrity.

26. SATURDAY. Tricky. Loved ones may be detached and withdrawn. Cancer people can have trouble finding out what is really going on in the hearts and minds of those closest to them. But badgering such people for answers and explanations can merely send them further into their shells. You may just have to be content to leave loved ones to themselves. In so doing, you can hope that they brighten up or find a way to speak about their troubles or moods. Difficulties may be brewing in your immediate vicinity and neighbors may have a lot to do with it.

27. SUNDAY. Happy. You should be feeling on top of the world now. You are likely to make a success of most things you turn your hand to today. There should be little doubt as to the love and support you are receiving from the people around you. Small jobs and undertakings can give great pleasure and satisfaction. You may have a bright idea for a money-making venture. Favorite hobbies or creative interests can be turned into viable commercial enterprises. Artists and designers can receive lucrative and interesting commissions.

28. MONDAY. Deceptive.   People may be playing hard to get. They can also deliberately keep you on tenterhooks by concealing vital news or information. It is unlikely that you will receive the help, support or encouragement that would enable you to make a success of your undertakings. Cancer men and women may have to stand completely on their own two feet and this can give them a chance to test their own strength and abilities. Loved ones may have their heads in the clouds. There's not much chance of realistic answers from them. Your motives may be misunderstood.

29. TUESDAY. Mixed.   Thoughts and feelings are more easily expressed in words. Today is especially good for letting romantic partners know the depths of your feelings for them. Cancer people can find themselves in a more poetic vein. Today is also especially good for creative writing and other artistic enterprises. Excitement and enthusiasm can build up to a peak, but Cancers will be able to put this kind of energy to good use. There's not much chance of emotions getting out of hand today. You will have much greater control and mastery of yourself. Take nothing for granted where funds are concerned.

30. WEDNESDAY. Disquieting.   It is best to play things safe now, whether in romantic, financial or other affairs. Conditions are too unpredictable to break with the old or to stray into unknown territory. Putting money on the line is a recipe for loss. Children's needs and demands can prove costly. Don't give in to their every whim and fancy. Youngsters probably need to learn that money doesn't grow on trees. But there are also likely to be essential expenses that cannot be avoided. While loved ones may be in an irritable and provocative mood, Cancer people should do all they can to avoid arguments and quarrels.

31. THURSDAY. Sensitive.   Do your best to keep your options open where the future and finances are concerned. You may be taking on more than you can handle by signing financial agreements today. Your own feelings and hunches are likely to be more accurate than the advice or suggestions received from others. Too much hesitation or lassitude can mean the loss of valuable opportunities, particularly where money is concerned. Parents may be demonstrating a more overbearing attitude to their offspring than they realize. Encourage children to express their own views, feelings and ideas more.

NOVEMBER

1. FRIDAY. Good. The month gets off to a lively start for Cancer people. Exciting new developments are about to get under way. Influential people can open new doors for you or may have a proposal or even a surprise up their sleeves. It's a good day for talking over future possibilities with your boss. Publishers can be in a more open and receptive mood. Manuscripts can be accepted for publication. Cancers may receive commendations for their written work. A few words of encouragement can make all the difference to loved ones. Give them a helping hand.

2. SATURDAY. Fortunate. You can relax and enjoy a very happy day for romance. A whole new chapter can begin in your love life. Important relationships can start from fairly casual beginnings. Trips and outings with loved ones can be most enjoyable. It's a good day for sharing common interests with your nearest and dearest. And it's another day when you should have no trouble expressing your deepest thoughts and feelings. Love letters will be well received, especially if delivered in person. Help with an important or heartfelt scheme can come from influential quarters.

3. SUNDAY. Fair. You may simply be building up additional resistance if you try to force yourself to break with bad habits or restrictive patterns. It is probably best to let traits that you now find unacceptable in yourself drop away in their own time. No good will really come from wearing a hair shirt or sleeping on a bed of nails. Changes in your immediate environment may not be much to your liking. Household members may decide to move on, leaving you feeling lonely and bereft. You seem to have influential people very much on your side at the moment.

4. MONDAY. Challenging. It seems you still have much to learn and absorb where recent and past events are concerned. You might try rereading diaries or sifting through memories in an attempt to get your experience into better perspective. But it's a good day for following research and inquiries through to the bitter end, no matter how much waiting or difficulty this involves. More interesting jobs, with higher rates of pay, may be offered to you. It's also a good day for arranging or attending interviews in search of a better position. Cancer business people can set their sights high. Don't be shy about doing business with large firms.

5. TUESDAY. Variable.   It can be difficult for Cancer people to shake off a mood of depression and gloom. And it probably isn't just immediate problems and concerns that are giving you the blues. Deep questions concerning life, death and your purpose and direction may be causing deep discontent. You may have to turn to the teachings of philosophy or religion to regrasp a sense of meaning. Be more than ready to forgive others even though they continue to upset or irritate you. The more troublemakers see that you are not going to hold resentment for them, the quicker they are likely to pipe down and cease to be difficult.

6. WEDNESDAY. Satisfactory.   Hold to your own better judgment where money is concerned. People may try to tempt you into putting at risk any available funds you may have. If you are unsure about speculative enterprises, give them a miss. Youngsters may be in a rebellious or boisterous mood. Parents and teachers can have their work cut out for them just trying to keep children in hand. Once you get started on artistic or creative work, you probably won't want to stop. Originality will probably be pouring out of you. Solutions to long-standing problems can now be found.

7. THURSDAY. Profitable.   There may be exciting new developments in your love life. You can capture the heart of someone you have taken a fancy to. Use all the charm and capacity to attract that you can muster. Keep on your toes in occupational affairs. Situations can arise in which your skills and abilities are put to the test. Nevertheless you are likely to come through with flying colors. You can now win the highest praise from your boss and perhaps a financial bonus into the bargain. Any worries concerning your health can be calmed by medical checkups.

8. FRIDAY. Disturbing.   Remember that more haste can mean less speed. A thorough and painstaking approach must be adopted where all jobs and undertakings are concerned. Make sure that you avoid errors and mistakes that could mean that the work has to be done again. There's not much hope of receiving the help and cooperation you so much need from fellow workers. People upon whom you are relying can leave you in the lurch. Even people occupying responsible positions can be unreliable and erratic. The outcome of their actions places you in a very awkward position.

9. SATURDAY. Demanding. You may be feeling a bit low and depressed. Your reserves of energy are probably run down. A slight infection or other mild ailment may be further contributing to your discomfort. The best solution to your problems is to take it easy and get some rest. Don't push yourself to any limits. By all means avoid any jobs or chores that can be done another day or by other people. Later in the day you may feel more energetic and at least be able to attend to any really pressing undertakings or arrangements. Try to get someone to give you a helping hand.

10. SUNDAY. Useful. Let loved ones do things in their own unique way. They may seem to be doing it in a haphazard and time-wasting fashion, but they will at least get the job done. They will probably also enjoy themselves in the process if they are left to their own devices. Labor-saving devices can break down, but Cancer people may find they are handy at do-it-yourself work and get things functioning again quite soon. This is not a day for getting stuck indoors. You will enjoy being on the move, taking in new sights. It is good for joining in neighborhood activities.

11. MONDAY. Good. Here is another day when romance can blossom. Important and happy relationships can develop from mild flirtations or other casual beginnings. The achievements and insights of children can give Cancer parents something to smile and be thankful for. Teachers, too, can find that the children in their care are developing along the right lines. You may need professional help to sort out some legal complexities, but don't think that such problems are insurmountable. Advertising can make a great impact so sales should increase dramatically.

12. TUESDAY. Difficult. You may feel that certain people are deliberately setting out to disturb or upset you; and it could well be the case. Cancer men and women may have to put up with extreme provocation. Try not to be pushed into reactions that you will later come to regret. Don't go sticking your nose in places where it is not wanted. You may get more than you bargain for. Respect other people's privacy and feelings. There may be some disturbing news regarding your financial position. Bank statements can show that you are deeper into the red than you had realized.

13. WEDNESDAY. Disquieting. This is a good day for digging in and rooting around and getting down to the bottom of things.

Valuable information can be unearthed as a result of your investigations and inquiries. It is good for discussing problems with people who have already experienced situations that are facing you. Now is the time to do some checking up on pension and retirement programs. Employers or superiors may be able to put your mind at rest concerning future economic security. Any worries over health can be allayed by routine medical checkups.

14. THURSDAY. Confusing. Use today for getting priorities right and for putting your activities and interests in the right order. Attempts to combine professional and pleasure pursuits will result in confusion and dissatisfaction. Set your course for the day and then stick to your guns. Don't allow others to tempt you with distracting offers for relaxation or recreational activities. There's not much chance of your banker making loans available for risky ventures. He will want to know exactly how and when the money will be repaid. Children can get up to some mischief.

15. FRIDAY. Disconcerting. From your current vantage point it should be possible to get a clearer picture of what lies ahead. Cancer people should now be able to face the future with more optimism. Sharing a common aim and goals with loved ones can help to bring you both closer together. It's a good day for exploring new territory and for broadening your horizons. Journeys and adventures can be all the more enjoyable and exciting for having the companionship of someone you love. Stay on your toes where Scorpio people are concerned.

16. SATURDAY. Variable. Focus your attention today on current involvements and undertakings. You may just be dissipating your energies by attending to plans and arrangements for the future. It can prove impossible anyway to forecast such circumstances and possibilities with any accuracy. Any plans you do make will probably have to be completely revised as the time for action comes closer. It is best to double-check any news or information received from distant sources. Messages can become garbled in transmission. Don't sweep health problems aside.

17. SUNDAY. Successful. There is no point in resting on your laurels when there are opportunities for further adding to your good name and reputation. What you achieve today can increase your standing in the eyes of people who matter. You can even win a degree of fame and renown. Word-of-mouth publicity can stand you in good stead. Sunday walks and recreational activities can lead to chance encounters with useful business or professional contacts. Such people can put valuable information or new possibilities your way. You may find you have been following a false trail in research and investigative work.

18. MONDAY. Deceptive. Steer clear of any under-the-counter deals or transactions. Keep everything open and aboveboard. You may come to regret not keeping records of all financial exchanges. Any future official inquiries into your business or monetary interests can be made easier if you have the documentation to show. You just won't get away with a cursory handling of legal affairs. Such matters require a careful and thorough approach. Employers can engender more goodwill among the work force by improving working conditions and introducing incentive bonuses.

19. TUESDAY. Disturbing. You may feel that friends are taking unfair advantage of your long-standing relationship. It is probably best not to give into their demands for cash or favors. Cancer people themselves should try to get by without resorting to borrowing, especially where new business enterprises are concerned. It is only if you are in dire straits that borrowing should be considered. You may have no choice but to attend rather tiresome social events. In fact, invitations may be received on all sides. Romantic partners can be in a hypersensitive mood.

20. WEDNESDAY. Excellent. There seems to be scope for reducing overhead and making business activities run in a more streamlined way. Cancer business people should be more open to ways of cutting costs and so increasing profits. But the greatest success, where commercial interests lie, will probably come through advertising and public relations campaigns. Now is a good time for presenting a more attractive and even glamorous public image. New people can be added to your circle of friends. It will be easier to break the ice with strangers or casual acquaintances.

21. THURSDAY. Touchy. People in key positions or who have the final say can throw a monkey wrench into your works. Cancers may find they cannot make the hoped-for progress because influential people are making problems. You may even have to give up any hope of ever realizing a project that is dear to your heart. Friends can act in an insensitive and inconsiderate way. They may say things that you have expressly asked them to keep secret. It may prove impossible to translate high ideals into practical action. Official bodies can withdraw their support.

22. FRIDAY. Erratic. Cancer men and women may find themselves faced with impossible or threatening situations. Your self-confidence may be badly shaken or even undermined by testing circumstances. A mood of pessimism may come in to replace your former assurance and enthusiasm. But this particular cloud will probably have a silver lining. If you stand back from current involvements and undertakings, a greater sense of realism can be achieved. You may come to see that your former position was based on shaky foundations and had to lead to disappointments.

23. SATURDAY. Misleading. Your mind is likely to be on almost anything other than the job at hand. Cancer people will have to crack the whip over wandering thoughts if they want to make any progressive or constructive moves. If you approach jobs or undertakings with divided attention, you are almost certain to make mistakes. It is probably best to leave sick or lonely people to themselves for the time being. Hospital visits can have the opposite effect from the one intended. There's not much chance of others holding confidential information to themselves.

24. SUNDAY. Fair. Make sure that people are not asking the impossible of you before you make any attempt to carry out their wishes. If others have misguided ideas or expectations concerning you, there may be no way in which you can live up to them. There is no point in trying to be something you know you are not. No matter how much you would like to please someone, it would be a mistake to try to fit into a space that is either too small or the wrong shape for you. This is a good day for cultivating more friendliness and a cooperative spirit with neighbors.

25. MONDAY. Good. People should be more eager to go along with your plans and ideas. Cancer men and women should have little trouble in drumming up support and enthusiasm for their ideas. Obstacles that have been standing in the way of pet projects can now vanish or be sidestepped. Children may need a firm hand. If you let them get away with bad behavior, you will be inviting more of the same in the future. Hidden forces are working in your favor. You can afford to stick your neck out. Calculated risks can pay off. You may be reluctant to start creative work.

26. TUESDAY. Quiet. There won't be much in the way of interesting developments or events today. Cancer people are likely to find this a thoroughly humdrum day. Steady progress can be made with routine occupational and domestic affairs. Employers are likely to pile less on your back. This will mean that you can work along at a pace that suits you. With fewer distractions and disturbances, you should find it easier to concentrate on finicky and intricate undertakings, such as paperwork and accounting. Do not give material values a higher place than human ones.

27. WEDNESDAY. Ordinary. Now is a good time for buying furniture, kitchen equipment and other furnishings and fittings prior to moving into new homes with loved ones. Cancer people are probably in the mood to do some painting or wallpaper hanging in their own homes. Your innate love of homemaking can now come to the fore. Loved ones are likely to be genuinely appreciative of the extra touches of brightness and comfort you bring to shared surroundings. The boss can be impressed by the way you demonstrate your skills and abilities while under pressure.

28. THURSDAY. Variable. You may find yourself wriggling on the end of a hook held by an influential person. Cancer people can be placed in a no-win situation while key people jostle and maneuver for better positions or personal advancement. But trying to resist such situations may merely jeopardize your own position. It's a good day for making short trips and for running errands. Although you may have applied for an exciting job in plenty of time, other applicants are likely to be selected in your stead. It's a good day to join forces to achieve common ends.

29. FRIDAY. Uncertain. You seem to be in the mood for fun and enjoyment. That's fortunate, as today is a good one for attending parties and other social events. Cancer men and women will be happiest in the company of lively and cheerful people. Get your glad rags on and enjoy a night out on the town. Someone at work may have an exciting suggestion to make for an evening trip or an outing. Make sure you attend to your duties and tie up any loose ends before starting your weekend or getting your pleasure plans under way. Unfinished jobs will only nag at you and spoil your fun. Don't believe everything that colleagues say.

30. SATURDAY. Happy. Conditions are particularly favorable for making home improvements. Exciting plans can be drawn up for building on extensions or knocking down walls to make larger living areas. Following up lines of inquiry can at least put necessary and relevant information at your disposal. Research projects can be terminated on a triumphant note. Employers should be in a cooperative mood and may see no reason for your not taking work home to complete over the weekend. You are likely to do a good job if you work in familiar surroundings.

DECEMBER

1. SUNDAY. Deceptive. Past experience and precedents are unlikely to give you the guidance you need when faced with new and challenging situations. Cancer people will probably have to start from scratch and find totally new solutions to their problems. An extra degree of self-discipline may be required today. Your mind may be prone to going back over the past. Current difficulties or responsibilities may just be building up while you indulge in nostalgic musings. Try to stay within the present. You probably need to keep a tighter rein on your emotions.

2. MONDAY. Disquieting. This looks like a day when you may have to pay through the nose for your pleasure and enjoyment. You are certainly unlikely to get good times for nothing. Make sure your bank balance is up to your expensive tastes. Children may not be in the best of spirits. Their health may demand a day off from school. Give youngsters a chance to build up their strength and resistance. This is not a day for taking unnecessary chances or sticking your neck out. It's best not to rise to the bait if you feel romantic partners are looking for a fight.

3. TUESDAY. Good. There should be no shortage of creative and original ideas for artists, designers and others who use their imagination in their work or hobbies. Brilliant solutions to long-standing problems can now occur to you. Jot down any brainwaves that come and keep on file any that cannot be acted upon immediately. They are all too easily forgotten otherwise. Artists may receive a lucrative and interesting commission. You can make the day for loved ones by giving them a special surprise. The time is right for planning a trip away with mates or spouses.

4. WEDNESDAY. Enjoyable. Although this may be something of a slow-moving day, Cancer people can take advantage of the easygoing conditions to get in some extra rest and relaxation. You should now be able to catch up on personal needs and activities. Employers are likely to be in a friendly mood. They may even let you have some time off work to get ahead with your Christmas shopping. It is a day when shops and stores may be a little less busy than usual. It's good for buying clothes and shoes. You may be able to afford something you have been saving for.

5. THURSDAY. Variable. Interesting and well-paid jobs may be up for grabs. Nonetheless it is advisable for you to stay calm and not get overexcited, no matter how promising these new situations are. If prospective employers see that you are over-eager, this may jeopardize your chances or be reflected in the amount of money they agree to pay you. You will also need to keep cool and collected to spot any loopholes or drawbacks contained in new occupational offers. This is not the best day for taking complaints or suggestions to employers.

6. FRIDAY. Frustrating. If nothing else, today is favorable for patching up differences with others. Apologies will be accepted with good grace. People are unlikely to hold your mistakes or shortcomings against you. In fact, you should get any help you need to put wrongs to rights. But it is unwise to put too much faith in influential people. Their promises can prove to be merely hollow words when it comes to the crunch. Penalties for dangerous or careless driving can be heavy. Be more cautious and alert on the roads if you want to hold on to your license.

7. SATURDAY. Rewarding. There may be some exciting new developments in your love life. Single Cancers can meet someone they really take a fancy to. Important and happy partnerships can grow from hesitant beginnings. Love and trust are likely to increase in existing relationships. Let loved ones know the depth of your affection and appreciation. They will probably treasure a small gift or special treat. Today is especially good for writing love letters and for sending flowers to someone special. Stubborn people can be won over to your point of view.

8. SUNDAY. Tricky. You seem to be restricting the freedom of action and choice of loved ones to an unnecessary degree. It is foolish to chide mates and spouses simply because they do not approach things just as you do. Let them handle their own affairs and work things out in their own way. Remember that they probably have interests and attitudes that may not seem important to you, but are vital to them. Swallow your pride. Encourage others to develop their own skills and abilities. New people may be added to your circle of friends.

9. MONDAY. Disturbing. You are unlikely to have things all your own way now. Cancer men and women will have to meet other people at least halfway. Try to be more flexible and accommodating. You may have no choice but to give way in the face of fierce and concerted opposition. Be ready to adapt your plans and preconceived ideas in the light of changing circumstances. It is probably wisest not to travel too far from home or workplace. Journeys can involve you in complications and problems. Try to bring a single-minded focus to all jobs and undertakings.

10. TUESDAY. Fair. Now you can track down any facts and information you are seeking by making extensive inquiries. Your researches and investigations can throw light in dark places. It should be possible to forecast future trends and possibilities on the basis of knowledge acquired today. Don't be put off the trail by bad-tempered officials or others who block your path. A review of the terms of insurance policies may be in order. Make sure all your needs are still covered by existing arrangements. Leave nothing to chance where property and possessions are concerned.

11. WEDNESDAY. Exciting. At last you are given a favorable day for approaching bankers. You can now arrange loans and credit instruments on reasonable terms. Don't bother with small fry in business dealings. Cancer business people should be aiming at trading with the larger firms and organizations. Lucrative contracts can be won. Any worries concerning future job and economic security can be put to rest by employers. They should now be in a position to outline future prospects and plans. You can probably plumb the depths of riddles where others merely draw a blank.

12. THURSDAY. Quiet. With fewer responsibilities to worry about, Cancer people should take this opportunity to stand back from all current affairs, involvements and undertakings. They should endeavor to view them all at arm's length. Problems and difficulties can dissolve into nothingness when you see them in true perspective. Let others stir up trouble for themselves if they want to. There is no need for you to get involved or to feel implicated. There should be opportunities for some quiet reflection and contemplation. Cancer people may feel a need to read or think.

13. FRIDAY. Disquieting. You can now discover mistakes and errors you have made before anyone else notices them. It's a good day for putting wrongs to right so that other people are none the wiser. With quick thinking, Cancer men and women can ensure that their reputations remain unsullied. It is probably advisable to obtain a second opinion in medical matters. Earlier diagnoses can be put in a broader perspective the second time around. But you may be easier in your mind where physical ailments or discomforts are concerned.

14. SATURDAY. Slow. This should be a relaxed and easy-going start to the weekend. Cancer people may wish to relax by the fire with a good book for part of the day. Your mind is likely to stray to business and professional concerns in quiet moments. It's a good day for outlining plans and proposals in rough form. You should now have sufficient distance and detachment from professional activities to understand what the real issues are. Distant contacts may have some important news or information to pass along. Cancers may discuss serious aspects of life and death.

15. SUNDAY. Changeable. Rouse yourself and try to get out and about today. Valuable opportunities can be lost if you give in to lazy feelings and spend the day indoors. Sunday walks or other recreational activities can bring you into contact with people who can advance your business or professional interests. Do what you can to give others a helping hand. Kindheartedness and generosity can help to improve your reputation in ways that are difficult to conceive. Give loved ones the support and encouragement they need to face difficult and challenging situations.

16. MONDAY. Good. Your past hard work and loyalty in occupational affairs can now pay off in unexpected ways. Your employer may invite you to fill a vacant position, giving you a more interesting and responsible job at a higher rate of pay. Keep an open mind to any new business or financial propositions. You may be on to a winner. Cancer people can fall head over heels in love today. Someone you meet can prove irresistible. Today is good for dating a prospective romantic partner for the first time.

17. TUESDAY. Misleading. You may feel that friends are taking unfair advantage of your close relationship. They can make heavy or unreasonable financial demands or play on your generosity in other ways. Cancer people should not be afraid to draw the line, even if this seems to jeopardize friendship. It will be up to you to lay down the conditions on which the acquaintanceship continues. Try to get by without borrowing in business activities. Loans can become a heavy stone around your neck. Recreational activities can be spoiled by the membership fees or expenses.

18. WEDNESDAY. Variable. Here is another upbeat day when conditions are most encouraging for love and romance. Chance encounters or casual contact can mean the start of an exciting new love affair. Cancer people may find themselves drawn into amorous adventures before they quite know what is happening. And there probably won't be any complaints when you finally do catch up with events. Mates or spouses seem to have luck very much on their side at the moment. Things can work out just as they had hoped. Loved ones will thoroughly appreciate a little gift or treat.

19. THURSDAY. Pleasant. Cancer people should have the satisfaction of seeing justice done. The law or circumstances should now catch up with someone who has wronged you or who has been getting away with murder. People not seen for some time can reappear with the intention of repaying a financial debt or favor. Help can come from unexpected quarters. Your energy reserves may not be as high as you think. Don't take on too much. Keep your rushing about to a minimum. Get all the rest and relaxation possible. Romance is endowed with a special quality.

20. FRIDAY. Disconcerting. You must try to be more considerate of others' feelings and needs. Beware of making hurtful or cutting remarks. Cancer men and women should substitute more tact and diplomacy for an overly blunt and direct approach. People may be able to take only so much honesty at one time. If they feel they are cornered, they may go for your throat. It may be necessary to make ultimatums to people, but it would be unwise to nag and pressure them insistently. You need warm clothing and regular nourishing food as additional protection against infection.

21. SATURDAY. Confusing. People in positions of power and authority may give the impression of being open and honest. They are probably, in fact, keeping important knowledge totally to themselves. You may feel that you are not receiving the guidance you really need from people who could show you the way. Instructions and orders can fall far short of the mark, so that you hardly know where to begin. Don't take the law into your own hands. Call on the authorities if there is a breach of the peace. Cancers may be harboring an unnecessary fear or suspicion of the police.

22. SUNDAY. Fair. Don't be slow about responding generously to the requests and needs of others. Do what you can to help friends or acquaintances out of a jam. People are likely to be deeply appreciative of any assistance you give, though they may find it difficult or embarrassing to voice their gratitude. Be ready to be of service without expecting anything in return. Loved ones may prefer to remain sitting on the fence, rather than make their position plain on important issues. There is no point in trying to force a definite answer from them.

23. MONDAY. Mixed. Money matters can take you into deep waters. You may find yourself at loggerheads with others involved in financial transactions and negotiations. Discussions may have to be called off when it is seen that stalemate situations are unlikely to produce breakthroughs. You may now be thankful that you have put some money by for domestic purposes. Household bills can be higher than anticipated. Cancer employees may be faced with challenging situations that put their abilities to the test.

24. TUESDAY. Disquieting. You are probably in an energetic and industrious mood. If so, keep your nose to the grindstone in routine work activities. Don't be disheartened by the amount of work you have to do, or by certain difficulties facing you. You will finish work at a faster rate than you thought possible and solve problems relatively easily. Don't waste any time in idle chatter. Let workmates know that you mean business. But outings or entertainment trips that you have been looking forward to may have to be sacrificed to meet other commitments or demands.

25. WEDNESDAY. MERRY CHRISTMAS! Everything is likely to fall into place today. Cancer men and women should be feeling at one with themselves, the people around them and the world in general. This is the traditional day when you find that you probably derive more pleasure and satisfaction from giving than you do from receiving. It's good for letting the people nearest to you know what is going on in your innermost feelings. Don't keep yourself to yourself. Others are likely to respond in a like manner if you are open and outgoing. Gifts can give great pleasure on both sides. You may meet important leaders while attending parties.

26. THURSDAY. Manageable. You will probably feel all the better for getting out and about and walking off some of that Christmas cheer. A lot of rich food and drink may have left you feeling distinctly jaded. But there's probably nothing wrong that some fresh air and gentle exercise will not put right. Don't, however, push yourself to the limit. Leave any heavy jobs or work until another day. Cancer people can feel closer than ever to their mates, spouses or romantic partners. You will probably be feeling extremely supportive and protective of your loved ones.

27. FRIDAY. Sensitive. There's not much chance of making speedy progress with property transactions. Unexpected legal complications can crop up to slow down proceedings in a most irritating way. You may receive a cry for help from family or household members who have fallen foul of the law. You may have to vouch for the character of people you are close to. Influential people may feel awkward and uncomfortable if invited as guests to your home. There should be fewer tensions and difficulties if such guests are entertained on more neutral territory.

28. SATURDAY. Deceptive.   The farther you stray from home territory today, the more unhappy and insecure you are likely to feel. You probably need the peace, quiet and protection of familiar and safe surroundings. Energetic spouses, friends or family members may insist on going about their business, leaving you at home alone. But this is probably the best option to follow. You probably need to refuel your tanks after the recent excitements and revelries. Some quiet hours alone will soon have you feeling your old self again. But you may face broken agreements.

29. SUNDAY. Quiet.   There can be a strong temptation today to indulge in nostalgic and sentimental feelings. But once you have turned on this particular tap it may be difficult to stop the flow. Too much introspection and brooding over the past can produce profound feelings of sadness and discontent. Talking about past events and people may merely stir up happy memories, but it is when nostalgia becomes obsessive that you should worry. Cancer people will be at their happiest in the bosom of the family. It's a good day for inviting many members around to your home or attending their gatherings elsewhere.

30. MONDAY. Good.   You may have a bright idea for a money-making venture. Cancer men and women may now see ways of turning hobbies or creative pursuits into commercial enterprises. But you may need the advice and guidance of experienced or influential people if you are really going to make a success of such projects. Good news can be received from employers or colleagues. The holiday period may be extended for a day or two longer. The achievements of youngsters can give parents or other family members something to smile about.

31. TUESDAY. Uncertain.   Be wary of being taken in by outward appearances. Remember that all that glitters is not gold. Financial propositions or speculative enterprises seem promising enough at first, but may reveal glaring drawbacks. Gambling activities can result in heavy losses. It's best to play it entirely safe where money is concerned. Minor disagreements can build up into serious quarrels or disturbances in romantic affairs. Youngsters can get out of hand, but are probably only asking for more love and attention. Prepare for welcoming 1992!